FOREWORD SIR GEOFFREY PALMER

# Alcohol:
## a dangerous love affair

An in-depth study of the effects of alcohol on users,
the community, the nation of New Zealand,
and globally

George A. F. Seber

D. Graeme Woodfield

WSP
WILD SIDE PUBLISHING
real stories. real hope.

wildsidepublishing.com

**WSP**
WILD SIDE PUBLISHING
real stories. real hope.

Published by George A. F. Seber in association with
Wild Side Publishing, PO Box 33, Ruawai 0549, New Zealand
www.wildsidepublishing.com

Co-writer, D. Graeme Woodfield
Cover design, Janet Curle | wildsidepublishing.com
Text layout, George A. F. Seber

Cataloguing in Publication Data:
Title: Alcohol: A dangerous love affair
ISBN: 978-0-473-50321-5 (pbk)
ISBN: 978-0-473-50322-2 (epub)

Subjects: New Zealand Non-Fiction, Alcohol, Addiction, Social Effects, Crime, Alcohol Industry, Health, Healthcare Delivery, Health Policy, Medical Ethics, Medical Law & Legislation, Biology, Genetics, Disease

First printing 2020
International listing 2019 www.ingramspark.com

# FOREWORD
## Sir Geoffrey Palmer

New Zealand has a long and troubled history with alcohol. Colonial New Zealand was awash with booze. Prohibition was almost adopted in 1918.

Few areas of public policy are as resistant to researched based solutions to solve the problems created as the alcohol industry in New Zealand. Rational thinking gives way to prejudice and lobbying by vested interests evidenced-based policy must be the best approach and public opinion will favour a new look at our alcohol laws.

As president of the Law Commission I was privileged to lead a comprehensive review of New Zealand's alcohol laws that reported in 2010. A new law did finally emerge from the parliament in 2013 but the most potent measures recommended to control the abuse of alcohol were not adopted. The issue will not go away.

Fortunately, in New Zealand there is a community of scholars who research in this area and have shone bright lights to illuminate what is wrong. There is considerable research on New Zealand alcohol policy now and it makes a persuasive case for change.

When I was first exposed to these issues as MP, and later as Minister of Justice, there was little research. Now there is a prodigious amount, and it points clearly to what is needed to be done.

Now the learning from all the available research both New Zealand and overseas has been brought together and explained in a book with admirable clarity and precision. It sets out the evidence in an objective and scientific way that is hard to argue with. The extensive comparative material from other countries is used to help explain and put in context the New Zealand situation.

People who want to know about the dangers of the consumption of alcohol, its health effects, the social consequences, the heavy drinking culture of New Zealand, the organisation of the industry and its techniques to grow the market can find it all here. This book deserves to be a bible for policy makers.

The authors, George A. F. Seber and D. Graeme Woodfield are highly quali-fied, the first a former professor of statistics and the second as a doctor, expert in blood types and transfusion. These distinguished and experienced scientists bring a wealth of relevant expertise to this troubled subject. The book is rigor-ous but written in plain English. It should be of great help to anyone who wants to be fully and reliably informed concerning almost any aspect of alcohol in New Zealand.

Some of the messages are bleak and the following quotations from the text will provide a flavour from the stunning assembly of evidence marshalled so well in this book:

"Unfortunately in New Zealand we have a culture where heavy drinking has become normalised, and where almost half the alcohol consumed in heavy-drinking situations."

"It is an addictive psychotropic drug."

"New Zealanders spend more than $4 billion per year, and NZ households spent, on average, the same on alcohol as on fruit and vegetables."

"We state right from the outset that overall there is no safe level of alcohol con-sumption."

"New Zealand has the fifth highest prevalence of female drinkers at 88%, while the men did not feature in the top 10 in the study."

"Alcohol is widely misused by children and young people in New Zealand…"

"Worldwide, 3.3 million die every year due to the harmful use of alcohol."

"In New Zealand, alcohol contributes to violence, suicide, and injuries with more than 62,000 physical assaults and 10,000 sexual assaults occurring every year that involve a perpetrator who had been drinking."

"It appears that the link between alcohol and cancer is not well known amongst drinkers."

"Alcohol abuse and depression are linked."

"The less a person drinks the healthier they will be, with a reduction of the rela-tive risks of such things as heart disease, cancer, hypertension, diabetes, and mental illness."

"The consumption of alcohol has a range of harms to people other than the individual drinker."

"Alcohol marketing in recent years has greatly increased in complexity, innovation and diversification over a range of media and new technology."

"Young New Zealand adults tend to see heavy drinking as part of a national identity."

"Sport, in particular, has been the focus of the alcohol industry..."

"Alcohol is an excellent product for making money, and yields huge profits for the alcohol industry."

The book is treasure trove of information about alcohol itself, the effects on health and on society, and its contribution to criminal offending. There is even extensive information on hangovers. Good advice is provided on how to moderate drinking.

There is much about the detailed behavior of the alcohol industry, its marketing techniques and its lobbying power with politicians.

The message is clear. New measures must be taken to reduce the harm from alcohol and the alcohol industry must be reined in. I hope the parliament can be persuaded to take up the issue.

Alcohol law is an area of policy failure in New Zealand. That is the inevitable conclusion to be drawn from the evidence canvassed in this book.

~**SIR GEOFFREY PALMER** KCMG AC QC PC
New Zealand lawyer, legal academic, and past politician, who was a member of Parliament from 1979 to 1990. He served as the 33rd Prime Minister of New Zealand for a little over a year, from August 1989 until September 1990, leading the Fourth Labour Government (Wikipedia).

# CONTENTS

# PREFACE

Writing about alcohol is not a popular subject in New Zealand. We prefer to cover up our attitudes to it under a veneer of humour and obscure some of its known problems. We tend to ridicule the wowsers, teetotallers and non-drinkers as spoilsports and being somehow abnormal, and not in contact with modern thinking. So to embark on writing a book on this subject is a little daunting as some would consider any effort to ridicule or expose the alcohol industry is too much like "tilting at a windmill" and not likely to have any effect. After all, a huge number of people are employed by the alcohol industry, and exports of alcohol overseas has reached a new peak. One can almost say that New Zealand has become a major drug exporter and the government supports this, as it produces export overseas funds.

Unfortunately in New Zealand we have a culture where heavy drinking has become normalised, and where almost half of all alcohol is consumed in heavy-drinking situations. This has resulted in an enormous damage to individuals, families, and communities. Alcohol is really the sabotage of so much of New Zealand society, although few really appreciate the damage it does. We are so focussed on not disturbing the average or moderate drinker that we do not realise the insidious effect that alcohol is really having on our society.

And it is not just New Zealand. The world seems to have an alcohol crisis, though many people are slow in coming to believe it! It has been impossible to write only about New Zealand aspects without referring to the situation in other countries, and we make no excuse for this. Lessons are to be learnt from other parts of the world and we have realised that many other individuals and organisations have similar worries and concerns about alcohol involvement as we have. People have been frustrated in their attempts to change governmental legislation with regard to alcohol.

Alcoholic beverages have been consumed by humans for thousands of years for religious, social, and cultural reasons. It has played various roles, especially in places where good drinking water is a problem. Globally, spirits, wine, and beer are the most commonly consumed types of alcoholic beverages, although, in some parts of the world, locally or home-produced beverages contribute significantly to daily consumption. Every society seems to have its own popular version. For example we have arrack in the Middle East, sake in Japan, and kava in the Pacific Islands.

In Judaism, over two thousand years ago, there were strict rules about drinking alcohol; drunkenness was definitely not the in-thing. When it comes to religious arguments about alcohol, people might say Jesus turned water into wine and used wine in communion, so it must be okay. Some people will argue that the problem is not so much with alcohol itself but how it is dispensed. These days a drunk behind the wheel is more dangerous than a drunk on a camel! Today we have fortified drinks such as whisky where the alcohol concentration has been substantially increased.

A profit driven alcohol system is unlikely to promote the public good and we now feel that unless the corporations can be controlled they will continue to make huge profits from unsuspecting and naive individuals. Although personal responsibility and self-control is the ideal solution, this is hard to maintain when alcohol has been imbibed as this undermines logical thought. A new attitude to drinking is required. Alcohol is not essential to life, though some may think so, and the ideal must be to encourage sobriety rather than some artificial minimal intake of the drug. The essential role of government cannot be ignored as one of their roles is to protect the general public from harm either by regulation or statute through its legal or public health departments.

A common factor in the love affair with alcohol we have in New Zealand is the central role of advertising and promotion of alcohol. Some of the cleverest minds in New Zealand are enticed to develop attractive and often humorous ways to encourage drinking. Nearly always they obscure the real results of alcohol intake and emphasise the social benefits of taking part in this activity. Their profits are enormous so they can afford to spend huge amounts in advertising, promotion and sponsorship to brainwash populations into accepting alcohol as essential to modern society.

We cannot ignore the fact that a major problem with alcohol is that it can be very addictive irrespective of a person's status in life. Alcohol is no respecter of persons, and the reader may be aware of people where alcohol has destroyed relationships and turned some people into paupers. However, some argue that alcohol in moderation is good for us so that we should not condemn it because some people misuse it.

This book represents a compendium of verified data on alcohol, examining nearly every aspect of its involvement in our community. There has been much that has not been included, but the many references listed will provide further information to an enquirer. The data available is enormous and we are left with the impression that our political peers have conveniently ignored this elephant in the living room.

Who is our audience? The book is written for anyone interested in alcohol, either on their own behalf or on the behalf of relatives, friends, or the wider community. We have tried to approach the subject with an open mind and look carefully and extensively at the documented research related to the effects of alcohol on our health and society. We shall refer to similar debates that occur overseas about alcohol, but we shall use New Zealand as our main example as we are very much a drinking nation. What is clear is that there is a general lack of knowledge about health aspects of alcohol, which we hope to provide in this book so that readers can make an informed choice as to their relationship with alcohol.

In chapter 1 we look at the chemical nature of alcohol and what happens to us in our bodies when we drink it, whether we are male or female, young or old. The concept of a standard drink plays an important role. We consider questions like: "Is there a safe level of drinking?", "What are the health risks with alcohol?, and "What is an appropriate parental role with regard to alcohol and youth?"

Chapter 2 looks in detail on alcohol and the individual, and what health and mental issues alcohol can affect a person, of which there are many. The age-old question and the source of much debate is "Are there any beneficial effects of alcohol?" As alcohol is mainly a social drink we look in chapter 3 as to how alcohol affects our society in terms of different ages, hospital admissions, crime, the economy, the role of the media, and sport.

Chapter 4 focuses on the alcohol industry, its tactics and industry messages, and its attitude towards social responsibility. In New Zealand there is some interesting history about the development of alcohol in New Zealand, and how the government has responded to alcohol issues and legislation. This is considered in chapter 5.

As this book is about alcohol, an addictive substance, it would not be complete without chapter 6 on addiction, looking at the nature of an addiction, why alcohol is so addictive, and along with some discussion on having low-risk drinking. We also describe some medications for alcohol use disorder, and consider the question of giving up alcohol altogether. In chapter 7 we ask the question "Where to now?" by looking at proposals from the New Zealand Medical Association in detail to reduce harm, and also consider an international perspective.

We then have an Appendix covering some miscellaneous topics such as some questionnaires relating to alcohol consumption, some help resources, and what the Bible has to say about wine (for the reader who might be interested, as it is a controversial topic). A lot of research has gone into this book so that there are about 440 references to articles from established medical journals and to some books. Throughout this book we also refer to the occasional news item.

We would like to thank Alcohol Health Watch in New Zealand for its regular emails on alcohol issues around the country, and also thank Dave Hookway from the Northern District Health Board for his regular and informative "Take Five ..." circular letters giving recent developments on alcohol.

Finally, our special thanks goes to Amy Hendrickson who has allowed GAFS to use her LATEX computer package, and has provided help on occasions.

GEORGE A. F. SEBER

*Auckland, New Zealand*

D. GRAEME WOODFIELD

*Hamilton, New Zealand*
*November, 2019*

# CHAPTER 1

# HOW MUCH IS TOO MUCH?

## 1.1 INTRODUCTION

The New Zealand Medical Association (NZMA) in a 2015 report said that alcohol (ethanol, ethyl alcohol) should be viewed as "no ordinary commodity". This is emphasised by an important book with that title produced by a consortium of international experts (Babor, Caetano et al., 2010). The NZMA noted that alcohol, among its many properties, has three important characteristics that differentiate it from other beverages, namely:

(1) It is an intoxicant that produces functional impairment in psychological and psychomotor performance.

(2) It is a toxin that has direct and indirect effects on a wide range of body organs and organ systems. It may contain carcinogenic contaminants such as nitrosamines, polycyclic aromatic hydrocarbons, and mycotoxins, as well as a wide variety of esters, phenols and other compounds derived from interac-

tion between the original plant material and the production processes.

(3) It is an addictive psychotropic drug; though not all heavy drinkers develop dependence.

Not a very exciting list! Some people do not recognise alcohol as a drug, even though it is classed as a "sedative hypnotic" drug. This means it acts to depress the central nervous system at high doses, while at lower doses it can act as a stimulant. Calling alcohol a drug is important (Kypri and McCambridge, 2018) even though drinkers might feel unfairly judged if labelled as drug users. But pretending that alcohol is anything but a drug is doing drinkers an equal disservice. It is a negative label not liked by the alcohol industry, which is not surprising. Some will say alcohol helps them to relax and therefore cope with stress. A New Zealand Listener article (Bowden, 2019) referred to a Scottish psychiatrist RD Laing who described drinking as "a way of coping that makes you less able to cope."

What about "organic" wine? It is wine made from grapes grown in accordance with principles of organic farming, which typically excludes the use of artificial chemical fertilizers, pesticides, fungicides and herbicides. However, its legal definition varies from country to country. The main difference relates to the use or nonuse of preservatives during the winemaking process. Irrespective of whether the wine is organic or not, it still has alcohol along with its harmful effects discussed in this book.

### Non-communicable diseases

Anderson, Harrison, et al. (2011), in discussing ways of healthier living, noted that the spread of noncommunicable diseases (NCDs)—in particular, heart disease, stroke, diabetes, cancers, and chronic respiratory diseases—presented an ongoing global crisis (Beaglehole, Bonita et al., 2011). They said that:

> Globally, two thirds of all deaths result from NCDs, with three fifths of these deaths occurring in the world's poorest countries, where NCD death rates are already higher than those in wealthier countries. Half of all disability in the world arises from NCDs, and they are the major adult health issue, particularly among the working-age population.

The main risk factors for NCDs for individuals are well known and similar in all countries. These are alcohol, a diet high in saturated and trans fats, salt and sugar, physical inactivity, and tobacco. According to the World Health Organization, (2013), they

> cause more than two thirds of all new cases of NCDs, with alcohol being the world's number one risk factor for ill health and premature death

among the core working-age population, i.e. those who are 25–59 years old.

Scocciantia, Cecchini, et al. (2015) stated that alcohol consumption was the third leading risk factor for disease and mortality in Europe.

Alcohol has long been recognised as a leading risk factor for disease burden, and has been linked to 60 acute and chronic diseases via a multitude of mechanisms, both through cumulative consumption and acute intoxication. In fact ethanol has been classified as a Group 1 carcinogen (highest rating for carcinogens) by the World Health Organisation's International Agency for Research on Cancer (IARC) since 1988, along with substances such as asbestos and formaldehyde (see, for example, Secretan, Straif et al., 2009 for other substances as well). In past days when people were asked what are you drinking they sometimes used the alternative question "What is your poison?" It seems they were better informed than expected! Because of these properties that contribute to individual and social harms, the sale and supply of alcohol is regulated in every country. As we shall see in chapter 3, alcohol also has a major social impact as described by Smyth, Teo, et al. (2015). They provided an overview of different harms involving a sample of 114,970 adults across countries at different levels of income. They found that:

> Alcohol consumption is estimated to be the third most important modifiable risk factor for death and disability worldwide.

### *The situation in New Zealand*

In New Zealand, with a population of 4.9 million people, 476 million litres of alcohol were consumed in 2017 (97 litres per person, including adults and children), consisting of 289 million litres of beer, 111 million litres of wine, and 77 million litres of spirits. New Zealanders spent more than $4 billion per year, and NZ households spent, on average, the same on alcohol as on fruit and vegetables. We find that 75% of all alcohol was sold from off-licences (bottle stores, supermarkets, grocery stores), with supermarkets selling around 30% of all beers, and 60% of all wines (Alcohol Healthwatch, AHW, 2018:12). Alcohol is freely available from supermarkets, especially with the extent of their advertising. AHW reported that there were significant reductions in overall consumption between 2006–2011 probably because of the economy, but not in later years apart from young people people (see later). Almost half of all alcohol in New Zealand is consumed in heavy drinking occasions.

### 1.1.1   Men, Women, and Alcohol

Women have a higher blood alcohol concentration (BAC) after drinking the same amount of alcohol than men due to difference in size as well as differences in metabolism and absorption, and such factors as body fat and water content. Women have a higher fat-to-water ratio and alcohol has more contact with the brain and other organs. Men therefore have, on average, more fluid in their body to distribute alcohol than women have. They both have a lifetime risk of death not only increasing with the number of daily drinks, but increasing at a much faster rate for women as compared with men. In addition, women appear to eliminate alcohol from the blood at a faster rate than men.

These findings may be explained by women's higher liver volume per unit of lean body mass, because alcohol is metabolised almost entirely in the liver. When dosage is calculated on the basis of total body water, rather than on total body weight, the age and sex differences virtually disappear (Kalant, 2005).

Some ethnic groups have different levels of a liver enzyme responsible for the breakdown of alcohol. Sometimes there is also a cultural aspect to alcohol consumption. For example, Zhang, Casswell, and Cai (2008) found that to be the case in China at the time when the peak volume of alcohol consumed occurred at 50–59 years of age. This reflected cultural norms around the use of alcohol in which it is expected that older men will drink both for pleasure and during the course of business. However, this was in contrast to what happens in Chinese youth where there are no expectations of drinking for a number of reasons (e.g. study, lack of independent finance, more time at home, or in educational pursuits).

### *Binge drinking*

Binge drinking is a world-wide problem. Its definition depends on the definition of a standard drink (see below) that varies among countries. However, it is 50 gm or more of alcohol, which is generally five or more "standard" drinks (World Health Organisation and New Zealand), or in the US a five ounce glass of wine at 12% of alcohol, or a 1.5 ounce of spirits 80% proof, or a 12 ounce can of approximately 4% beer. Binge drinking continues to be a public health concern, for example in the US with tens of millions of Americans drinking at dangerously high levels, particularly among subgroups such as women, older adults, racial/ethnic minorities, and the socioeconomically disadvantaged, thereby constituting a public health crisis (Grant, Chou, et al., 2017). Saitz, Heeren, et al., (2019) found that "approximately half of drinkers exceed low-risk limits." They also found that 73 % of those drinking risky amounts were still doing so two to four years later, while 15% of those not drinking risky amounts began to.

In 2014 it was found that in Sweden 40% of all alcohol is consumed by the top 10% of drinkers by volume; in Switzerland the top 8% accounted for 50% of all alcohol consumed; and in Brazil the top 2.5% consumed 14.9%. The Irish Times (June 29, 2019) reported that more than half of Irish men binge drink once a month. According to the Globe (2014, issue 2, page 3), about 11.5% of drinkers world-wide have weekly binge drinking episodes with men outnumbering women by four to one. Binge drinking is also more common in poorer countries, among single individuals, and those with lower educational achievement.

### New Zealand consumption

Alcohol consumption is common in New Zealand with 79% of individuals 15 years and over reporting drinking alcohol in the past 12 months (Ministry of Health, 2017). Women's drinking patterns have increasingly become more like those of men, with drinking to intoxication, binge drinking, and the consumption being common across all ages, particularly with young women. In 2017, 75% of New Zealand women reported drinking alcohol in the past 12 months, compared with 84% of men. What is serious is highlighted in a study by Wall and Casswell (2017) that looked at young females and their consumption of RTDs (Ready To Drinks). Those under the age of 24 who purchased RTDs ("alcopops") were shown to consume on average 24 litres of alcopops per year, which is double what the female age group above them consumed and more than the heaviest male-drinking group. They like it because it contains twice the alcohol content of a standard beer, and the sweetness of the drink disguises the alcohol taste. Also they are heavily targeted through social media and Facebook promotions. In 2018, Coca-Cola launched in Japan its first alcoholic drink, a lemon flavoured alcopop, in a bid to tap new markets and consumers. The product is aimed at a growing market of young drinkers, especially women (BBC news, 28 May 2018).

After an initial decline in New Zealand consumption rates for hazardous drinking from 2006–2011 due to an economic decline, the rate has increased each year in every age group that was over the age of 18 years from 21.6% to 26.6% for males and 8.6% to 12.3% for females, for the period 2011–2016. The heaviest drinking group were females with a mean age of 24 who consume 23 litres of absolute alcohol per year, compared with 9 litres for the general population. They had the dubious honour of making it into the top five countries when it comes to the highest number of female alcohol drinkers per head of population. What is concerning is that 46% of all alcohol sold is consumed on very heavy drinking occasions (Viet Cuong, Casswell, et al., 2018: Fig.1). There is a similar problem in Australia, where 35% of men and 20% of women drank to long-term risk; an average of more than two standard drinks per day (Callinan, Livingston, et al., 2018).

### 1.1.2  Under-Reporting

It should be noted that the under-reporting of alcohol consumption, particularly with self-reporting surveys, has been known to be a problem for some time due to non-response bias and memory problems (e.g., Wilson, 1981; Crawford, 1987). International surveys of alcohol consumption among the general population are known to underestimate the alcohol available for consumption (from government tax or sales data) by substantial amounts (e.g., around 50% in the US according to Kerr and Greenfield, 2007). This is supported by research that found that as people consumed more alcohol, they increasingly underestimated the amount they had consumed (a fuzzy memory?). Heavy drinkers are thought to be more difficult to contact and are less likely to respond to surveys (Goddard, 2001). Boniface, Kneale, and Shelton (2014) concluded that heavy drinking and non-routine drinking patterns may be associated with greater under-reporting of alcohol consumption, and estimates of drinking above recommended levels are likely to be disproportionately under-estimated. Also the under-estimation will vary with demographic or consumption-based subgroups of the population (Livingston and Callinan, 2015).

Boniface, Scholes et al. (2017) used the so-called continuum of resistance model to develop a method to correct for non-response bias in survey estimates of alcohol consumption in England. They mentioned a number of international studies relating to the problem of nonresponse in alcohol surveys. For example, a study by Meiklejohn, Connor, and Kypri (2012) found similar problems in New Zealand. A summary of some studies on the topic of non-response bias is given by Dawson, Goldstein, et al. (2014). Stockwell, Zhao, and Macdonald (2014) described methods of estimating the under-reporting. They found that Canadians substantially under-reported their drinking compared to sales data (spirits by 65.9%, wine by 38.4%, and beer by 49%). However, Casswell, Huckle, and Pledger (2002) developed a methodology that seemed to avoid under-reporting. They concluded that:

> The New Zealand National Alcohol Survey 2000, using within-location beverage-specific consumption questions, respondent-friendly coding procedures, and a CATI (computer-assisted telephone interviewing) system

with a relatively high response rate, has demonstrated that population-based surveys have the ability to account for the majority of taxable alcohol available for consumption in certain contexts.

A comprehensive sample of 40 cohort studies from 18 countries involving 1,876,046 participants was carried out by Stockwell, Zhao, et al. (2018). They found that the underestimation of alcohol consumption in cohort studies was less than in typical population surveys, and varied considerably with country (e.g., Russia 70.8%, Japan 3.5%). It was felt that the usual recommendation to use a global 20% under-reporting in general seemed reasonable for the time being. This allowed also for nonresponse bias. The authors also found that spirits consumption was underestimated by 65.9% compared with sales data, wine by 38.4%, and beer by 49%. Alcohol consumption was underestimated significantly more by younger drinkers, and by low-risk more than high-risk drinkers. Under-reporting did not differ by gender.

### 1.1.3 Standard Drinks

Before proceeding further we need to define what we mean by a standard drink, as labels on containers of alcohol (bottle, cans, and casks) in New Zealand are legally required to give the number of standard drinks they contain. Guidelines for standard drinks (units) are given on the internet, depending on the country. According to World Health Organisation guidelines, a standard drink contains 10 gm of pure alcohol (ethanol), and is the amount of alcohol the average person can process (metabolise) in the liver in one hour. However, a standard drink varies considerably with country, for example countries like Ireland, Italy, Poland, and Spain have the same as New Zealand with 10 gm, UK has 7.9 gm, Canada has 13.6 gm, the US has 14 gm (along with the Philippines, Chile, Grenada, and Mexico), Japan has 19.75 gm, and Austria has 20 gm. Kalinowski and Humphreys (2016) considered a pool of 75 countries that might have definitions for a standard drink, with 37 identified as definitely having adopted a definition. Most used the WHO recommendation of 10 gm. Because of the variations it is hard to make some country comparisons, especially when it comes to criteria.

The number of standard drinks in a container will depend on the size of the container and the alcoholic strength. The latter is defined internationally in terms of the percentage of alcohol by volume (ABV). The strength of alcohol in drinks varies considerably, as seen in Table 1.1.

For the strongest spirits, the term *proof* is used (and this has nothing to do wth mathematical proof!), which is simply twice

Table 1.1     Alcohol Percentages (ABV)

| Drink | Percentage alcohol |
| --- | --- |
| Beer | 2–6 |
| Cider | 4–8 |
| Alcopops | 4–5 |
| Wine | 8–20 |
| Tequila | 40 |
| Rum | 40 or more |
| Brandy | 40 or more |
| Gin | 40–47 |
| Whisky | 40–50 |
| Vodka | 40–50 |
| Liqueurs | 15–60 |

the ABV at 60 degrees Fahrenheit; for example 80 proof = 40% ABV. In practice the maximum proof value is 191-proof, as not all of the water can be distilled from ethanol. Compulsory labelling with the number of standard drinks in New Zealand only applies to drinks with alcohol volumes of more than 0.5% alcohol. (See http://www.foodstandards.govt.nz/code/userguide/Documents /Guide to Labelling of Alcoholic Beverages.doc for information about labelling.)

The blood alcohol concentration (BAC) rises and the feeling of intoxication occurs when alcohol is drunk faster than the liver can break it down. In New Zealand, a 330ml can of beer at 4% is one standard drink, or 0.7 standard drinks for lite beer at 2.4%; 30ml of spirits at 42% is a standard drink, and a 750 ml bottle of beer at 4% is 2.4 standard drinks. A 100 ml glass of wine (which is a small glass) at 12.5% is one standard drink, while a 750 ml bottle of sparkling wine at 12% is 7.1 standard drinks. If a bottle of wine contains 8 standard drinks and it yields four glasses, then each glass contains two standard drinks. In pubs or bars, the serving sizes are usually consistent.

Most people do not know why the standard drink is important. Nor do many drinkers know how much alcohol they have drunk on a particular occasion, nor how fast it is processed, nor how to pour a standard drink. In fact drinkers usually overestimated the size of a standard drink (e.g., in Australia, Callinan, 2014). According to the newspaper NZ Herald 8 December 2016 commenting on a research report, some people thought a glass of whatever size, even if it contains a third of a bottle of wine, was a unit (a standard drink). A 250ml glass of wine can contain as many as 3.5 units. A New Zealand survey confirmed that New Zealanders do not know how big a standard drink is, or how long it takes for the body to process one (Newshub, 2 February, 2019). They were also confused about how many standard drinks are in a glass (Stuff news, February 6, 2019).

A survey of 2000 middle-aged British women found many believed a pint of beer or large glass of wine was the equivalent of just one unit, when a strong pint of beer can contain three units (as noted above the UK unit is just 7.9 gm). The report also stated that middle-aged women were drinking three times as much alcohol as they should be.

Diluting alcohol does not change the amount (gms) of alcohol actually drunk. The amount of drink in litres multiplied by the percent by volume of alcohol multiplied by 0.789 (which is the density of ethanol at room temperature) equals the number of standard drinks. For example 330 mls at 4% gives us $1/3 \times 4 \times 0.789 = 1.05$, which is close to 1 standard drink (10mg).

### 1.1.4  Measuring Alcohol in the Blood

Before proceeding further we briefly consider how the concentration of alcohol in the blood is generally measured (e.g., in drink-driving incidents). We are familiar with so-called breath testing and the testing of a sample of blood. Since ethanol is exhaled with breath, a great deal of research has been done concerning breath alcohol concentration (BrAC), measurement of BrAC, and its relationship to blood alcohol concentration (BAC). Background to this and some history is given by Pavlic and Grubwieser (2005). In general, two types of breathalyser are used. Small hand-held breathalysers are reliable enough to justify an arrest, but are not reliable enough to provide evidence in court. They are generally based on electrochemical platinum fuel cell analysis. Larger desktop breathalyser devices found in police stations can then be used to produce court evidence. These generally use infrared spectrophotometer technology, electrochemical fuel cell technology, or a combination of the two. How the devices are used legally depends on the jurisdiction. Such instruments need careful calibration and there needs to be an awareness of the presence of any interfering compounds such as acetone for example.

## 1.2  IS THERE A SAFE LEVEL OF DRINKING?

We state right from the outset that overall there is no safe level of alcohol consumption (Burton and Sheron, 2018). Our general message echoes the words of a Guardian editorial (Sun 26 Aug 2018), namely drinking less alcohol is good for you. A massive study showed that consuming any amount of alcohol has health risks. An international consortium carried out a combined analysis of individual-participant data from three large-scale data sources in 19 high-income countries (Wood, Kaptoge et al., 2018) involving 599,912 current drinkers in 83 prospective studies and concluded that the recommended limits for drinking alcohol are too high in many countries. The study found that those who consumed more than five to six UK glasses of wine or beer (100 gm) a week had a greater risk of death from stroke, coronary disease, heart failure, fatal high blood pressure, and fatal ruptures of arteries in the chest. An interesting fact from the study is that they estimated that the long-term reduction of alcohol consumption for men from 196 gm per week (the upper limit recommended in US guidelines) to 100 gm per week or below was associated with about 1–2 years of longer life expectancy at age 40 years.

Dietary guidelines for Americans in 2010 defined moderate drinking as up to one drink per day (14 mg) for women and up to two drinks per day for men. Heavy alcohol drinking in the US is defined as having more than three drinks on any day or more than seven drinks per week for women, and more than four drinks on any day or more than 14 drinks per week for men. These recommendations are the same for the US Dietary guidelines of 2015-2020. The above suggested levels are in conflict with most health guidelines, like those which espouse health benefits associated with consuming up to two drinks per day. In fact, as we shall see later, the level of consumption that minimises health loss is zero.

### New Zealand standards

In New Zealand, where a standard drink is 10gm, the Health Promotion Agency (HPA) recommends no more than three standard drinks a day or 15 a week for men, and no more than two standard drinks a day or 10 a week for women; also two alcohol-free days a week for everyone. To reduce injury risk, the HPA recommends no more than five standard drinks on any single occasion for men and four for women (https://www.alcohol.org.nz/help-advice/advice-on-alcohol/low-risk-alcohol-drinking-advice). However, the New Zealand Cancer Society recommends an average of no more than two standard drinks a day for men, and an average of no more than one standard drink a day for women. These numbers treated as daily maximums are supported by the World Cancer Research Fund and the American Institute for Cancer Research. (They are also the new guidelines introduced in Switzerland by the Federal Commission on Alcohol Issues in 2018, replacing the 2015 guideline of no more than three standard drinks a day for men.) In a recent article in a local newspaper (NZ Herald, July 11, 2019), nutritionist Nikki Bezzant, who endorsed the message that no amount of alcohol is good for you, recommended the "123 rule", which involves one standard drink a day, no more then two standard drinks at any one time, and no more than three times a week. This means a low-risk of harm, but of course not zero risk.

Professor Jürgen Rehm, who advises the World Health Organisation, said drinkers should have no more than one unit a day (half a glass of wine) or risk dying from alcohol-related diseases. Also he said that the guideline of a maximum of 14 units of alcohol a week for both sexes should be cut to seven. A UK unit equates to half a pint of regular lager or half a 175ml glass of wine (IOL News, 21 November 2018). An article by Hartz, Oehlert, et al. (2018) raised a further issue. Two data sets with self-reported alcohol use and mortality follow-up were analysed involving 340,668 individuals from the National Health Interview Survey (NHIS) and 93,653 individuals from the Veterans Health Administration (VA) outpatient medical records. They concluded that daily drinking, even at low levels, is detrimental to one's health. Bowden (2019), in a NZ Listener article referring to research literature concerning women, highlighted:

> At more than one drink a day, the risk of breast, brain, stomach and pancreatic cancers increases, as does the risk of high blood pressure and strokes.

These health issues are discussed in more detail in the next chapter.

### 1.2.1 The GBD Study

A New Zealand news item (August 2018) and an article in The Guardian (26 August 2018) referred to a study (Griswold, Fullman et al., 2018) by a huge number of collaborators that gave the most comprehensive estimate of the global burden of alcohol use to date. The particular study is referred to as the Global Burden of Diseases, Injuries, and Risk Factors Study (GBD) 2016, and mentioned that alcohol consumption is responsible for 2.8 million deaths per year across the globe, with cancer the leading cause of alcohol-related death among people aged 50 years and older. It used information from 195 countries, 694 data sources, and 592 prospective and retrospective studies involving 28 million individuals on the risk of alcohol use from 1990–2016. It has two extensive appendices giving data and graphs for each country. (https://www.stuff.co.nz/national/health/106528251/experts- conclude -theres-no-safe-level-of-alcohol-consumption-after-global-study.)

It should be noted that the GBD study is not a new trial but a combination of a large number of previous observational studies, which is referred to as a meta analysis. A further recent extensive review of alcohol harm is given by Rehm, Gmel, et al. (2017).

The GBD study found that, globally, one in three people drink alcohol, including 25% of women and 39% of men. A standard way of reporting how much ill health is caused by a risk factor is the disability-adjusted life year (DALY). This gives an estimate of how many years of life are lost as a result of this exposure, either from death or ill health. Alcohol use was the seventh leading risk factor for both deaths and DALYs in 2016, accounting for 2.2% of age-standardised female deaths and 6.8% of age-standardised male deaths. Another study that also included drug consumption using the GBD data was given by Degenhardt, Charlson, et al. (2018), and globally found that alcohol dependence was the most prevalent of the substance-use disorders.

Among the population aged 15–95 years, the GBD study showed that alcohol use was the leading risk-factor in 2016, and is linked to one in 10 deaths in this age group. This goes up to one in 5 when fatalities from drunk driving are included. Also, the risk of all-cause mortality and of cancers specifically rose with increasing levels of consumption. For example, for one year, in people aged 15–95, drinking one alcoholic drink a day increased the risk of developing one of 23 alcohol-related health problems by 0.5 per cent compared with not drinking at all. This rose to 7% with two drinks a day, and 37% with five drinks a day. Before we proceed further we need to look at the concept of "risk."

### Absolute and relative risks

It should be noted that the previous percentages about alcohol refer to relative risk and not absolute risk; the latter could be quite low. For example, if the absolute risk (probability) of developing a certain disease is 1 in a 1000 (0.001), then increasing this by 0.5% (a relative risk) means that the absolute risk (0.001005) is still small. In statistical jargon, a difference can be statistically significant, but not clinically or physically significant. However, the increase is not zero and can contribute to increased health costs in a large country when multiplied up by the number of drinks and the population size. This is the case for example with driving accidents, where the probability of having an accident might be small. If we are very careful, we can reduce the risk, which for some might be whether or not to drive at night (because of night vision), or driving in the early hours of the morning after drinking. However, we may have to drive whether we want to or not (e.g., going to work, dropping off children at school), but we do have a choice to avoid risky situations. Even with a low risk of a driving accident, the number of drivers is very large thus giving rise to a substantial economic burden from accidents.

## *Is alcohol protective?*

The GBD study said that:

> Failure to address harms from alcohol use, particularly at high levels of consumption, can have dire effects on population health. For example, the mortality crisis in Russia is a striking example, where alcohol use was the primary culprit of increases in mortality starting in the 1980s and led to 75% of deaths among men aged 15–55 years.

New Zealand has the fifth highest prevalence of female drinkers at 88%, while the men did not feature in the top 10 in the study.
The lead author Griswold of the GBD study said:

> Previous studies have found a protective effect of alcohol on some conditions but we found that the combined health risks associated with alcohol increase with any amount of alcohol. The strong association between alcohol consumption and the risk of cancer, injuries and infectious diseases offset the protective effects for ischaemic heart disease in women in our study.

This is interpreted as no level of alcohol consumption improves health. The idea that even low levels of alcohol use on a regular basis pose health risks has been known in the literature for some time, but this information does not seem to have filtered through to the general public. Previous research suggested that low levels of consumption could have a protective effect against heart disease and diabetes, but, as noted in the above quote, this effect is outweighed by other health issues such as different types of cancer (colorectal and oesophageal cancer, and cancers of the breast, larynx, liver, and nasal and oral cavities), liver disease, tuberculosis, and road injuries. These harms are discussed in detail in chapter 2. The research about low levels of consumption having a protective effect is considered later.

We mention another study (De Pirro, Lush, al., 2019) that claimed that a single glass of wine or pint of beer may have a major impact on one's appropriate behaviour, i.e., inhibiting self-control and leading to being overconfident, including both the decision to perform any given action or to resist certain behaviours in light of possible consequences. This can potentially lead to unacceptable behaviours that may put people in danger.

### Reducing alcohol harm

In discussing the above GBD study, Burton and Sheron (2018) commented that the most effective and cost-effective means to reduce alcohol-related harms are to reduce affordability through taxation or price regulation, including setting a minimum price per unit (MUP), closely followed by marketing regulation, and restrictions on the physical availability of alcohol. Furthermore:

> Any of these policy actions would contribute to reductions in population-level consumption, a vital step toward decreasing the health loss associated with alcohol use.

Similar recommendations proposed by the New Zealand Medical Association are considered later in chapter 7. The Guardian editorial (26 August 2018) said:

> The report is right that many people should drink less than they do. Almost everyone should drink less than they want to. Perhaps the real benefit of moderate drinking is not that it protects the heart, but that it requires a little self-discipline.

In summary, the harm that alcohol can do in various ways may come as a shock to the drinker.

The primary damage in poorer countries is through tuberculosis. With more developed countries, where there is more drinking, the damage shifts to cancer and heart disease. The above study found that the increased risk of cancers outweighed any possible reduced risk of heart disease among middle-aged moderate drinkers. An interesting single finding is that two-thirds of the world's population do not drink alcohol at all. Alcohol is not so essential for living!

Given the variation of guidelines and the dependence of government policies on them, Casswell (2012b) asked the question of whether we need guidelines at all. In the UK, for example, there has been a focus on "safe limits" and subsequently "sensible limits", often in partnership with alcohol producers. This is without any policy aimed at reducing access, affordability, or restricting the marketing of alcohol. Guidelines may be useful, but they should not be regarded as a means of changing drinking behaviour, and thereby reducing any harm.

### 1.2.2 Future Standards for Drinking

The above findings mean that the New Zealand guidelines should come down, though in the interim they might at least give heavy drinkers something to aim for. Health Promotion Agency guidelines are to be reviewed in 2019. It is unlikely that the above findings will encourage many people to stop drinking altogether as it has been previously argued that many things in life are not risk free, with no safe level (e.g., driving and going on holiday). For example, although driving has a risk, it does not mean we should give up driving. However, driving does not have the same social problems discussed in chapter 3 that alcohol has, and, as mentioned above, for many people driving is not a choice while alcohol is. What we can conclude from the above discussion is that if people reduce their drinking, they will generally improve their health, especially for heavier drinkers. Like smoking, alcohol is very addictive, and the government should be proactive to encourage less drinking as it has been with endeavouring to reduce smoking as much as possible both through legislation, price rises, as well as education.

## 1.3   WHAT'S IN ALCOHOLIC DRINKS?

Having talked about harms from alcohol we now need to see why alcohol has this bad reputation. The type of alcohol in the alcoholic drinks we drink is a chemical called ethanol. To make alcohol, one needs to put grains, fruits, or vegetables through a process called fermentation when yeast or bacteria react with the sugars and starch in food giving up by-products of ethanol and carbon dioxide.

Wine and cider are made by fermenting the sugar in fruit, while fermenting the sugars in cereals such as barley and rye form the basis of beer and spirits. A drink's alcohol content is affected by how long it is left to ferment.

Vodka comes from the sugar in potatoes, beets or other plants. Spirits also go through a process called distillation, where a proportion of the water is removed, leaving a stronger concentration of alcohol and flavour.

Alcohol is also included in some medicines, mouthwashes, household products, and essential oils (scented liquids taken from plants). It can also be used as a disinfectant.

### Carcinogen exposure

Unfortunately alcohol drinking results in exposure to acetaldehyde derived from the oxidisation of ethanol. A WHO working group concluded that this acetaldehyde is carcinogenic to humans (Group 1) and confirmed the Group 1 classification of alcohol consumption and of ethanol in alcoholic beverages. This problem is discussed further in section 2.2.1 (*Acetaldehyde from alcohol.*) Alcoholic beverages may also contain a variety of carcinogenic contaminants that are introduced during fermentation and production, such as nitrosamines, asbestos fibres, phenols, hydrocarbons, and ethyl carbamate (urethane), a frequent contaminant of fermented foods and beverages. Lachenmeier, Przybylski, and Rehm (2012) list 15 known and suspected human carcinogens, namely acetaldehyde, acrylamide, aflatoxins, arsenic, benzene, cadmium, ethanol, ethyl carbamate, formaldehyde, furan, lead, 4-methylimidazole, N-nitrosodimethylamine, ochratoxin A, and safrole occurring in alcoholic beverages that were identified based on monograph reviews by the International Agency for Research on Cancer.

### Drug harms

Nutt, King, and Phillips (2010), in a study on drug harms in the UK, scored 20 drugs on 16 criteria; nine related to harms to the individual and seven to harms to others. They found that heroin, crack cocaine, and methamphetamine were the most harmful drugs to individuals (harm scores 34, 37, and 32, respectively), whereas alcohol, heroin, and crack cocaine were the most harmful to others (46, 21, and 17, respectively). Overall, alcohol was the most harmful drug (overall harm score 72), with heroin (55) and crack cocaine (54) in second and third places, respectively. With regard to harms to others, the Guardian (10 May, 2019) quoted a survey of 5000 over-16s across England that found that one in five people in England have been harmed by others drinking alcohol over the past year. It said:

> The most commonly reported harms related to less serious issues, such as being kept awake (8%) or feeling anxious or uncomfortable about another person's behaviour at a social occasion (7%). But nearly one in 20 people reported experiencing aggression—being physically threatened or hurt—or being pressurised into something sexual.

The numbers in the subgroups were small so care in interpretation is needed. Harm from other's drinking is discussed further in chapter 3.

### 1.3.1  What Happens to Alcohol in the Body?

As already noted at the beginning of the chapter, alcohol is classed as a "sedative hypnotic" drug, which means it acts to depress the central nervous system at high doses. At lower doses, alcohol can act as a stimulant, inducing feelings of euphoria, talkativeness and even aggressiveness as a person becomes less inhibited. After a drink is swallowed, the alcohol is rapidly absorbed into the blood (about 20% through the stomach and 80% through the small intestine), with effects felt in the brain within 5 to 10 minutes after drinking. Alcohol artificially stimulates the nucleus accumbens, or the pleasure centre in the brain, producing two main chemicals (neurotransmitters), dopamine, which is responsible for desire and craving, and serotonin, which is responsible for the feelings of satiety, and inhibition. In a healthy brain there is a delicate balance between the two, which is thrown off balance towards dopamine by alcohol.

Alcohol affects just about every biological system because it's a small molecule that goes everywhere in the body. If there is food in the stomach, alcohol stays in the stomach longer so more is absorbed through the stomach. An enzyme in the stomach also has time to break down some alcohol before most of the alcohol moves down into the intestines. Alcohol usually peaks in the blood after 30–90 minutes, and is very quickly moved around the body in the blood stream to all parts of the body, and stays circulating in the blood until the liver is able to break it down. Most (90%) of the metabolism, or breaking down, of alcohol to water, carbon dioxide, and products the body uses for energy, is performed by the liver. The rest is excreted through the lungs (allowing alcohol breath tests), through the kidneys (into urine), and in sweat. The liver can only break down alcohol at an average rate of one standard drink per hour. The kidneys filter blood, balance the amount of fluid in the body, and remove wastes (into urine). Alcohol makes the kidneys work harder and they produce more urine, with up to 10% of alcohol leaving the body in the urine.

Although not drinking to the point of becoming drunk is a common way people gauge how much they should drink, it can be inaccurate. Researchers who study alcohol abuse find that people with high tolerance to alcohol and do not feel the effects of alcohol after they drink several alcoholic beverages, are actually at a higher risk for alcohol-related problems. It is also important to note that even though a person may not feel the effects of alcohol they still have the same amount of alcohol in their body as someone who starts to feel intoxicated after one or two drinks. Their lack of response to the alcohol may be related to an increase in their body's alcohol tolerance over time. Some people are born with high tolerance; many people develop a tolerance with regular drinking (the nature of addictions).

It should be realised that alcohol has a greater effect for those over 40 years as the organs that metabolise alcohol, such as the liver and stomach, shrink as they get older, so alcohol stays in their system longer. As the total fluid in the body becomes less as we get older (due to dehydration), the alcohol distributed in the blood will be more concentrated. It will not be broken down as quickly as it would in the bloodstream of say a 20-year-old.

### 1.3.2 Number of Calories

A standard medium 175 ml glass of 13% ABV red wine contains as many as 160 calories; that is the equivalent of a slice of Madeira cake. And to burn off those calories a person would need to do approximately 16 minutes of running. A large 250 ml glass of 13% red wine can contain as many as 228 calories, which is more than a jam doughnut. So a person would need to run for around 23 minutes to burn it off. It is not hard to see that drinking alcohol can lead to weight gain!

### 1.3.3 Biology of a Hangover

We cannot talk about alcohol without mentioning what happens with after-effects and a so-called "hangover" after drinking. After a night of alcohol consumption, a drinker will not sleep as soundly as normal because the body is rebounding from alcohol's depressive effect on the system. Initially alcohol targets the GABA (gamma-aminobutyric acid) receptor, which sends chemical messages through the brain and central nervous system to inhibit the activity of nerve cells so that it calms the brain, reducing excitement by making fewer neurons fire. After more drinking, alcohol inhibits glutamine, which is one of the body's natural stimulants. When a person stops drinking, their body tries to compensate by producing more glutamine than it needs so that they end up with unnaturally low GABA function and a spike in glutamate, a situation that leads to anxiety. This also stimulates the brain while the drinker is trying to sleep, and stops them from reaching the deepest, most healing levels (stages 3 and 4) of sleep. This lack of deep sleep is a large contributor to the fatigue felt with a hangover (see section 2.3.7 for further comments about sleep and the stages of sleep). The severe glutamine rebound may be responsible for tremors, anxiety, restlessness, and increased blood pressure.

Alcohol also causes a small rise in noradrenaline, known as the "fight-or-flight " hormone. Initially, noradrenaline suppresses stress when one first takes it, and increases it in withdrawal, so that severe anxiety can be considered a surge of noradrenaline in the brain. The post-drinking feelings of guilt and stress have come to be known colloquially as "hangxiety (Guardian, 27 January, 2019, "Hangxiety": why alcohol gives you a hangover and anxiety").

Because alcohol is absorbed directly through the stomach and is a toxin, the cells in the stomach lining become irritated and the secretion of hydrochloric acid is promoted. Also, alcohol slows down how fast the stomach empties its contents into the small intestine, meaning food and fluid sit in the stomach for longer. These effects eventually lead to the nerves informing the brain that the stomach's contents are hurting the body and must be expelled through vomiting. This has the advantage of reducing hangover symptoms in the long run by getting rid of the alcohol in the stomach and reducing the number of toxins the body has to deal with. Finally, it is noted that it is not a good idea to drive when hungover.

### 1.3.4 Alcohol Used in Cooking

The use of alcoholic beverages in cooking has the purpose of adding flavour to the food but it may also change the texture of foods. Because of the low boiling point of alcohol (ethanol) relative to water ($78.5°C$ vs $100°C$), alcohol has generally been assumed to evaporate from foods during cooking. This is not the case. In fact Augustin, Augustin, et al. (1992) found that the six alcohol-containing recipes in their study retained from 4% to 85%, where it was believed that the differences were associated with the degree of severity of heat treatment. One very common use of alcohol is as cooking liquid in meaty dishes or as an ingredient in a sauce.

Recently one of the authors (GAFS) saw a TV programme which indicated that when alcohol is used in cooking a surprisingly large amount remains in the food. Despite starting to boil much sooner than water does, alcohol does not just evaporate away the instant it is heated. No other cooking liquid does, either. Cooking with alcohol can be tricky, and not everyone wants it as an ingredient. It is not always appropriate if you are going to be serving the dish to children, pregnant women, drivers, recovering alcoholics or to alcohol abstainers. Substitutes are available for alcohol and are available on the internet (e.g., search on "Cooking With Alcohol: Substitute Ingredients").

To determine the amount of alcohol left in food after cooking one has to consider both the amount of alcohol in the choice of alcoholic beverage used, the heating applied, the utensil used, and the cooking time. Predicting the rate of loss through cooking is therefore not simple, and there seems to be more alcohol left after cooking than one might expect. Ryapushkina, Skovenborg, et al. (2016) stated that for the samples used involving beer:

> The highest estimated amount of ethanol per serving was accordingly 1.28 gm which would be of little concern to most people.

However it is generally not zero and, as noted above, 10 gm is the standard drink for most countries.

With regard to wine, which has a higher alcohol content, the amount retained can be much higher. Mateus, Ferreira, and Pinho

(2011) found that for fish stew cooked for 45 min in a covered pan where the wine was added in cold ingredients, alcohol retention was 30%. However, for beef bib and hunter rabbit with red wine added to boiling ingredients and then cooked for 1 hour in a covered pan, the ethanol retention was 5%. An interesting table giving retention rates is given by the Office of Alcoholism and Substance Abuse Services at https://www.oasas.ny.gov/AdMed/FYI/FYI-Cooking.cfm which shows surprisingly high percentages of alcohol retained under a variety of preparation and cooking conditions. Using a flame to burn the alcohol will still leave a substantial percentage of the alcohol behind (Hansen, Kwasniewski, and Sacks, 2012)

There is also the question of food preparation with alcoholic ingredients that involves no heat application or that involves temperatures below the boiling point of alcohol. Alcohol's presence in significant amounts affects the energy value of a food as it contributes 6.93 kcal/gm of alcohol; a factor important to dieticians.

## 1.4 EFFECT OF ALCOHOL ON YOUTH

### 1.4.1 Alcohol and the Young Brain

As noted by Blakemore (2019), adolescence is a time of many changes, both physical and mental. She noted that many mental illnesses, including depression, anxiety, eating disorders, substance use disorders, and psychosis, first appear before the age of 24 years, and can persist throughout adult life. In the past two decades, large-scale longitudinal studies using magnetic resonance imaging (MRI) have revealed that the human brain undergoes substantial and protracted development throughout adolescence and into adulthood. Different types of tissue in different brain regions show varying patterns of maturational development. Adolescents are more likely to take risks and experiment when they are with peers than when they are alone. Their hypersensitivity to the opinions of other teenagers and social exclusion might lead adolescents to make decisions to avoid the risk of social rejection, even if it means taking health and legal risks. Alcohol can add to such risks. One of the problems is the use of words that have become derogatory such as "tee-totaller", "spoilsport", and "on the wagon" may encourage young people to drink even when they may not want to. We hear the terms "wowser" and "nanny state" also used a lot by adults in New Zealand.

Some young people begin to use alcohol during the period from the age of 10 to 15 years. This is not a good time as these adolescents experience dramatic changes in their biological, cognitive, emotional, and social development as well as in their physical and social environments. There are also physiological and psychological changes associated with puberty, further brain developments, and social changes within family, peer, and romantic relationships. In fact right throughout their teens and into their twenties, the brain continues to grow and change as the synapses that connect all the different neurones become more complex and efficient. Research shows that drinking alcohol while the brain is developing might stall or alter this process (cf.https://www.steppingstonecenter. com/how-alcohol-affects-the-adolescent-brain/). This could leave the young person with potential brain damage that they will carry with them throughout the rest of their lives.

### Effect on the hippocampus

Alcohol can damage or even destroy the cells that make up the hippocampus, that part deep inside the brain that is responsible for learning and memory. This is why some people experience fuzzy memories or "blackouts" after drinking. How well the hippocampus functions will affect how well a young person can learn and store short term memories, which could affect performance at school, work, hobbies, and when learning new skills like driving a car. Several studies have found links between alcohol consumption and significantly smaller left hippocampus volumes in teenagers and young adults. Also, Heikkinen, Niskanen, et al. (2016) found that excessive alcohol use during adolescence appears to be associated with an abnormal development of the brain grey matter.

### Effect on the pre-frontal cortex

The pre-frontal cortex is also affected by the consumption of alcohol. This part of the brain is implicated in planning complex cognitive behaviour, personality expression, decision making, and moderating social behaviour. This is why people who have been drinking might become irrational, overly confident or less inhibited. When a developing adolescent brain comes into contact with alcohol, not only is the pre-frontal cortex still in the process of maturing, but the alcohol might damage these brain cells. Pre-frontal cortex damage could affect how well a person makes judgements as they move into adulthood. The basic activity of this brain region is considered to be the orchestration of thoughts and actions in accordance with internal goals. What is unfortunate is that under most laws, young people are recognised as adults at age 18. However, a growing body of science says that we mature much later than this. Critical parts of the brain involved in decision-making are not fully developed until years later at age 25 or so. A female brain matures a couple of years earlier than a male brain (Lim, Han et al., 2015).

## Effect on the rewards system

Another part of the brain that is different in adolescence is that the brain's reward system becomes highly active right around the time of puberty and then gradually goes back to an adult level later. One of the side effects of these changes in the reward system is that adolescents and young adults become much more sensitive to peer pressure than they were earlier or will be as adults. This means that a 20 year old is more likely to do something risky if two friends are watching than if he is alone.

## Binge drinking

Binge drinking has been all too common with young people. One problem with this is that it is usually characterised by repeated episodes of heavy drinking, which leads to a great elevation of blood alcohol levels, followed by periods of moderate or null consumption. Such a a practice can lead to even more important brain alterations than regular alcohol intake. Teenagers who only binge drink infrequently (4–5 drinks once a month) have brain cells in 18 parts of the brain that are found to be thinner and weaker with less protective coating leading to poor, inefficient communication between brain cells. Persistent binge drinking is associated with verbal memory and monitoring difficulties (Mota, Parada, et al., 2013).

Adolescents are less sensitive than adults to some adverse effects of alcohol, such as the motor impairing, anxiolytic effects, and to hangover discomfort so that they can consume more alcohol before they feel the aversive effects (Gil-Hernandez, Mateos, et al., 2017). However, young people are more vulnerable to other effects of alcohol than adults for a number of reasons.

In addition to problems with brain development we have the following (Scott and Kaner, 2014): a typically lower body mass and less-efficient metabolism of alcohol; psychoactive effects of alcohol affecting motor control and coordination, which increases the likelihood of accidents and trauma; a typically low-frequency, high-intensity drinking pattern that leads to intoxication and risk-taking behaviour; and the fact that young people generally have less experience at dealing with alcohol effects and fewer financial resources to buffer them. As mentioned above, heavy alcohol drinking in adolescents brings a certain dysfunction of prefrontal circuits. Although this is not so clearly demonstrated in the neuropsychological tests used by Gil-Hernandez and Garcia-Moreno (2016), it was observed in the performance of daily activities.

An Australasian study (Silins, Horward et al, 2018) of about 9000 adolescents across Australia and New Zealand found that adolescents who drink weekly before age 17 are two to three times more likely to binge drink, drink drive, and be dependent on alcohol in adulthood compared with peers who do not drink. One of the problems is with special events. For example Lam, Liang, et al. (2014) refer to the drinking that goes in with school-leaving celebrations in Australia, where 17–18 year olds reported an average consumption of 18 standard drinks in males and 13 in females, which was greater than typical drinking levels. Moreover, 87% of them reported at least one negative outcome attributed to alcohol and/or other drug use. Piano, Burke, et al. (2018) found that American young adults who frequently binge drink were more likely to have specific cardiovascular risk factors such as higher blood pressure, cholesterol, and blood sugar at a younger age than non-binge drinkers.

A further discussion on the role of social media with youth is given in section 3.5 along with the youth association of alcohol with sport (section 3.5.1).

### 1.4.2 Other Effects of Alcohol

Excessive alcohol use in adolescence and is associated with academic failure, violence, injuries, unprotected sexual intercourse and later excessive use, alcoholism, and early mortality. For example, young adults who frequently binge drink were more likely to have certain risk factors for cardiovascular disease than non-binge drinkers. Those under 15 years of age are at the greatest risk of harm from drinking alcohol, and not drinking in this age group is critically important. With young people aged 15 to 17 years, the safest option is to delay drinking for as long as possible. For this reason, parents introducing young people to alcohol at an early age is NOT protective of future alcohol-related harm. If 15 to 17 year olds do drink alcohol, they should be supervised, drink infrequently, and at levels usually below and never exceeding the lower adult daily limits. After about 21, alcohol does not generally change the structure or architecture of the brain, though there can be other adult issues later.

For older youth (greater than 18), a survey of 289 students who satisfied the criterion of binge drinking (six or more drinks on one occasion) in the past 30 days (Sharma, Anyimukwu et al., 2018), indicated that initiating a change to drink responsibly or abstain from drinking would first require them to be convinced of the immediate advantages to health, relationships, and school grades. In addition, participants noted that confidence in their ability to change, either from a belief in themselves or a higher power, as well as a change in their physical environment such as moving out of a fraternity house where drinking is prevalent, would be necessary for change. In brief there is a need to get the health message across and encourage avoidance of a drinking environment.

One of the problems is the use of alcohol to deal with mental problems. For example, the Irish Times (May 21, 2019) stated that almost two-thirds of people under 25 years of age in Ireland drink alcohol as a coping mechanism. The coping mechanisms cited were: "to cheer you up when you are in a bad mood or stressed"; "to forget about your problems"; or "because it helps you when you feel depressed or anxious".

### 1.4.3 New Zealand Scene

Alcohol is widely used and misused by children and young people in New Zealand, with estimates suggesting that over 1 in 3 young people aged 12 to 16 engage in binge drinking (Fortune, Watson et al., 2010), and a similar fraction of young people aged 16 to 21 engage in hazardous drinking (Wells, Baxter, and Schaaf, 2007). These data are particularly alarming, as mentioned above, young developing brains are far more susceptible than adults to the harmful effect of alcohol, so that alcohol can cause irreparable damage. We shall see later that there appears to be a reduction in these statistics.

A New Zealand survey of 16- to 29-year-olds by Huckle, Gruenewald, and Ponicki (2016) about context-specific drinking concluded that bars/nightclubs are inherently risky contexts for drinking by young people and improved controls are required. Drinking at others' home, private motor vehicles, and outdoor public places were also associated with consequences, and the authors suggested the need for increasing the price and reducing the availability of takeaway alcohol to reduce the consequences.

Another study, by Huckle, Huakau, et al. (2008) involving 1179 teenagers 12–17 years (under the minimum purchase age), examined the relationship between physical, socio-economic and social environments, and alcohol consumption and drunkenness. It was found that:

> Alcohol outlet density was associated with quantities consumed among teenage drinkers in this study, as was neighbourhood deprivation. Supply by family, friends and others also predicted quantities consumed among underage drinkers and both social supply and self-reported purchase were associated with frequency of drinking and drunkenness. The ethnic status of young people also had an effect.

Here "neighbourhood deprivation" is a measure of how a particular census area unit is deprived (Hay, Whigham, et al., 2009). People living in poor areas suffer higher mortality than those in wealthy areas. Environmental factors partly explain this association, including exposure to pollutants and accessibility of healthcare.

### 1.4.4   Some Recent Developments

Misuse of alcohol by children is an international problem. According to Bellis, Phillips-Howard, et al. (2009), pan-European studies reported that between 35% (Isle of Man) and 2% (Armenia) of 15–16 year olds have been drunk at least once in the past 30 days, and give a number of other negative statistics. However in spite of these gloomy statistics, there are some positive signs. A study by Oldham, Holmes, et al. (2018) analysed data from the 1988-2016 surveys on Smoking, Drinking and Drug Use amongst Young People in England, and the 2001-2016 Health Surveys for England. Both are nationally-representative surveys of young people in England, and covered respondents aged between eight and 24. They found that there has been a sharp decline in youth drinking across all age groups over the last 15 years. This indicates that young people are now less likely to drink and, if they do drink, they start doing so later, drink less often, and consume smaller amounts.

For example, 61 percent of 11–15 year-olds had previously consumed a full alcoholic drink in 2003 but this dropped to 38 percent by 2014 when the last comparable data were collected. For 8–12 year-olds, this fell from 25 percent in 2002 to just four percent in 2016. Also the average age at which 11–15 and 16–17 year-olds reported having their first alcoholic drink increased by up to a year for each group. Apparently one reason for drinking less alcohol is the constant social-media surveillance along with the need for control. Nights out are documented through photos, videos, and posts across social media where it is likely to remain for the rest of their lives, so that over-drinking is therefore something many seek to avoid. Nobody likes looking stupid on social media.

A study by Pennay, Holmes, et al. (2018) showed that over the past 15 years adolescent drinking has declined in more than 30 high-income countries. For example, in Australia, past-week alcohol consumption among 12–15 year olds went down by more than half between 2002 and 2014, while abstention rates more than doubled among 16–17 year olds between 2004 and 2013. Adults under 30 were most likely to reduce their consumption to improve their lifestyle, get more enjoyment out of social situations, and avoid violence. Those aged 18–23 were also most likely to stop drinking altogether because they didn't like the taste and found it too costly. Older adults found that avoiding drink driving was also a major consideration.

In the US, a study by Hingson, Zha, and Smyth (2017) of those aged 18 to 24 found that the percentage of college students who reported binge drinking (five or more drinks on an occasion at least once in the last 30 days) rose from 42% to 45% from 1999 to 2005, but then declined to 37% by 2014. For those not in college, binge drinking rose from 36% to 40% between 1999 and 2014. Those in college who reported driving under the influence of alcohol rose from 27% to 28% from 1999 to 2005, but this fell to 17% by 2014. For those not in college, driving under the influence declined from 20% to 16% between 1999 and 2014. The authors suggested two possible reasons for the reduction: (1) the economic recession of 2008, when less disposable income meant less money to spend on alcohol, and (2) the passage in every state of the 0.08% legal limit for blood alcohol concentration for drivers in 2005. However, in this age group there have been increases in overdose hospitalisations and deaths involving alcohol, both alone and in combination with other drugs.

### 1.4.5   Early Exposure

According to the World health Organisation (WHO), the average age internationally at which drinking alcohol first occurs is 12 years. About 80% of young people begin drinking alcoholic beverages regularly at age 15 or younger. Exposure to marketing of various sorts has been shown both to reduce the age of the onset of drinking and to increase consumption by young people (e.g., Anderson, de Bruijn et al., 2009). We have also seen the introduction of pre-mixed drinks (referred to as alcopops, ready to drinks (RTDs), or flavoured alcoholic beverages). These were introduced in the 1995 in New Zealand, and many are sweet and packaged to appeal to the young. Huckle, Sweetsur, et al. (2008) found that RTDs were most popular among young people aged 14–17 years, "entry-level" drinkers, and females. RTDs predicted higher alcohol consumption on typical occasions and heavier drinking more accurately than any other beverage for females aged 14–17 years. For the other age and gender groups, other beverages predicted higher quantities and frequencies consumed. This study and overseas ones (e.g., from Scotland, Wales, and the UK generally) showed that alcopops encourage heavier drinking. Young people often have problems in recognising alcohol in alcopops.

Early initiation into alcohol use is a risk factor for alcohol-related harm in young people, and for heavy drinking and alcohol dependence in adulthood. Also, early-exposed adolescents had significantly more criminal convictions as adults than non-early-exposed adolescents (Zeigler, Wang et al., 2005). Data from the Dunedin Multidisciplinary Health and Development Study in New Zealand (Odgers, Caspi, et al., 2008) showed that adolescents with no history of illegal conduct problems, when exposed to alcohol and other drugs before the age of 15 years developed problems. They were two to three times more likely than non-early exposed adolescents at age 32 to be substance dependent, to have herpes infection, to have had an early pregnancy, and to have failed to obtain educational qualifications.

We also know that drinking is one of the biggest risk factors for youth suicide (e.g., stuff news, Sept 13, 2012; Norström and Rossow, 2016; and the discussion paper https://www.pmcsa.org.nz/wp-content/uploads/17-07-26-Youth- suicide-in-New-Zealand-a-Discussion-Paper.pdf).Young people who have low mood, depression, or are feeling distressed are far more likely to act impulsively on those feelings and take their own life if they have alcohol in their system.

### 1.4.6  Association with Adult Drinking

Bendtsen and Damsgaard et al. (2014) carried out a cross-sectional study on 13- and 15-year-olds in 37 countries, totalling 144,788 children, who participated in the Health Behaviour in School-Aged Children (HBSC) Study in 2010. Their aim was to analyse how adolescent drunkenness and frequency of drinking were associated with adult drinking patterns and alcohol control policies, and their study appeared to be the first multi-level study of this kind. Although there was considerable variation among countries, they found that, cross-nationally, high levels of adult alcohol consumption and limited alcohol control policies are associated with high levels of alcohol use among adolescents. Their alcohol use is influenced by the context in which they live so that each person tends to adjust his or her alcohol consumption to other people within the same culture, i.e. the population tends to behave collectively. This is probably the problem in New Zealand, where there is a tendency to have a binge drinking culture that extends through both age and sex.

## 1.5  ROLE OF PARENTS

Based on surveys in 2013 and 2015, Huckle and Romeo (2018) reported that parents are still the major suppliers of alcohol to young people in NZ (for under 18s, 49% by parents and caregivers, 28% by other relatives, 22% by friends, and less than 1% by strangers). On average, suppliers usually supplied seven standard drinks. The report's lead researcher Dr Taisia Huckle said:

> The quantities supplied to friends and their under-age children are still too high, which reinforces the need for affirmative action on social supply at the policy, family and whanau and wider community level.

An Australian study (Mattick, Clare, et al., 2018) strongly refuted the idea that the parental supply of alcohol promotes safer drinking, thus rejecting the popular "European" model which says that introducing young people to alcohol at an early age reduces future harmful alcohol use. In fact the study found that the parental supply of alcohol to teens is associated with subsequent binge drinking, alcohol-related harm, alcohol use disorder symptoms, and increased access to alcohol from non-parental sources. Alcohol consumption is the leading risk factor for death and disability among young people age 15 to 24 years globally. Parental supply, which aims to introduce alcohol in a safe, supervised environment with the aim of moderating a child's drinking, is not associated with any benefit.

This finding is reinforced by another Australasian study (Silins, Horword et al., 2018), which incorporated four long-running longitudinal studies with up to 9453 participants between the ages of 13 and 30. This study showed in a series of appendices that those who drank at least once a week from age 13 were more than twice as likely than their peers to binge drink, drive while intoxicated, and have other problems related to alcohol once they became adults. Also those who drank at least weekly before age 17 had rates of alcohol dependence in adulthood that were three times higher than those who did not drink before age 17, and their risk of smoking cigarettes in adulthood increased by 60%. The answer is that parents should not supply alcohol to children.

A stronger view was taken by Colder, Shyhalla, and Frndak (2018) in a US study, who stated that even sipping and tasting alcohol with adult permission is risky behaviour. They found that allowing this is associated with more frequent drinking and an additional drink per drinking episode later on. It embeds the children in a social context that supports drinking. A European review by Tael-Öeren, Naughton, and Sutton (2019) using 29 combined articles from 7471 articles involving 16,477 children and 15,229 parents found that children whose parents had less restrictive attitudes towards their child's alcohol use were more likely to start drinking alcohol than their peers. They also drank and got drunk more frequently.

With regard to underage drinking in South Korea, Asante, Chun, et al. (2014) analysed data from 247 high schoolers aged 16-18 years old as part of the International Alcohol Control Study. They found that more than 56% of high schoolers who participated in the International Alcohol Control Survey had been supplied alcohol at least once. Of this number, approximately 59% were males. Parents (especially fathers) and friends were the main suppliers, with friends contributing greater volumes of alcohol. Of the number of students provided by mothers, 52% of them were females while 73% of respondents provided by friends were males. The most significant place for alcohol supply was at special events. The prevalence of underage drinking remains high in the United States. According to the 2015 Monitoring the Future survey, almost two thirds of 12th graders have tried alcohol, and more than one third reported drinking in the past 30 days (Miech, Johnston et al., 2016).

### Alcohol in the home

Parents need to be good role models. For example, they can minimise drinking at home, and have social events where they do not serve alcohol at all. Dr Kathy Stephenson (stuff.co.nz, June 12, 2018) said:

> If you're hosting a party, or your teenager is heading out to one, make sure you know the rules. As mortifying as it is for my son, I always make contact with the host's parents to check out who is supervising, what the expectations are around alcohol, and so on— usually by phone, but occasionally a text or email if I'm confident that it's well planned.

### 1.6  POLICING OF ALCOHOL RETAILERS

From frequent local new items we have found that in New Zealand there is a regular occurrence of retailers being found selling alcohol to underage buyers. For example, choosing a few news items at random, it was found that three out of 15 off-license premises failed a recent controlled purchase operation by selling alcohol to a minor (Auckland Council News, 26 June, 2019). Some New Zealand wineries selling wine online have been failing to check if the buyers are over 18 (Stuff news, 8 July, 2019). More than 31% of on-license premises selling alcohol in Auckland failed in selling to minors during Controlled Purchase Operations carried out in the past five months (One News Now, July 24, 2019).

Schelleman-Offermans, Knibbe, et al. (2012) carried out a longitudinal study in the Netherlands using a cohort of 1,327 adolescents (aged 13–15 years at baseline). They investigated whether intensified inspections on alcohol retailers, combined with a policy of withdrawing liquor licenses if retailers are fined twice per annum, is effective in reducing adolescents' probability to initiate weekly drinking and drunkenness. It was found that intensified enforcement was effective in preventing adolescent drunkenness. Also, effectiveness of enforcement could be increased by adopting enforcement methods with a high likelihood of apprehension, increasing social support for restrictive measures, and mobilising the community to be more outspoken against adolescent (heavy) drinking. An earlier study by Gosselt, van Hoof, et al. (2007) concluded that

> supermarkets and liquor stores generally fail to see the need for extra care when young customers try to buy alcohol. Legal age restrictions without enforcement and facilitation clearly do not suffice to protect adolescents from early exposure to alcohol.

## 1.7 CONCLUSION

In this chapter we have looked at what is in alcohol, what happens when we drink it (including the effect of a hangover), and the important role of the standard drink (which varies among countries) that enables a drinker to keep track of how much they are drinking. Men, women, and the aged are affected differently by alcohol. Binge drinking seems to be a universal problem and questionnaires endeavouring to find out about people's drinking habits tend to be plagued by under-reporting.

From very extensive research across many countries, the conclusion is that no level of alcohol is safe, but keeping the amount drunk small will keep any health risks low, though zero risk would be better. In this respect, current standards generally for "healthy" or "moderate" drinking are too high and need to be lowered. Alcohol can provide too many calories leading to weight gain, and a surprising amount can be left when it is used for cooking, rather than all evaporating.

Considerable attention is given to the effect of alcohol on youth, especially with regard to the developing brain. The role of parents and the question of early exposure to alcohol are considered in detail. Underage drinking is a universal problem and the chapter closes with the importance of keeping retailers honest in this regard.

# CHAPTER 2

# PHYSICAL AND MENTAL EFFECTS OF ALCOHOL

## 2.1 STATISTICAL OR CAUSAL RELATIONSHIP?

Since statistics plays a prominent part in our discussions, we need to consider an important concept briefly that can lead to some confusion and misunderstanding. It should be noted that a statistical relationship does not necessarily mean a causal one, an argument used in the past by the tobacco industry. For example, if the number of doctors was plotted versus accidental deaths for each year in order of year, there will be some sort of trend suggesting an increasing statistical relationship. However would it be a causal one? For example, both could be caused by an increasing population, which could cause absolute numbers of both doctors and deaths to increase together. Alternatively, as the number of deaths increases, this could cause more doctors to be trained. A skeptical person might say that an increase in the number of doctors has caused an increase in the number of deaths!

How then do we separate causality from just a a statistical relationship? In the case of alcohol we first identify substances that might be harmful, as we identified carcinogens in smoking cigarettes when the argument was originally put forward that there was just a statistical relationship between smoking and cancer and not a causal one. Then, secondly, we demonstrate possible harmful effects of alcohol that are consistent across a wide range of illnesses, and over different populations and ages. Thirdly, we look for a dose-response effect where an increase in the amount of alcohol consumed is related to an increase in the degree of sickness. These three conditions would provide very strong evidence that would be foolish to ignore.

### 2.1.1   Deaths Due to Alcohol

Worldwide, 3.3 million people die every year due to the harmful use of alcohol (World Health Organisation, WHO, 2014). This represents 5.9% of all deaths, and alcohol is also estimated to account for approximately 5% of the global burden of disease and injury. According to WHO, the number of deaths and limitations caused by alcohol exceeds those caused by tobacco use. In 2018 WHO said in their launch of SAFER, a new alcohol control initiative, that every 10 seconds a person dies from alcohol-related causes including cancers, heart disease, traffic crashes, and violence.

In the WHO Global Status Report on Alcohol and Health, 2018, an estimated 2.3 billion people are current alcohol drinkers, but consumption varies across regions. More than a quarter (27%) of all 15 to 19 year-olds are current drinkers, with rates of current drinking highest among this age group in Europe (44%), followed by the Americas and the Western Pacific (both 38%). Alcohol is consumed by more than half of the population in three WHO regions, namely the Americas, Europe, and the Western Pacific. Current trends and projections point to an expected increase in global alcohol per capita consumption in the next 10 years.

WHO said that some countries have implemented and enforced policies to reduce alcohol use already. For example, states in the US that increased the legal alcohol consumption age to 21 saw a 16% median decline in motor vehicle crashes. In Brazil, reducing the opening hours of bars from 24 hours a day to closure at 11 pm was associated with a 44% drop in homicides.

### *Alcohol and life expectancy*

Alcohol disorders have a big effect on life expectancy. For example, Westman, Wahlbeck et al. (2014) found that in Norway, Finland, and Sweden, people hospitalised with an alcohol-use disorder had an average life expectancy of 47–53 years for males,

50–58 years for females, and die 24–28 years earlier than people in the general population.

A large extensive study of 48,557 adult Russian deaths found that more than half at ages 15–54 years were caused by alcohol (Zaridze, Lewington, et al., 2009). In fact alcohol, mostly consumed as spirits like vodka, killed an estimated 600,000 Russians per year at the time (Parfitt, 2009). However Starodubov, Marczak, et al. (2018) noted that following rapid decreases in life expectancy after the collapse of the Soviet Union, life expectancy at birth in Russia improved after 2006. In 2016 it was 65.4 for males and 76.2 for females, and this disparity between the sexes was the greatest of any country worldwide. They found that in contrast to the previous study, they estimated that of those aged 15–49 years 34.4% of deaths in males and 20.1% of deaths in females were attributable to alcohol. Russia (together with other former Soviet republics, particularly Ukraine continues to be among the countries with the highest alcohol-related mortality globally. The authors noted that the association between mortality, alcohol, and social stress is notable for its enduring role in trends in the burden of disease in Russia.

In commenting on the above study, Rehm and Ferreira-Borges (2018) suggested that the reductions in alcohol use described above are likely to have resulted from policy measures (including the most effective policies; the "best buys") instituted over the past decade, such as the gradual raising of the minimum price on spirits since 2010. They noted that the differences between the above studies reflected different methodologies; however, both studies indicated that a high proportion of premature mortality in Russia was due to alcohol. Also they suggested that alcohol exposure and attributable burden statistics might be underestimated by both studies.

### Other countries

According to Bellis, Phillips-Howard, et al. (2009), Europe had higher levels of alcohol consumption per person than any other global region, amounting to 6.1% of all deaths. Rehm, Zatonski, and Taylor (2011) concluded that in Europe:

> The absolute risk of dying from an alcohol-attributable disease and injury (accounting for a protective effect for ischaemic diseases) increases with increasing daily alcohol consumption beyond 10g alcohol per day.

Also:

> About 25% of the difference in life expectancy between western and eastern Europe for men aged 20–64 years in 2002 can be attributed to alcohol, largely, but not exclusively, as a result of differences in heavy episodic drinking patterns.

In the UK alone, alcohol-related hospital admissions increased by 41% between 2003 and 2013 (Health and Social Care Information Centre, 2013). A large UK study by Roberts, Morse, et al. (2019) involving 1,657,614 patients from 124 studies concluded that about 1 in five patients in the UK hospital system used alcohol harmfully and one in 10 were alcohol-dependent.

Roberts and Drummond (2019), in referring to the previous study mention that there were more than 1.2 million alcohol related admissions to hospitals in 2017/18. Also the government's cuts to addiction services have placed an even bigger burden on the National Health Service (NHS) hospital system. People in England now have effectively less than half the level of access to specialist alcohol treatment compared to either Wales or Scotland. It is false economy as specialist care saves over £3 for every £1 spent. New Zealand may need to take note of this.

In Norway, three consecutive cross-sectional studies showed a marked change in drinking patterns (Bratberg, Wilsnack et al., 2016). On the positive side, intoxication (among recent drinkers) has decreased in both genders, but more in men than in women. However, abstaining had become rarer, while consumption and rates of recent drinking and problematic drinking had increased. Most changes were in the same direction for men and women, but women have moved towards men's drinking patterns in abstaining, recent drinking, problematic drinking, and consumption. As already mentioned, such trends seem to be global. For example in Thailand, where liberal alcohol laws were introduced because of vested interests and a growing economy, consumption of alcohol had since increased dramatically along with associated harms, especially road traffic injury (Thamarangsi, 2006).

### Heavy drinking

Scott and Kaner (2014), in looking at the heavy price paid by populations for heavy drinking, remind us that

> excessive drinking is not just the preserve of the young, and that public health interventions need to reach across the entire population and include middle aged drinkers, women and those living in conurbations where alcohol outlet density is often greatest.

As an aside, according to a news item from the Drink Business (17 January 2019), US alcohol sales across beers, wines, and spirits increased by 5.1% in 2018 but the US population is drinking less as a whole so that that an aging (60+) population is helping to grow the alcohol industry.

An extensive study by Rehm, Guiraud, et al. (2018) also considered some statistics for EU countries involving women and men with alcohol dependence and very high risk drinking level (VHRDL) defined as drinking more than 60gm and more than 100gm of ethanol per day, respectively. The estimated prevalence of VHRDL in the 13 EU countries examined was 0.74-0.85 %, with a disease and injury occurrence risk of 13.5 per 100 people with VHRDL per year. For a subset of nine EU countries, VHRDL caused 53.6 percent of all liver cirrhosis, 43.8 percent of all pancreatitis, and 41.1 percent of oral cavity and pharyngeal cancers. They concluded that:

> These results indicate that the health burdens of VHRDL are potentially large, and interventions targeting VHRDL should be considered when formulating public health policies.

In New Zealand, 802 deaths in people aged less than 80 years were attributable to alcohol (5.4% of all deaths), and 13,769 years of life lost (Connor, Kydd et al., 2015). As is consistent with other high-income countries, alcohol use in New Zealand is responsible for just under 4% of the total health loss (net of its so-called protective effects against cardiovascular disease), and is the largest risk factor for injury (Ministry of Health, 2016a). The figures are likely to be conservative because of the way they are recorded.

The BBC news (7 May, 2019) said that Northern Ireland officially recorded alcohol deaths are just the "tip of the iceberg" according to a coroner, and referred to an earlier BBC news item (14 August, 2018) entitled "Alcohol misuse 'biggest health problem in Northern Ireland'."

Although not generally mentioned in the literature, accidental alcohol poisoning is a cause of death. However, the numbers involved tend to be underestimated because the real cause is not always mentioned on a death certificate (Rehm, Gmel, et al., 2017: 971).

### 2.1.2 Alcohol Disorders and Harm

Rehm, Baliunas, et al. (2010) in a literature review provided evidence of a causal impact of average volume of alcohol consumption for over 23 major diseases, both chronic and acute, and injuries. We begin by looking at what has happened in several different countries.

### *US data*

Lundberg (2018) stated that:

> Of every 100 Americans who drink (140 million), about 12 (16 million) are considered in need of treatment for an alcohol use disorder (AUD), and eight will become chemically dependent on alcohol. Of those eight, one will become addicted very early, even after the first drunken episode.

He then goes on to say that a person might argue that if the odds are roughly 90% that they can drink without worrying about becoming an alcoholic, then they are pretty good odds. However, if you knew that when going to an airport to get on an airplane that there was a 1-in-10 chance that the plane would crash, would you fly?

Piano, Burke et al. (2018) examined high blood pressure (BP), cholesterol, blood sugar and other cardiovascular risks in 4,710 adult Americans aged 18-45 who responded to the 2011–2012 and 2013–2014 US National Health and Nutrition Examination Survey. They found that high-frequency binge drinking was reported by 25.1% of men and 11.8% of women. Binge drinking 12 times a year or less was reported by 29.0% of men and 25.1% of women. They concluded that:

> Compared with young adult women, repeated binge drinking in men was associated with an elevated systolic BP, and greater frequency of binge drinking in men was associated with a more unfavourable lipid profile. In young adults with elevated systolic BP, practitioners should consider the possible role of binge drinking and address the importance of reducing alcohol intake as an important cardiovascular risk reduction strategy.

Another recent study (American College of Cardiology, 2019) of more than 17,000 US adults showed that moderate alcohol consumption — seven to 13 drinks per week — substantially raises one's risk of high BP. This study is among the first to suggest moderate drinking harms, rather than protects, heart health. At present the US has a declining life expectancy and an exorbitantly expensive health care system.

### Australia

A study of 1608 aged 18+ Australians by Dietze, Room, et al. (2011) found that 10% reported experiencing either alcohol related life-area problems and/or physical/ emotional/legal problems as a result of their drinking in the previous year. Around 4% reported getting into a fight after they had been drinking and 6% reported adverse effects of alcohol on their physical health. There were a number of age variations. For example, 17% of the sample aged under 25 reported being injured or injuring another. Tobin, Moodie, and Livingstone (2011) considered further aspects of alcohol in Australia beginning with the statement that the consumption of alcohol in Australia is high by world standards. They found that 83% of Australians aged 14 years and over consume alcohol, one-in-five regularly drink at levels which risk short-term harm, and one-in-ten at levels which risk long-term harm. Furthermore:

> In addition to increased personal risk of morbidity and mortality, alcohol-related harm to third parties have become so common that the term 'passive drinking' has been coined to denote the impact of drunken behaviour on others.

## South Africa

Parry, Trangenstein, et al. (2018a) carried out a survey of South African households in the Tshwane Metropole using complete data from 949 adult drinkers. They found that 49% reported symptoms of alcohol problems, as a proxy for Alcohol Use Disorder (AUD), with white persons having 74% lower odds of symptoms of alcohol problems compared to Black Africans. Also people who reported stressful life events in the past 6 months were four times more likely to report symptoms of alcohol problems. Those whose primary drinking location was a pub/bar/tavern and "other club" were more than twice as likely to have symptoms of alcohol problems than persons who drank at home, while those whose primary beverage was wine were 74% less likely to have symptoms of alcohol problems compared to beer drinkers. They concluded that a substantial part of alcohol-related harm was accounted for by the drinking context, including where the drinking occurred.

As South Africa is considering a range of alcohol policy reform, Parry, Trangenstein, et al. (2018b) endeavoured to determine the amount of public support for 13 alcohol policies in the Tshwane Metropolitan Municipality and whether this varied by demographic factors and heavy drinking status. They found that public support from adult drinkers for a range of alcohol policies is extensive and, as found elsewhere, was strongest for raising the minimum drinking age (to 21) and lowest for increasing prices. The sample included 1920 drinkers aged 18–65 years and 53% of the sample were found to be heavy drinkers.

## South Korea

Along with a high consumption rate by world standards there has been a significant growth of alcohol-related harms in South Korea. According to World Health Statistics 2013, alcohol consumption (litres L of pure alcohol per person per year) among Korean adults aged 15 years or more was 14.8 L, twice as much as the world median of 6 L and highest among Western Pacific Regional Countries: for example, Australia 10.21 L, New Zealand 9.99 L, Japan 7.79 L and China 5.56 L. Compared to world statistics, the 1-year prevalence of AUD (Alcohol Use Disorder) was also high at 6.6% and 2.1% among Korean males and females, respectively. Another survey indicated that the weekly binge-drinking rate is steadily increasing, particularly among women from 12.7% in 2011 to 14.8% in 2012. There was a rapid increase of high-risk drinkers from 14.9% in 2005 to 19% in 2008. The social and economic cost of alcohol in Korea is significant, accounting for 3.3% of GDP, greater than other high and middle income countries.

Seo, Chun, et al. (2015) surveyed 2510 people, aged 15–65 and living in geographically diverse regions, who completed a questionnaire asking the support of 12 alcohol control measures. They found that female, old, and married people are more supportive than males, young, and single people, and targeted measures were more popular than universal. Most opposition of universal policies came from binge and frequent drinkers, which is not unexpected. The two most strongly supported policies were raising the purchase age to 20 (64.1%) and more controls on drink-driving (e.g., more random breath testing, 64.6%, and lowering the blood alcohol limit (0.05 to 0.03) for drunk driving, 49.2%). Some of the other policies scored reasonably well such as the restriction on the number of outlets (41.3%), earlier closing times for bars and night clubs (39.4%), and restrictions on alcohol marketing (41.1%). Part of the problem has been the reluctance of the government to introduce policies that are well known to be effective.

## China

In section 1.1.1 it was mentioned that in China there is an entrenched drinking culture, and binge drinking has been on the rise, especially among the middle aged where it tends to increase with age. According to Li, Jiang, et al. (2011), what does not help is the overwhelming popularity of spirits over wine, the profusion of alcoholic advertisements, and the fact that there is no age limit on buying alcohol. The authors found that of almost 50,000 people surveyed across China, 55.6% of men and 15% of women were current drinkers. Among current drinkers, men averaged 47.8 gm of pure alcohol per day which was just below the binge drinking level of 50 gm or more in a day, and had a true binge about once every two months. For women the daily average was 19.1 gm with binges about once every 5 months. They concluded that

> Excessive drinking, frequent drinking and binge drinking behaviour have reached epidemic proportions among current drinkers in China, and culturally appropriate public health strategies to reduce hazardous drinking behaviour are needed.

In an article in the Guardian (Branigan, 22 August, 2011) entitled "The rise of binge drinking in China" said "Binge-drinking is increasingly common for Chinese professionals—often it's even in the job description." The author mentions one advertisement for a security business that says, "Candidates with good drinking capacity will be prioritised."

## Japan

Higuchi, Matsushita, and Osaki (2006) said that for the last several decades, alcohol consumption in non-traditional drinking populations, such as women and young people, has been on a steep rise. Alcohol policy and prevention programmes, however, had not developed to adequately control these problems. Availability of alcoholic beverages, including to underage populations, remains very high. Legislation related to alcohol control has not been well enforced, with the exception of the Road Traffic Law. The significant fact about alcohol and drinking in Japan is that alcohol has never been regarded as a major social problem, and few measures against its production or use have been taken. In this respect Japan stands nearly alone in the industrialised world (Partanen, 2006).

Sake, Japanese rice wine, with about 15–16 % alcohol, has traditionally been the beverage of choice in Japan. The traditions of sake reach back to the beginning of rice cultivation and have been closely linked with it ever since. Religious meanings have always been attached to sake. Milne (2002) said that:

> Sixty percent of problem drinkers are salaried businessmen who claim that getting drunk with clients or coworkers is part of their job and a mark of company loyalty. To refuse a drink from the boss is a terrible insult that can damage a career. And although alcohol consumption is now decreasing in most industrialised countries, it has quadrupled in Japan since 1960.

Japan lags far behind Western countries in recognizing and treating alcoholism. Unlike many Westerners, the Japanese do not regard alcohol as a drug. The country's liberal attitude toward drinking means that alcohol can be found almost anywhere at any time of day. Alcohol is glorified in Japanese culture.

### 2.1.3 Alcohol in New Zealand

A common statement we often read is that the vast majority of New Zealanders that consume alcohol do so in a responsible way, without self-harm or harming others. However, as noted by the NZ Law Commission (2010:72), the statement is wrong as

> one-in-five drinkers and half of young drinkers usually drink enough to double their risk of injury; nearly one-in-three drink over the daily recommended maximum and so face a greater than 1:100 risk of dying of an alcohol-related disease or injury.

Boozing has become normalised in New Zealand. The lifetime risk of death attributed to alcohol increases with every drink for both females and males. In section 1.1.1 we described how alcohol affects men and women differently, and the effect on youth in section1.4.

## Age and alcohol

The following data is from a survey report by the Ministry of Health (2016b) and a helpful summary and graphs from the AHW (Alcohol Healthwatch, 2018). In terms of prevalence of past-year drinking, the percentage of adults dropped from 83.6% in 2006/07 to 79.5% in 20011/12, perhaps due to the downturn in the economy. The percentage then slowly increased and flattened out around 79.5% with 79.3% in 2017/18. For the age groups 15-17 and 18-24 there were downward trends from 2011/12 with 56.3% and 83.7% respectively in 2016/17; though still high percentages, we have decreasing trends, which is positive.

The story is very different with hazardous drinking, which has increased every year in every age group over 18 years from 2011/12 to 2016/17. As noted in section 1.1.1, for men, the increase was from 21.6% to 26.6%, and for women from 8.6% to 12.3%; overall 19.8% in 2017/18, involving 775,000 people. Also, 38.1% of young men (aged 18 to 24 years) were hazardous drinkers. The heaviest drinking group was females with a mean age of 24, consuming 23 litres of absolute alcohol per individual per year (compared to 9 litres for the general population). Much of this was from buying RTDs (alcopops) from off-licences. During the 2016-2017 financial year, 4070 people were hospitalised due to their alcohol consumption; some more than once.

## Older age groups

There is some concern for older age groups where prevalence and hazardous drinking have been increasing, being higher in the latter among older adults who were male, healthier, and wealthier. As far as prevalence is concerned, Towers, Sheridan et al. (2018) found that of those 50 or more years old, 83% were current drinkers. With hazardous drinking (Alcohol Healthwatch, 2018), the increases from 2011/12 were 50% (45–54 years), 75% (55–64 years), and 100% (65–74 years). In fact New Zealanders 50 and over were drinking more excessively and frequently than adults in some other countries.

## Heavy drinking occasions

In chapter 1 we noted that in New Zealand, we spend an average of about $85 million a week or $4.5 billion a year on alcohol (about the average spent on fruit and vegetables). This represents about 476 million litres of alcoholic beverages, or an average of 2 standard drinks per day for every person aged 18 years and over. Also 46% of all alcohol sold in New Zealand is consumed in very heavy drinking occasions, and there are many countries with higher percentages (Alcohol Healthwatch, 2018). Clearly this is where the profit from alcohol lies. In section 1.4 we considered the relationship of youth with alcohol, but we see from the above statistics that it is not just about youth, as there is an appalling drinking culture of middle-aged and older New Zealanders.

### Hospital injuries

Cherpitel, Witbrodt, et al. (2018) looked at data from 14,390 injured patients arriving at the Emergency Department within 6 hours following injury in 62 emergency departments in 28 countries covering five regions. They found that the more restrictive the alcohol policy in a country, the lower the rate of alcohol-related injury. New Zealand was ranked second for the number of injuries.

### Adolescent behaviour

While younger age groups have far more hazardous drinkers than age groups over 50, it was noted above that the proportion of hazardous drinkers in younger age groups (under 18 years) is dropping over time, while the proportion in age groups aged 45 and over is increasing. We find similar statistics in Australia where, according to the 2010 National Drug Strategy Household Survey, risky drinkers make up 30% of the Australian population aged 16 or over (Callinan, 2014). More recently adolescent alcohol, tobacco and cannabis use from 1999 to 2015, and was associated with similar reductions in parent favourable attitudes and availability of substances. They said it was plausible that the reduced tendency for parents and other adults to supply adolescent alcohol are implicated in the reductions in adolescent alcohol use observed across Australia. There is also evidence from 28 countries from 2002 to 2010 that adolescent weekly alcohol use in Europe and North America is decreasing (de Looze, Raaijmakers, et al. (2015).

### Weekend heavy drinking

Weekend heavy drinking is commonplace, and this occurs in many established market economies including the United Kingdom, some Nordic countries, Australia, and New Zealand. In New Zealand, it is common for drinkers to intentionally drink to become intoxicated, and this behaviour is widely viewed as socially acceptable (McEwan, Campbell, and Swain, 2010).

### Physical and economic harm in New Zealand

In New Zealand, alcohol contributes to violence, suicide, and injuries with more than 62,000 physical assaults and 10,000 sexual assaults occurring every year that involve a perpetrator who has been drinking. Of these, 10,500 incidents required attention and 17,000 involved police (Connor, You, and Casswell, 2009)). Apparently about one third of people that committed suicide have alcohol in their system. Alcohol also contributes to approximately 60 medical conditions, and is responsible for over 1000 deaths and 12,000 years of life lost each year (Stewart, Das et al., 2014). Some of these medical conditions are discussed in detail below.

Car crashes involving someone else's drinking were responsible for an annual average of 5,535 injuries to innocent victims, including 60 deaths. In a year, 147,500 adults take one or more days off work or school due to their alcohol use (Connor and Casswell, 2012). This harm costs New Zealand about $7.5 billion dollars per year (2018), which is far more than what is spent purchasing the alcohol or the tax collected ($1,012 million for Feb 2017–Jan 2018, NZ Treasury). Hungover employees could be costing New Zealand businesses more than $1.65 billion a year (Sullivan, Edgar, and McAndrew, 2019), which is said to be the tip of the iceberg. Researchers from the University of Otago surveyed 800 employees and 227 employers online across a range of industries to estimate the cost of lost productivity associated with drinking. They found employees calling in sick or coming in to work glassy-eyed and fatigued after a night out cost an average of $1100 in lost productivity per employee, per year. Clearly drinking has a huge cost on New Zealand workplaces both financially and socially. The alcohol producers must be doing fine as they spend approximately $400,000 each day or $150 million each year in promoting alcohol (https://tttpho.co.nz/wp-content/uploads/2016/10/10-Facts-A3.pdf).

### 2.1.4  Racial Differences in New Zealand

Alcohol also contributes to health inequalities as Māori (the indigenous people of New Zealand) as they have higher rates of hazardous drinking (31%), and are therefore at greater risk of some alcohol-related harm than non-Māori (Ministry of Health, 2016b). For example, the standardised alcohol-attributable death rate for Māori overall is about 2.5 times the rate for non-Māori. Likewise, the age-adjusted alcohol-attributable years of life-loss rate for Māori is about 2.7 times the rate for non-Māori. We note in passing that road traffic injuries were the most common cause of alcohol attributable deaths in Māori and non-Māori males, while breast cancer was the most common cause of alcohol attributable deaths in Māori and non-Māori females. Given the conservative methods used to derive the above figures, the net health harms of alcohol use in New Zealand may be even greater than those estimates (Wilson and Blakely, 2015).

Alcohol-related harms are disproportionately high not only with Māori, but also with Pacific and lower socio-economic population groups. Huakau, Asiasiga, et al. (2005) found that 57% of Pacific peoples living in New Zealand were drinkers compared with 85% of the general New Zealand population (the figures of course differ for males and females). However, that group of drinkers drank more on average (21 litres per year) compared with the general population (11 litres per year). Thirty-three percent of Pacific drinkers consumed enough to feel drunk at least weekly compared with 9% of drinkers in the general New Zealand population. The study concluded that:

> Pacific peoples drinking patterns appear to be more harmful with greater proportions of Pacific peoples reporting violence and injury from other people's drinking, and greater proportions of Pacific drinkers reporting problems from violence and serious arguments as a result of their own drinking compared with the general New Zealand population and general New Zealand population drinkers.

These harms may not simply be reflecting existing inequalities between ethnic groups, but may actually be driving inequalities. For example, there was a landmark report on the social determinants of health that listed alcohol (and other drugs) as one of 10 major contributors to inequalities that can be influenced by public policy (Wilkinson and Marmot, 2003; New Zealand Medical Association, 2011). Particularly outside of New Zealand, many Pacific Islanders seemed to lack understanding of cancer, including breast cancer. For example, inaccurate general cancer knowledge continues to overlap with traditional beliefs about cancer among Samoans; the same applies for Tongans (Mounga and Maughan, 2012).

## 2.2 ALCOHOL AND DISEASE

We saw in chapter one that ethanol is initially converted to a carcinogen acetaldehyde, and there can be other harmful substances in an alcoholic drink. It is therefore perhaps not surprising that alcohol consumption contributes to over 60 diseases and globally is the fifth leading risk factor for disease (Lim, Vos, et al., 2012). In fact alcohol has an even wider effect as it is causally linked to over 200 different diseases, conditions, and injuries, as specified in the International Classification of Diseases, Revision 10 (ICD-10), and described by Rehm, Gmel, et al., 2017). We list some of the main ones below.

## 2.2.1 Cancer

It appears that the link between alcohol and cancer is not well known amongst drinkers. For example, Cotter, Perez et al. (2013) concluded that in Australia:

> Less than half (48%) of the participants were aware that drinking alcohol could cause cancer and 51% were aware that limiting alcohol intake helps prevent cancer.

Also a report published from a survey of 2100 adults in England in 2016 commissioned by Cancer Research UK and led by researchers from the University of Sheffield (Gulland, 2016) estimated that 87% of people in England do not associate drinking alcohol with an increased risk of cancer. Yet there is an established link between alcohol and at least seven types of cancer (WHO news, 2 February, 2018): bowel (colon and rectum), breast, gullet (oesphagus), larynx, liver, mouth, and upper throat (see also Secretan, Straif, et al., 2009). The best evidence we have is for mouth and throat cancers where alcoholic drinks directly damage cells in these tissues. Moderate and even light drinkers are not exempt from some cancers as we shall see below.

Zhao, Stockwell, et al. (2016) found that alcohol is also linked to prostate cancer with a significant dose-response relationship between the level of alcohol intake and risk of prostate cancer, starting with low volume consumption. The relationship is stronger in the relatively few studies free of drinker misclassification error. Dickerman, Markt et al. (2016) found that binge drinkers were at a significantly increased risk of prostate cancer compared to non-binge drinkers. For some general statistics see Praud, Rota, et al. (2016).

A recent news item by the NZ Herald (29 May, 2019) based on a British study said that for men, drinking a bottle of wine a week increased the absolute lifetime risk of cancer that was equivalent to smoking five cigarettes weekly, while for women it was equivalent to smoking 10 cigarettes a week, mostly due to an increased risk of breast cancer caused by alcohol.

A study by Bates, Holmes et al. (2018) of 2100 adult residents in England indicated that support for alcohol policies was greater among individuals who are aware of the link between alcohol and cancer. As already noted, a large proportion of people are unaware of the alcohol-cancer link so that increasing awareness may be an effective approach to increasing support for alcohol policies. The New Zealand Cancer Society said that:

> The level of public awareness of the relationship between alcohol and cancer is not known in New Zealand.

We now look at some European studies.

## European studies

A large study, which is still ongoing, called the European Prospective Investigation into Cancer and Nutrition (EPIC) study with 109,118 men and 254,870 women, mainly aged 37–70, was carried out in eight countries (France, Italy, Spain, UK, the Netherlands, Greece, Germany, Denmark) to investigate the relative risk of cancer incidence for former and current alcohol consumption (Schütze, Boeing, et al., 2011). Assuming causality, 10% of men and 3% of women attributed the total cancer incidence to former and current alcohol consumption. This includes considerable proportion of the most common and most lethal cancers. The data was broken down to different types of cancer.

A substantial part of the alcohol attributable cancer cases was associated with consumption of more than two standard drinks per day for men or more than one for women. Many cancer cases could have been avoided if alcohol consumption was limited to two standard drinks per day in men and one standard drink per day in women, which are the recommendations of many health organisations. We find then that even moderate drinking increases the risk of cancer and the risk increases with every drink. The British Million Women Study (Allen, Beral, et al., 2009) showed that just one drink a day significantly increased the risk for cancer. It appears that among women the major cause of death by far during their middle years is cancer.

An article by the Guardian (3 July 2017) entitled "Britons are among most at-risk in Europe for alcohol-related cancers" said that

> Britons consume an average of 2.1 alcoholic drinks every day, just above the two drinks threshold that significantly increases the risk of being diagnosed with either bowel or oesophageal cancer. Those two drinks are enough to raise a person's risk of getting bowel cancer by 21%. Anyone having four or more drinks a day is at risk of three other cancers: liver, gastric and pancreatic cancer.

It has been suggested that a heavy drinker should be screened for liver cancer regardless of age.

The average across 28 EU nations was 1.9 standard drinks per day. The Alcohol Health Alliance was quoted in the article as saying that as awareness of the link between drink and cancer is so low at just 10%, alcohol manufacturers should be forced to put health warnings on the labels of cans and bottles. We believe that warning panels should also be on advertisements for alcohol.

A very big meta-survey involving a total of 572 studies published between 1956 and 2012 involving a total of 486,538 cancer cases and 22 cancer types that met the inclusion criteria, was carried out by Bagnardi, Rota et al. (2015). The study showed the pervasive affect of alcohol, and that the risk of developing these cancers appears to show a dose-risk response, meaning the more a person drinks the greater the risk. For example, a heavy consumption of alcohol appears to increase the risk of gastric and pancreatic cancer. A meta-analysis concluded that "moderate" (2-3 standard drinks per day) and "heavy" ($\geq 4$ standard drinks per day) consumption of alcohol was associated with an increase in the risk of colorectal cancer of 21% and 52%, respectively (Fedirko, Tramacere et al., 2011). Further details of cancer risk are given in the review by Zhou, Zhen, et al. (2016). The Cancer Society of New Zealand recommends that people limit the amount of alcohol they consume or do not drink alcohol at all if they wish to reduce their risk of developing cancer.

### US studies

Two large prospective studies in the US (88,084 women and 47,881 men) by Cao, Willett, et al. (2015) concluded that:

> Light to moderate drinking is associated with minimally increased risk of overall cancer. For men who have never smoked, risk of alcohol related cancers is not appreciably increased for light and moderate drinking (up to two drinks per day). However, for women who have never smoked, risk of alcohol related cancers (mainly breast cancer) increases even within the range of up to one alcoholic drink a day.

A further US study (Gapstur, Drope, et al., 2018) estimated that more than 1.7 million people will be diagnosed with cancer, and more than 600,000 will die of the disease in 2018. They listed modifiable risk factors for cancer risk and reduction, namely tobacco, alcohol, excess body weight, poor diet, and physical inactivity. Also alcoholic beverage consumption is a major contributor to cancer among women (6.4%) and men (4.8%). One study referred to found that, compared with lifelong abstention, heavy drinking ($\geq 3$ US standard drinks per day) was associated with increased risk for five cancer types: upper airway/digestive tract, lung, female breast, colorectal, and melanoma, with light-to-moderate drinking related to all but lung cancer.

### Some global statistics

Stokowski (2015) has an extensive article where she also gives a good general description of some of the problems with alcohol and some fact and figures. For example, the World Cancer Report released in 2014 highlighted the role of alcohol in cancer, finding that alcohol accounts for 3.5% of cancers (about 1 in 30 cancer deaths) globally. Recent data indicate that the proportion of cancers attributable to alcohol worldwide has increased. For example, in 2012, alcohol consumption was found to have caused 5.5% of all cancer cases and 5.8% of all cancer deaths. This increase is believed to be attributable primarily to an increase in the prevalence of drinkers and in the amount of alcohol consumed, particularly by women. The increased risk for cancer appears to be significant at lower levels of alcohol consumption in women than in men. Total alcohol consumption rather than regularity of drinking or heavy episodic drinking seems to drive the association between alcohol consumption and risk for cancer.

Alcohol may increase the risk of cancer in ways described below (cf. Sherafatmanesh, Ekramzadeh, and Akbarzadeh, 2017 for some technicalities). We first begin with the formation of acetaldehyde.

### Acetaldehyde from alcohol

Ethanol is oxidised to acetaldehyde, the first and most toxic metabolite of alcohol metabolism. This is a highly reactive toxic chemical with mutagenic and carcinogenic effects that can damage both DNA and proteins, and cause gross chromosomal aberrations discussed further below. Acetaldehyde can also interfere with DNA repair mechanisms. It is similar in structure to the poison formaldehyde. Acetaldehyde concentrations in different alcoholic beverages might explain some of the variations in cancer risk associated with beverage types. The highest acetaldehyde concentration is generally found in fortified wines (118 mg/L), followed by spirits (66 mg/L), wine (34 mg/L) and beer (9 mg/L) (Zhou, Zheng, et al., 2016). Acetaldehyde gets broken down in the liver by a second enzyme acetaldehyde dehydrogenase (ALDH) into acetate, which human cells can use as a source of energy. This means that provided there is not too much alcohol, acetaldehyde does not usually have time to build up or last long enough to cause significant DNA damage. However, this protection mechanism can be overwhelmed once alcohol is in the bloodstream, meaning it does not work properly.

Acetaldehyde can cause errors in DNA called point mutations where one base (or "letter") in a gene is swapped for another, and trigger larger-scale changes to our DNA by interfering with entire chromosomes by causing bits of chromosomes to break off and to swap around. It has also been shown to bind to DNA forming clumps called adducts that are another type of mutation, which can play havoc with how the DNA works. For further information about the chemical reactions involved see Seitz and Becker (2007) and Seitz and Mueller (2015). There are other cancer-causing mechanisms that we are still learning about. A study by researchers at Rutgers University (Gangisetty, Sinha, and Sarkar, 2019) found that binge drinking can trigger genetic changes, particularly to two genes that make people crave alcohol even more. It suggests that alcohol use causes epigenetic changes that may reinforce addiction, and these changes can be hereditary.

Some people develop a distinctive facial flush after drinking alcohol, when their face turns either slightly or very red. The red facial flush happens because the blood vessels in the face dilate in response to these toxins. In some people, this can happen after very little alcohol. If a person is sensitive to alcohol or has a lot to drink, their body may not be able to manage all of those toxins, and acetaldehyde can begin to build up in the body. This side effect of drinking alcohol is more common in people of East Asian descent. Although it does not cause immediate health problems, it may signal an increased risk of some serious health issues, such as high blood pressure and certain types of cancer.

## Further cancer risks from alcohol

(1) There is an accumulation of acetaldehyde in the saliva and intestinal contents during and after the consumption of alcohol, which limits the ability of oral microbes and mucous membranes to detoxify it.

(2) Alcohol generates reactive oxygen species or ROS (chemically reactive molecules that contain oxygen), which can damage DNA, proteins, and lipids (fats) through a process called oxidation.

(3) Alcohol impairs the body's ability to break down and absorb a variety of nutrients that may be associated with cancer risk, including vitamin A; nutrients in the vitamin B complex, such as folate; vitamin C; vitamin D; vitamin E; and carotenoids.

(4) Alcohol increases blood levels of oestrogen, a sex hormone linked to the risk of breast cancer.

(5 Ethyl carbamate (urethane) is a frequent carcinogenic contaminant of fermented foods and beverages (including alcohol).

## Red wine and cancer

A question sometimes asked is "Can drinking red wine help prevent cancer?" Researchers conducting studies using purified proteins, human cells, and laboratory animals have found that certain substances in red wine, such as resveratrol, have anticancer properties (Athar, Back, et al., 2007). Grapes, raspberries, peanuts, and some other plants also contain resveratrol. It transpires that the amount in red wine is negligible, and clinical trials in humans have not provided evidence that resveratrol is effective in preventing or treating some cancers (e.g., Patel, Scott, et al., 2011).

Studies looking for a positive or negative association between moderate red wine consumption and cancer in humans are still ongoing. For example, Chao, Hague, et al. (2010) found that moderate red wine consumption was not associated with reduced risk of colorectal cancer in a population of middle-aged men. On the other hand, Vartolomei, Kimura, et al. (2018) found that consumption of white wine increased the risk of prostate cancer, whereas moderate consumption of red wine had a slight protective effect. There is growing evidence that any health benefits of red wine are related to its nonalcoholic components. When it comes to white wine or red wine, red wine tends to have more sulphites, a preservative in wine, and that can irritate those who suffer from asthma or migraines. .

## What if I stop drinking?

Another question of interest is whether cancer risk declines after a person stops drinking alcohol. Most of the studies relating to this question have been focused on head, neck, and oesophageal cancers. They have found that stopping alcohol consumption is not associated with immediate reductions in cancer risk; instead, it may take years for the risks of cancer to return to those of never drinkers. For example, Rehm, Patra, and Popova (2007) carried out a pooled analysis of 13 case-control studies of cancer of the oral cavity and pharynx combined and found that alcohol-associated cancer risk did not begin to decrease until at least 10 years after stopping alcohol drinking. Even 16 years after they stopped drinking, the risk of cancer was still higher for ex-drinkers than for never drinkers. In the case of oesophageal cancer, a pooled analysis of five case-control studies found that the risk of oesophageal cancer did not approach that of never drinkers for at least 15 years after stopping alcohol drinking.

Park, Ryu, and Cho (2017) analysed cohort data from 9001 Korean participants aged 40–69 years old to see whether health changes affect cessation of alcohol consumption and to compare the health status of former drinkers and abstainers. They found that there was a significant association between disease onset or treatment and alcohol cessation for cancer cases, but not for cardiovascular disease or chronic disease cases. Sex, age and worsened perception of health were significantly associated with cessation of drinking.

### 2.2.2  Cardiovascular Disease

A common belief is that red wine in moderation provides some cardiovascular protection (Lippi, Franchini, and Guidi, 2010), and people have been particularly referred to what has been happening in France. Some studies have suggested that moderate drinkers live longer than abstainers. The problem here is that the relationship between alcohol and cardiovascular disease is complex as alcohol has a number of physiological effects on the cardiovascular system. For example, moderate regular consumption can increase high-density lipoproteins and inhibit platelet activation and fibrinolytic factors—effects that may contribute to a cardio-protective association, though this is debated. Episodes of heavy drinking increase blood pressure, fibrinolytic factors, and ventricular arrhythmias, which increase the risks of cardiovascular disease and may counter any cardio-protective effects of low to moderate consumption. However, the so-called protective effect of alcohol and related studies have come up for criticism. This question is considered in more detail in section 2.6 below.

Wood, Kaptoge, et al. (2018) carried out a study involving almost 600,000 current drinkers without previous cardiovascular disease from 83 prospective studies using three large-scale data sources in 19 high-income countries. They concluded that very moderate drinking, about 100gm a week (10 New Zealand standard drinks a week or one standard US drink a day), lowers the rate of certain kinds of heart attacks but raises the risk of other cardiovascular problems. In particular:

> For cardiovascular disease subtypes other than myocardial infarction, there were no clear thresholds below which lower alcohol consumption stopped being associated with a lower disease risk. These data support adoption of lower limits of alcohol consumption than are recommended in most current guidelines.

### 2.2.3  Liver Disease

Liver diseases caused by alcohol consumption are collectively called alcoholic liver diseases. The first of these to appear is fatty liver, characterised by increased fat inside liver cells. Fatty liver develops in 90% of those who drink more than 16 gm (about half an ounce) of alcohol per day, and is usually symptomless and fully reversible. In heavy drinkers, binge drinking may cause the liver to become inflamed. In worst case scenarios, liver cells die and get replaced with scar tissue, leading to a serious condition called cirrhosis. This is irreversible and associated with many serious health problems. In advanced cirrhosis, getting a liver transplant may be the only option. Part of the problem is that cirrhosis is not always obvious as people can look normal, have normal blood tests, normal ultra sounds and CT scans and still have cirrhosis (North and South, September, 2018, "What's your poison?"). For a review see Rehm, Taylor, et al. (2010). It has been suggested that a heavy drinker should be screened for liver cancer regardless of age.

### 2.2.4   Breast Cancer

Jung, Wang, et al. (2016) analysed data from the followup of 1,089,273 women from a number of countries (Australia, Japan, Netherlands, US, and Sweden, and various ethnicities) during a maximum of 6–18 years and concluded that alcohol consumption was positively associated with risk of breast cancer, even among women with high folate intake. Associations were similar for alcohol intake from beer, wine, or liquor.

Breast cancer is the leading cause of alcohol-related death for both Māori and non-Māori New Zealand women. From the World Cancer Research Fund (2018), New Zealand was ranked the 10th highest country for breast cancer with an age-standardised rate per 100,000 of 92.6; Australia is the 7th highest with 94.5. The highest countries are Belgium (113.2), Luxembourg (109.3), and the Netherlands (105.9). (cf. https://www.wcrf.org/dietandcancer/cancer-trends/breast-cancer-statistics).

It has been known for some time that just one standard drink per day can increase the risk of breast cancer in women, and there is a 10% increase in the risk of breast cancer for each extra standard drink consumed per day, with no known safe threshold. These figures from Key, Hodgson et al. (2006) were based on a so-called meta-analysis of 98 studies involving 75,728 cases in drinker versus non-drinker, and 60,953 cases for dose-response analyses. Consumption of three or more standard drinks per day was estimated to increase the risk of breast cancer by 40-50%.

In another paper involving a large meta-analysis of global studies reviewed to November 2011 by Seitz, Pelucchi et al. (2012) on light alcohol drinking came up with similar conclusions, namely: (1) there is a significant increase of around 4% in the risk of breast cancer for those drinking up to one alcoholic drink per day, and (2) there is an increase of 40–50% for those drinking three or more drinks per day. These numbers translate into up to 5% of breast cancers attributable to alcohol in northern Europe and North America for a total of approximately 50,000 alcohol-attributable cases of breast cancer worldwide. Also up to 1–2% of breast cancers in Europe and North America are attributable to light drinking alone.

A study by Romieu, Scoccianti, et al. (2015) involving 10 European countries found that using 0 to 5 gm per day as a reference point, alcohol intake of greater than 5 to 15 gm per day was related to a 5.9% increase in breast cancer risk. Also:

> Breast cancer risk was stronger among women who started drinking prior to first full-time pregnancy. Overall, our results confirm the association between alcohol intake and both hormone receptor positive and hormone receptor negative breast tumors, suggesting that timing of exposure to alcohol drinking may affect the risk.

Connor, Kydd, et al. (2017) found that around 20 New Zealand women die each year from breast cancer linked to consuming no more than two standard drinks a day on average. It is recommended that women should not exceed one standard drink per day. Alcohol increases oestrogen levels, and oestrogen may exert its carcinogenic effect on breast tissue either via the oestrogen receptor, or directly. Other mechanisms may include the effects of acetaldehyde, oxidative stress, epigenetic changes due to a disturbed methyl transfer, and decreased retinoic acid concentrations associated with an altered cell cycle (Seitz, Pelucchi et al., 2012).

What is concerning is the number of women who do not know the link of alcohol with breast cancer. For example, a recent UK study (Sinclair, McCann, et al. (2019) found that less than one in five women attending a mammogram knew of the risk of alcohol. Even the staff had knowledge gaps, with less than half of the staff at the breast screening centre able to identify alcohol as a breast cancer risk factor. For some New Zealand statistics and practical information about breast cancer see:
https://breastcancerfoundation.org.nz/Images/Assets/22648/1/
BCFNZ-ABC-Report-2018-REPRINT-10.2018.pdf?_ga=2.88576601.
3390831.1550383201-4a0027b8-c1b1-4401-8b53-a0a1e7964da8.

## 2.3  ALCOHOL AND GENERAL HEALTH

Up till now we have just looked at some specific diseases, but now we look at some general effects of alcohol on health. To begin with, heavy drinking results in uncontrolled iron absorption into the body, putting strain on vital organs and increasing the risk of death (Schutte, Huisman, et al., 2019). Obad, Peeran, et al. (2018) noted that the effect of alcohol on body organs extends beyond the liver where it is metabolised to include the central nervous system, cardiovascular system, kidneys, lung, gastrointestinal tract, pancreas, and the immune system. Because alcohol has the ability to distribute throughout most fluid compartments of the body, the chronic consumption of it leads to cell injury in nearly every tissue, specifically cardiac tissue. The authors also refer to alcoholic men and women having significant shrinkage of their brains compared to non-alcoholic subjects as well as cerebellum changes and affects on the integrity of blood-brain barrier. Chronic alcohol consumption also causes impairment of the memory learning abilities.

Premenstrual syndrome (PMS) is a very common disorder worldwide. For example, Fernández, Saulyte, et al. (2018) considered 19 studies of eight different countries that met their inclusion criteria. They concluded that the relatively large number of studies conducted and the consistency of the results across study designs and settings provided substantial epidemiological evidence that alcohol drinking may be associated with an increase in the risk of PMS.

As an aside, we note that drinking more alcohol in very hot weather can lead to dehydration as the body runs out of water, and this can cause headaches, dizziness, and confusion. For example, drinking a pint of standard beer (560ml) will cause a loss of approximately 280ml of extra fluid. Add this up over the length of a night and this will leave a person with a huge water deficit. There is not only a loss of extra fluid, but alcohol's diuretic effect also depletes essential electrolytes, making one's kidneys work hard to keep the balance right.

### Immune system

Alcohol impacts the innate and the acquired immune system, especially with heavy drinking, and thus increases vulnerability to infectious diseases such as tuberculosis, HIV, and pneumonia. The overall impact of alcohol consumption on infectious diseases is substantial, especially in sub-Saharan Africa (Rehm, 2011). As a consequence, alcohol is one of the major risk factors for TB, especially in countries with high population densities and high infection rates of M. tuberculosis, with poverty being linked to both.

### Atrial fibrillation

We ask the reader, if a coffee drinker, whether you may have experienced a heart flutter after a strong drink of coffee because of the effect of caffeine. Well, the same thing can happen with alcohol after just one drink. Samokhvalov, Irving, and Rehm (2010) found a consistent dose-response relationship between the amount of alcohol consumed daily and the probability of the onset of atrial fibrillation (AF). Epidemiological criteria for causality were met to conclude a causal impact of alcohol consumption on the onset of AF with a monotonic dose-response relationship, which nontechnically means that the greater the amount of alcohol the greater the

AF. Voskoboinik, Pradhu, et al. (2016) examined data collected on almost 900,000 people and found a 7% risk increase for atrial fibrillation (heart palpitations) with each alcoholic drink consumed per day, e.g., by 14% with two drinks. Although alcohol might be beneficial for the "plumbing" or blood supply for the heart, it is not good for the "electrical" part of the heart or the heartbeat. On average, an AF diagnosis occurs in the sixties, with the condition being the leading cause of stroke in older people. For people who come to the emergency department with atrial fibrillation, between one and two-thirds of them have had palpitations triggered by alcohol.

Anybody with a history of atrial fibrillation should be especially vigilant about avoiding or limiting alcohol. Further evidence of this problem is given by Voskoboinik, Costello, et al. (2018) and Voskoboinik, Wong, et al. (2019). Also three standard drinks a day increases the risk of obstructive sleep apnea by 25% in men. A short study of 140 people found that by stopping drinking, or at least substantially lowering their alcohol intake, can lead to an almost 50% reduction in their chances of AF recurrence (Medscape, March 26, 2019). A study involving more than 3,000 people attending the 2015 Munich Oktoberfest found that the more alcohol a person drinks, the higher the heart rate goes up (Sinner, Drobesch, et al., 2018).

### Hair loss

This topic may raise some eyebrows. Alcohol has a net acidic affect on one's body, along with some foods, as it uses the protein called keratin to reduce the acidity. This protein is used to build hair follicles. Alcohol hydration can lead to dry, brittle hair, and can induce inflammation in the body, which promotes hair thinning and loss. Men and women who drink are at an increased risk of vitamin and mineral deficiencies, including vitamin B12, zinc, calcium, and folic acid absorption, all of which can impact hair health. Alcohol consumption has been linked to increased levels of the female hormone oestrogen in both men and women, which may contribute to hair loss.

### 2.3.1   Alcohol and the Adult Brain

Ethanol basically reduces communication between brain cells, a short-term effect responsible for many of the symptoms of being drunk. Binge drinking may even lead to a blackout, a phenomenon characterised by memory loss (amnesia) during a heavy drinking episode. These effects are only temporary, but chronic alcohol abuse may cause permanent changes in the brain, often leading to impaired brain function. The brain is very sensitive to damage caused by chronic alcohol abuse, which may increase the risk of dementia and cause brain shrinkage in middle-aged and elderly people. Alcohol impedes the ability of the microglia to keep the brain clear of amyloid beta and may contribute to the development of Alzheimer's disease (Kalinin, González-Prieto, et al., 2018). The authors Paul, Au, et al. (2008) found that

> moderate alcohol consumption was not protective against normal age-related differences in total brain volume. Rather, the more alcohol consumed, the smaller the total brain volume.

What is more, De Santis, Bach, et al. (2019) found that white matter changes through heavy alcohol exposure continued into early abstinence. Hence alcohol-induced brain damage does not stop when alcohol use ends; the harmful effects of alcohol may continue during abstinence. The effect of alcohol on the young brain is discussed in section 1.4.1.

### Dementia and lifestyle

Dementia is a prevalent condition, affecting 5–7% of people aged 60 years and older, and a leading cause of disability with people in this group globally. A stroke can double the chance of dementia (Hachinskia, Einhäupl, et al., 2019). The World Health Organisation (WHO, 2019) released guidelines favouring lifestyle over supplements to reduce cognitive decline and dementia. What is alarming is that in the next 30 years the number of people with dementia is expected to triple. They stated that there is a relationship between the development of cognitive impairment and dementia with lifestyle-related risk factors, such as physical inactivity, tobacco use, unhealthy diets, not maintaining healthy blood pressure, cholesterol and blood sugar levels, and the harmful use of alcohol.

### Dementia in France

Schwarzinger, Pollock, et al. (2018) analysed a nationwide retrospective cohort of adult patients twenty years or older (over 31 million) admitted to hospital in metropolitan France between 2008 and 2013, and looked at 1.1 million people diagnosed with dementia (according to ICD-10 codes of dementia). Of the 57,353 (5.2%) cases of early-onset dementia (before 65 years) most were either alcohol-related by definition (22,338 [38.9%]) or had an additional diagnosis of alcohol use disorders (10,115 [17.6%]). This gives 56.5% of cases of early-onset dementia related to chronic heavy drinking. It was suggested that for various reasons the numbers are under-estimates. The authors concluded that alcohol use disorders were a major risk factor for the onset of all types of dementia, and especially early-onset dementia. It was also found that although alcohol abstinence was expectedly associated with a lower risk of competing death compared with uncontrolled alcohol use disorders, the study findings show that the risk for dementia onset remained unchanged after abstinence. This finding corroborates recent results showing that alcohol use directly exerts lifelong brain damage.

The authors suggested that screening, brief interventions for heavy drinking, and treatment for alcohol use disorders should be implemented much earlier in primary care to reduce the alcohol-attributable burden of dementia. In commenting on this study, Ballard and Lang (2018) said that several issues still need to be addressed, in particular the relationship between alcohol use disorders and related comorbidities. They noted that alcohol use disorders are probably associated with poor diet and lifestyle, smoking, cardiovascular comorbidity, lower adherence to medical treatments, depression, and potentially social isolation.

### Depression

Alcohol abuse and depression are linked. People may start abusing alcohol due to depression, or become depressed from abusing alcohol. What happens is after a 20 minute high from a drink, which wears off, there is a depressive effect so that another drink is needed to combat the low mood caused by the first, and so on. Although alcohol can reduce self-consciousness and shyness, making it easier for people to act without inhibition, it can at the same time impair judgment and make people do things that they end up regretting.

### Alcohol and hypertension

It is well established that heavy alcohol consumption increases the risk of hypertension (HT). Roerecke, Tobe, et al. (2018) reviewed 20 articles involving 361,254 participants and concluded that any alcohol consumption was associated with an increase in the risk for hypertension in men. In women, there was no risk increase for consumption of 1 to 2 standard drinks/day, but an increased risk for higher consumption levels. They did not find evidence for a protective effect of alcohol consumption in women, contrary to earlier meta-analyses. Another review and meta-analysis was carried out by Roerecke, Kaczorowski, et al. (2017 ) involving 36 trials with 2,865 participants (2,464 men and 401 women). They found that for people who drank two or fewer drinks per day, a reduction in alcohol was not associated with a significant reduction in blood pressure; however, in people who drank more than two drinks per day, a reduction in alcohol intake was associated with increased blood pressure reduction.

Piano, Burke et al. (2018) examined high blood pressure, cholesterol, blood sugar and other cardiovascular risks in 4,710 adult

Americans ages 18–45 who responded to the 2011–2012 and 2013–2014 US National Health and Nutrition Examination Survey. They found that high-frequency binge drinking was reported by 25.1% of men and 11.8% of women. Binge drinking 12 times a year or less was reported by 29.0% of men and 25.1% of women. They concluded that:

> Compared with young adult women, repeated binge drinking in men was associated with an elevated systolic BP, and greater frequency of binge drinking in men was associated with a more unfavourable lipid profile. In young adults with elevated systolic BP, practitioners should consider the possible role of binge drinking and address the importance of reducing alcohol intake as an important cardiovascular risk reduction strategy.

One of the problems in diagnosing HT is that general practitioners (GPs) may consider alcohol as a relatively unimportant factor, as was found in a study of 867 GPs in Spain (Miquel, López-Pelayo, et al., 2018). These doctors also found it difficult to deal with alcohol problems. The three main barriers to implement screening for alcohol consumption in HT patients were the lack of time (50.0%), considering alcohol unimportant for HT (28.4%) and stigma (16.5%). As indicated by Alcohol Use Disorders Identification Test-C scores, 12.4% of GPs who responded were risky drinkers (21.3% of men versus 7.1% of women).

### 2.3.2 Alcohol and Tobacco

Epidemiological research shows that people who use both alcohol and tobacco have much greater risks of developing cancers of the oral cavity, pharynx (throat), larynx, and oesophagus than people who use either alcohol or tobacco alone. In fact, for oral and pharyngeal cancers, the risks associated with using both alcohol and tobacco are multiplicative; that is, they are greater than would be expected from adding the individual risks associated with alcohol and tobacco together (e.g., Hashibe, Brennan et al., 2013). This means that dependence on alcohol is correlated with dependence on tobacco. People who are dependent on alcohol are three times more likely than those in the general population to be smokers, and people who are dependent on tobacco are four times more likely than the general population to be dependent on alcohol (e.g., Eckhardt, Woodruff, and Elder, 1994).

The primary danger from drinking and smoking simultaneously is that, because one drug is a depressant and the other one is a stimulant, people may not realise how much the alcohol is affecting their bodies. This could cause them to drink more than they should because they do not feel drunk. As mentioned above, smoking and drinking together can increase the risk of throat and oesophageal cancer. This may be because the alcohol dissolves chemicals in the cigarette while they are still in the throat. This can cause carcinogens to become trapped against the sensitive tissues of the throat. Global statistics on alcohol, tobacco, and illicit drug use are given by Peacock, Leung et al. (2018).

### 2.3.3   Alcohol and Body Weight

Most people would not think of eating an excessive amount of junk food, yet many would easily drink its equivalent on a night out; alcohol can contribute to obesity because of its calorific content described below (see also section 1.3.2). In particular, binge drinking may be linked to weight gain, as studies have shown. It has been suggested that binge drinking for some may lead to unhealthy over-eating and lack of exercise, all contributing to weight gain or obesity. Drinking can suppress the hormone leptin, which controls appetite, so that people can overeat when drinking. As a sugar source, alcohol raises insulin and turns on fat storage by increasing fatty deposits in the liver and, in middle age, excess can lead to fat storage around the stomach leading to the so-called "beer belly". Drinking alcohol may lead to inflammation and irritation in the stomach that results in bloating.

Alcohol is the second most energy rich nutrient after fat, providing about 7 calories per gram (9 calories for fat). Beer contains a similar amount of calories as sugary soft drinks, ounce for ounce (cc for cc), whereas red wine contains twice as much. A 4% ABV (percentage of alcohol by volume) pint of beer can have as many calories as a slice of pizza (197 calories). A glass of 13% ABV wine can have as many calories as a slice of sponge cake (195 calories). But it is not the calories in the drink that makes one gain weight. Alcohol reduces the amount of fat one's body burns for energy. Because we cannot store alcohol in the body, our systems need to get rid of it as quickly as possible, and this process takes priority over absorbing nutrients and burning fat.

### 2.3.4   Pregnancy and Alcohol

It has been known for a long time that alcohol affects the foetus.In Carthage and Sparta the law made it forbidden for male and female newlyweds below the age of 30 to consume liquor in order to prevent the conception of defective children (Haggard and Jellinek, 1942). Plato stated that "children shouldn't be made in bodies saturated with drunkenness" (Burton, 1621). Similar statements were made by Aristotle, and there are texts in the Old Testament and the Talmud warning about drinking during pregnancy.

## Recent history

In 1726, the College of Physicians in Britain wrote to Parliament stating "parental drinking is a cause of weak, feeble and distempered children." In later years there were numerous references to the problem of children born to mothers who drank alcohol in excess, and these are outlined by Plant (1985).

Jones, Smith et al. (1973) first coined the phrase "fetal alcohol syndrome," (FAS, now FASD) and since that time the number of cases reported in the literature snowballed, particularly those with the clear physical features of FASD. By 1975, numerous American scientific studies indicated that more subtle harm may be caused by drinking during pregnancy. Plant (1985) summarised the literature up to 1985 on this subject by stating

> the literature..has produced a nearly unanimous conclusion that alcohol consumption in pregnancy is associated with foetal harm.

A systematic review of the effect of alcohol exposure and offspring mental health was published by Easy, Dyer et al. (2019). The review suggested

> that maternal alcohol use during pregnancy is associated with offspring mental health problems, even at low to moderate levels of alcohol use.

We discuss FASD in section 2.3.5 below.

## Teratogens

Alcohol is a teratogen, which is anything that interferes with the normal development of a foetus (unborn baby). Other examples are some environmental chemicals (e.g., hair spray, mercury, and tobacco substances), certain drugs and medications (e.g., dilantin, a medication to treat epilepsy; warfarin, a blood thinner; ACE inhibitors for hypertension; tetracycline, an antibiotic; selective serotonin re-uptake inhibitors for depression; some tranquilisers such as diazepam; illegal drugs), infections and diseases (e.g. chicken pox, shingles, hepatitis, German measles (rubella), HIV, Herpes, diabetes, sexually transmitted diseases); and ionising radiation (e.g., CT scan, X-rays). Some teratogens are dangerous throughout a pregnancy, and some are dangerous only at specific points of embryonic development.

Alcohol has its greatest effect in the early stages of pregnancy especially from heavy or binge drinking during this period. Women most at risk for drinking and binge drinking during this period are younger in age (16–24 yrs), and would suggest that they should be targeted for public health interventions (cf. Parackal, Parackal, and Harraway (2013) for references).

Binge drinking (4+ standard drinks per occasion) can increase the risk of physical problems and unusual facial features during the first trimester. Summing up, alcohol crosses the placental barrier and can stunt foetal growth or weight, create distinctive facial features, damage neurones and brain structures, and cause other physical, mental, or behavioural problems.

### Some pregnancy statistics

Lange, Probst, et al. (2017) estimated that 9.8% of women in the world population consume alcohol during pregnancy. This risky behaviour is also reflected in New Zealand statistics. For example, the Ministry of Health in New Zealand (Ministry of Health, 2009, 2015) believes the evidence suggests that about 50% of pregnancies in New Zealand are alcohol exposed (about 30,000 babies), and about 10% will be exposed to alcohol at high risk levels (binge drinking). Surveys suggest that around 50% of women (mistakenly) believe some alcohol in pregnancy is safe, and 28–36% of women continue to consume alcohol during pregnancy. According to midwives, the figure is closer to 80% for pregnant teenagers. The more frequently a woman drinks before pregnancy, the more likely she is to continue to drink. Over 70% of New Zealand women report drinking alcohol during the first trimester prior to being aware of their pregnancy, and over 10% continue to do so beyond the first trimester (Morton, Atatoa Carr, et al., 2010).

Fewer Māori women than non-Māori women drink frequently, but are more likely to drink hazardously and to intoxication. This reference to subpopulations raise some global questions. For example Popova, Lange, et al. (2019) carried out a review of special populations defined by service use and found that

> several global subpopulations of children in care, correctional, special education, specialized clinical, and Aboriginal populations have a significantly higher prevalence of fetal alcohol spectrum disorder compared with the general population, which poses a substantial global health problem.

The question is when should a person stop drinking.

### Stopping during pregnancy

Many women do reduce their alcohol use because of the pregnancy, but often only after they become aware of it. Parackal, Parackal, and Harraway (2013) looked at this question of stopping on early recognition of a pregnancy using a sample in 2005 of 1256 women aged 16–40 of which 127 were currently pregnant and 425 were previously pregnant. Half of currently pregnant women and 37% of previously pregnant women reported that they ceased drinking on recognising pregnancy. They noted that cross-sectional studies on representative samples of pregnant women in the US have reported maternal alcohol consumption prior to recognising pregnancy to be as high as 45%. Also, a Canadian study reported that even among women with planned pregnancies, 50% had consumed alcohol prior to recognising pregnancy. In Australia, a study of 1520 women found that 27% drank in the first trimester only, and another 27% continued to drink throughout pregnancy (Muggli, O'Leary, et al., 2016). Borschmann, Becker, et al. (2019) found that:

> For most women in their twenties and thirties, parenting a child < 1 year of age was associated with reduced alcohol consumption. However, this protective effect diminished after 12 months with drinking levels close to pre-parenthood levels after five years. There was little change in male drinking with the transition to parenthood.

More recently, Parackal, Parackal, and Harraway (2019) noted that nearly half of all pregnant women in the Western world drank prior to recognising pregnancy. This was in spite of the fact that current government guidelines in countries such as New Zealand, Australia, Canada, the US, and the UK include a recommendation of abstinence from all drugs when planning a pregnancy or thinking one could become pregnant.

The authors stated that pregnancy planning has been found to be associated with drinking patterns, but not with stopping drinking. They mentioned that a Swedish study found that only 10% of women changed their alcohol consumption patterns during the planning period, while a Danish study found no significant difference in the prevalence of binge-drinking in early pregnancy among women with a high degree of planning in comparison to those with a low degree of pregnancy planning. Also mentioned was that other studies confirmed that similar proportions of women with or without planned pregnancies continue to drink in the early stages of pregnancy (47% versus 53%), and women with planned/intended pregnancies were less likely to binge in early pregnancy in comparison to women with unintended pregnancies (19% versus 28%). Those with planned pregnancies drank significantly lower amounts of alcohol per occasion. Also, in contrast to information-seeking and the intake of folic acid, changing alcohol consumption was not a pregnancy planning behaviour. The authors also looked at risky drinking among non-pregnant sexually active women.

Finally, it should be noted that sometimes midwives are not fully informed and be able to give suitable advice, as shown for example by an English study from the Institute of Alcohol Studies (cf. www.ias.org.uk/uploads/pdf/IAS%20reports/rp37092019.pdf). It is clear that women need to be aware of what happens to alcohol when drunk during a pregnancy or breast feeding.

### Alcohol and the baby

Alcohol, once swallowed it is rapidly absorbed into the blood and moves to all parts of the body, including to an unborn baby. So while a woman drinks so does the baby! Alcohol can cross the placenta and directly affect foetal brain development by disrupting neuronal proliferation and migration, or by causing cell death. Lebel, Roussotte, and Sowell (2011) concluded that prenatal alcohol exposure has numerous effects on the developing brain, including damage to selective brain structure, reduced brain volume, and malformations of the corpus callosum connecting the left and right hemispheres of the brain. They also detected shape, thickness, and displacement changes throughout multiple brain regions, and concluded that almost the entire brain is affected. Donald, Eastman, et al. (2015) carried out a survey of 64 relevant articles and found that, overall, the articles reported smaller total brain volume as well as smaller volume of both the white and grey matter in specific cortical regions. The most consistently reported structural MRI findings were alterations in the shape and volume of the corpus callosum, as well as smaller volume in the basal ganglia and hippocampi. The hippocampus (we have two) is involved with long-term and spatial memory.

### No safe level

The Ministry of Health (2010) in New Zealand emphasised that there is no known safe level of alcohol use at any stage of pregnancy. There have been some confusing statements about so-called safe levels in news media in the past that are not correct. For example in Australia, Drinkwise, a "safe drinking" group almost entirely funded by alcohol companies, produced a poster with headline "It's safest not to drink while pregnant", and sent 2,400 posters to doctors. However, the text beneath included the words "It's not known if alcohol is safe to drink when you are pregnant", was considered misleading and inaccurate, and the posters had to be withdrawn from the walls of hospitals and GP clinics around the country and replaced by posters with the revised message "A very important choice you can make for the health of your baby is to abstain from alcohol while pregnant, planning a pregnancy or breast feeding."

It is well established that drinking alcohol while pregnant can cause a miscarriage, stillbirth, and a range of lifelong physical, behavioural, and intellectual disabilities that are permanent. Heavy drinking with at least four or more standard drinks *at a session* during early pregnancy, when a woman may not yet be aware she is pregnant, is considered the most harmful pattern (Maier and West, 2001; Strandberg-Larsen, Nielsen et al., 2008). O'Leary,

Nassar, et al. (2010) found a fourfold increased risk of birth defects observed after heavy prenatal alcohol exposure in the first trimester. It is drinking too much on one occasion that is particularly serious. The situation is even worse if drinking is combined with the smoking, given their compounding effect discussed above in section 2.3.2.

### 2.3.5  Foetal Alcohol Syndrome

We still do not know how many children are affected by Foetal Alcohol Syndrome (FASD) in New Zealand as statistics are not easy to obtain. International prevalence studies suggest FASD is conservatively estimated to occur in at least 1 out of every 100 live births and may be much higher in communities where binge and hazardous use of alcohol is prevalent. For example, May, Chambers, et al. (2018) in a US study had a conservative overall range of 1.1% to 5.0%, and 3.0% to 9% using a different method of estimation. The problem is that there can be a considerable proportion of children not diagnosed or misdiagnosed.

#### Physical and mental aspects

FASD is a range of physical, cognitive, and behavioural impairments, including some physical features, caused by exposure to alcohol during foetal development. These impairments pose major challenges for individuals with FASD across their lifespan, as well as for their families and a broad range of service providers. In developed countries, FASD is recognised as the leading preventable cause of developmental disabilities, but there is a paucity of reliable data in New Zealand. Nevertheless, based on international data and patterns of drinking in this country, it has been estimated that 600 to 3,000 babies a year or more are born with FASD in New Zealand (Sellman and Connor, 2009). According to the Ministry of Health, New Zealand (2018), there is no NZ data on the prevalence of FASD, but international studies suggest that around 3% of births may be affected. This implies that about 30,000 children and young people in NZ may have an FASD, with around 1800 more born each year.

As already mentioned, there is no known safe level of alcohol consumption at any stage of pregnancy. Since 2006, the Ministry of Health has recommended that women who are pregnant or planning to become pregnant do not consume alcohol. The problem is that a pregnant woman can have a drinking binge and then have a baby that seems perfectly normal at birth, but when the child goes to school the child might have learning issues or other defects.

### Large New Zealand study

The Growing Up in New Zealand study (Rossen, Newcombe, et al., 2018) followed nearly 7000 children from birth until they are aged 21 found that 71% of women drank alcohol before becoming pregnant, 23% percent continued through the first trimester and 13% percent continued to drink further into pregnancy. The above figures are startling as it means that these children may experience such things as intellectual impairment, learning difficulties, behaviour problems, and growth impairment. Clearly the messages around not drinking if a woman is at risk of being pregnant or while she is pregnant are not getting through to enough women. There is a paradox in that, on the one hand, early diagnosis of FASD and intervention have been identified as critical to improved outcomes and minimised secondary disabilities, but on the other hand individuals with FASD often go undiagnosed or are misdiagnosed (particularly without physical symptoms), are difficult to identify early, and may not receive appropriate early intervention. It has been described as a hidden or invisible disability.

### Diagnosis of FASD

As alcohol has broad and varied effects on brain development, there is apparently no unique clinical pattern of impairment that is sensitive or specific enough to confirm the diagnosis of FASD. Because of this there can be under reporting and a diagnosis may be overshadowed by conditions like attention disorders (ADHD), autism spectrum disorder (ASD), and mood disorders. (In fact related to the ADHA gene, LPHN3, could favour the likelihood to smoke, consume alcohol, cannabis, and other addictive substances, see Arcos-Burgos, Vélez, et al., 2019). Also the various diagnostic criteria involve a large number of categories. Then of course birth mothers may be generally reticent in identifying themselves because of the stigma attached to the diagnosis.

As already mentioned, early diagnosis and intervention from birth and in the first years of life can make significant differences to the developmental progress of the affected child, and better understanding of the condition can help parents and professionals cope more appropriately with the child's difficulties. However, a tool has recently been developed that can screen children for FASD quickly and affordably, making it accessible to more children in remote locations worldwide. The tool uses a camera and computer vision to record patterns in children's eye movements (Zhang, Paolozza, et al., 2019). It will be interesting to follow this development.

The usual FASD diagnosis can include:

- Prenatal exposure (the number of type(s) of alcoholic beverages consumed (dose), the pattern of drinking and the frequency of drinking in pregnancy should all be documented).

- Hereditary, prenatal and postnatal factors that may influence developmental outcome should be recorded. Family history must be reviewed and a three-generation family tree can be helpful.

- Medical assessment.

- Physical examination. Problems may include an abnormal appearance, short height, low body weight, small head size, poor coordination, low intelligence, behaviour problems, and problems with hearing or seeing. Standardised growth charts can be used.

- Three simultaneous sentinel (facial) features, namely short palpebral fissures, smooth philtrum, and thin upper lip, may or may not be present. However, it is well established that learning disabilities, inattention, social and executive function deficits can occur regardless of facial dysmorphology.

- Evidence of severe impairment in three or more of the identified neurodevelopmental areas of assessment (motor skills, neurophysiology, cognition, language, academic achievement, memory, attention, executive function including impulse control and hyperactivity, affect regulation, and adaptive behaviour, social skills or social communication).

- Growth impairment (e.g., low birth weight).

- Multidisciplinary assessment team.

- Management and follow up. Those affected are more likely to have trouble in school, legal problems, participate in high-risk behaviours, and have trouble with alcohol or other drugs. They are also more likely to become involved in criminal activity, and die prematurely from violence, accident or suicide.

Speaking to a mother, the risk of harm to the baby is likely to be low if they have drunk only small amounts of alcohol before they knew they were pregnant or during pregnancy. If a woman finds out they are pregnant after they have drunk alcohol during early pregnancy, they should avoid further drinking. For further background information see the clinical guidelines by Health Improvement Scotland called SIGN156 (www.sign.ac.uk/assets/sign156.pdf), set up in January 2019, and based on studies and reviews.

## Industry response to *FASD*

What does the alcohol industry say about FASD? We give an example from Australia. The Foundation for Alcohol Research and Education (FARE) analysed four alcohol submissions from the Winemakers Federation, the Brewers Association of Australia and New Zealand, the Distilled Spirits Industry Council of Australia, and the Australian Wine Research Institute. The analysis found that (Globe, 2012, Issue 2, page 150)

> between them, the alcohol industry bodies made a total of ten false or misleading claims regarding FASD, and the effectiveness of interventions to prevent FASD.

FARE commented that the industry submissions demonstrated a total lack of commitment to preventing FASD.

### 2.3.6 Breast Feeding and Alcohol

Before moving off the topic of pregnancy, we need to say something about breast feeding and alcohol, as alcohol can pass through the milk to the baby and affect growth and development. This is particularly relevant during the first month, when breastfeeding is being established with the baby. It is important to remember that alcohol reaches its peak about half an hour after drinking. It takes nearly two hours for a woman to rid herself of one standard drink, depending on a number of things such as weight. If a mother wishes to drink now and then, she needs to wait until after she has breastfed her baby, and then wait for two hours or longer until she breastfed again after drinking alcohol. It is also possible to plan ahead to express and store milk that does not contain alcohol and then discard milk after drinking alcohol in order to maintain supply. However current recommendations are not to drink at all when breast feeding. Feed Safe is a new phone app, which is now available on iOS and Android devices, and it contains answers to the most common questions about alcohol and breastfeeding. Some helpful contacts are given in the Appendix.

### 2.3.7 Alcohol and Sleep

Regular drinking can affect the quality of one's sleep, making one feel tired and sluggish. This is because drinking disrupts the sleep cycles that one goes through at night and affects melatonin production, a regulator of sleep-wake cycles. When a person drinks alcohol before bed they may fall into a deep sleep more quickly, which is why some people find drinking alcohol helps them drop-off to sleep. But as the night goes on they spend less time in this deep sleep and more time than usual in the less restful, Rapid Eye

Movement (REM) dream stage of sleep. This so-called "rebound affect" can upset the night's sleep and can leave one feeling tired the next day no matter how long one stays in bed. At night, over about 90 minutes, we go through several stages of sleep. First through two light sleep stages, then through two stages of deep sleep, then through one stage of light sleep, and finally to REM sleep. The latter is linked to memory and retaining information, and disruptions in sleep stages means we're causing issues for our cognition when we are awake. Our brainwaves can also be affected by alcohol as alpha and delta activity in the brain may inhibit restorative sleep. Having alcohol-free days can help, as a person should sleep better then and find it easier to wake up in the morning (see also section 1.3.3 about hangovers).

When a person drinks more than usual, they may have to get up in the night to go to the toilet. And it's not just the liquid they have drunk that they will be getting rid of as alcohol is a diuretic. This means it encourages the body to lose extra fluid through sweat too, making one dehydrated. Also, drinking can make a person snore loudly. It relaxes the muscles in the body, which means the tissue in the throat, mouth, and nose can stop air flowing smoothly, and is more likely to vibrate.

We see then that if a person is drinking alcohol, they should try to avoid it too close to bedtime. They need to give their body time to process the alcohol they have drunk before they try to sleep. As previously mentioned, on average it takes an hour to process one standard drink, but this can vary widely from person to person as well as the sex of the drinker. So having two standard drinks or more at night can upset sleep, with drinkers having a 23% more risk of having REM problems than those who did not drink at all.

Alcohol can affect the body's circadian rhythms governed by a master biological clock, a tiny region of the brain, and interferes with the ability of the clock to synchronise itself. As well as affecting sleep it also affects other bodily systems such as the liver's filtering action, the gut's unwanted permeability, and can exacerbate any depression.

### Alcohol-free months

If sleep is an issue or there are other problems, then alcohol free months can be tried as they are becoming popular throughout the world (e.g., dry January, dry July, dry October). There is evidence, including anecdotal stories from news articles, that a dry month can lead to substantial health benefits (e.g., BBC news, 3 October, 2018, https://www.bbc.com/news/health-45721671). A Guardian article (8 October, 2018) suggested the following ways of cutting back on alcohol to keep one drinking in moderation all year round, and it applies to someone trying to have a dry month or at least cutting back for a month, namely:

- find a solid reason for drinking less (e.g., health reasons)

- think about why you drink so much (perhaps relying too much on alcohol because of an underlying problem that you are not facing. Cutting back gives you a chance to see how much you are depending on the booze, and how much better you feel without it);

- find someone to do it with you (to be accountable to and to provide encouragement)

- avoid temptation (e.g., exercise instead of drinking, be a designated driver)

- reward yourself (if the rewards of better sleep, increased energy, and looking slightly less rough are not enough to persuade you to stay the course, put aside the money to be spent on booze and use it to buy something really wanted)

- tough it out, and deal with any unpleasant withdrawal symptoms

### 2.3.8 Alcohol and Medications

There are also some medications that interact with alcohol in potentially dangerous ways such as acetaminophen, antidepressants, anticonvulsants, pain-killers (e.g., tramadol), and sedatives. People taking sedative drugs (like diazepam/Valium) or antidepressants (like fluoxetine/Prozac) should avoid alcohol altogether. There are some antibiotics which simply do not mix with alcohol— drinking with these will make one vomit.

People taking long-term medications should be careful about drinking, as alcohol can make some drugs less effective, and long-term conditions could get worse. Examples of long-term medications include drugs for epilepsy, diabetes, or drugs like warfarin to thin the blood. Just because some medication does not require a prescription, that does not make it harmless. For instanceTylenol, a pain reliever and a fever reducer, contains acetaminophen which can cause liver damage if a user takes too much or combines it with alcohol. Other medications, such as cough syrup and laxatives, already contain as much as 10% alcohol, which can interact with just a drink or two.

There are two main reasons not to take alcohol with medication. Firstly, because alcohol is a depressant, it affects the way the brain works, numbing the senses so they do not operate properly. Some types of medication have the same effect so that if one is drinking alcohol there will be a conflict with increased problems of sleepiness and dizziness. It could also change the way the brain responds to the medication, making it less effective. If a person is taking a sedative drug, such as diazepam/valium, or any other drug that can make one drowsy, and they drink alcohol, their reaction times could decrease and they will get tired more quickly.

A second reason is that alcohol can affect the way drugs are absorbed by the body and broken down in the liver. Drinking alcohol regularly and especially in excessive amounts, causes the liver to produce more enzymes so that it can get rid of the alcohol more quickly. Those same enzymes might break down the medication being taken so it no longer has the same effect. An example of this is medications for epilepsy.

### 2.3.9   Alcohol and Antibiotics

When it comes to antibiotics, the message is slightly different than it is with sedative drugs. The National Health Service in the UK advises that people who choose to drink alcohol when taking most common antibiotics should do so within the weekly alcohol unit guidelines. However, there are some antibiotics like Metronidazole and Tinidazole with which one should not drink alcohol. Mixing them with alcohol can lead to nausea, vomiting, flushing of the skin, accelerated heart rate, or shortness of breath. This is because they can interfere with the breakdown of alcohol, leading to the production of unpleasant side effects.

There are many antibiotics available, with penicillin and amoxicillin being the most widely used. These can have different interactions with alcohol, and, as with any medication, a person should always consult their doctor or pharmacist about guidelines regarding alcohol consumption. A list of antibiotics and the effect of alcohol is given by Medical News Today (17 April, 2019) at https://www.medicalnewstoday.com/articles/324991.php.

### 2.3.10   Statins and Alcohol

Statins are drugs which are taken to lower the levels of cholesterol in the blood. High levels of "bad cholesterol" (LDL) can increase the risk of developing cardiovascular disease due to fatty deposits building up in the arteries. According to the UK National Health Service, there are no known interactions between statins and alcohol. However, consumption of statins can occasionally result in an increase in liver enzymes, which if left unchecked can lead to liver damage. It is therefore important for those taking statins to stay within the government's low risk alcohol unit guidelines (of no more than 14 standard drinks per week for both men and women, those could be seen as too high) and to have their liver function tested periodically. As with any medication, a doctor should always be consulted about consumption guidelines.

### 2.3.11 Alcohol and Fitness

The acute effects of alcohol on exercise performance mean that not too many people try and combine the two as they are less coordinated, have reduced power, and their eye-hand co-ordination is compromised. A late night out may mean that an early workout is cancelled. Too much alcohol slows down the absorption of water and increases urine output, which would both lead to dehydration. The effects wear off as a hangover subsides. While the short-term impact on fitness levels from a few drinks may only be reduced energy levels at the next workout, for the 20% of New Zealanders that report a potentially hazardous alcohol consumption pattern, there is likely to be a negative effect on fitness gains and overall health in the medium to long term.

Alcohol also affects fertility and the pregnancy success rate for for women, while for men excessive alcohol consumption lowers testosterone levels and reduces sperm quality and quantity.

An item from Medicalxpress entitled "Why alcohol after sport and exercise is a bad idea" and research from Massey University, New Zealand, (June 2, 2018), came to the following conclusions (medicalxpress.com/news/2018-06-alcohol-sport-bad-idea.html): (1) after vigorous sport and exercise, athletic qualities such as strength, power and endurance can be depleted for several days after an intense workout; (2) even moderate amounts of alcohol affect recovery from athletic performance, with muscle performance loss doubled in those who drank alcohol; (3) alcohol slows down the repair process of exercise-induced muscle damage by inhibiting the functions of hormones that usually aid this process (such as testosterone); (d) for athletes with a soft tissue injury, it is even worse, as alcohol opens up the blood vessels and encourages swelling at the injury site; (e) in a hot or humid environment, the body also loses a large amount of fluid from sweating, reducing the blood volume, and since alcohol is actually a diuretic that promotes fluid loss it contributes to dehydration. Therefore if a person drinks even moderate levels of alcohol after strenuous use of their muscles they are impairing their ability to recover. If a person is serious about their sport, they should not be drinking alcohol in the post-match or recovery period. For further comments on sport, alcohol, and advertising see section 3.5.1.

### 2.3.12  Alcohol and the Aging Process

The following information is summarised from a booklet by the Health Promotion Agency (2015b) in New Zealand.

As a person ages they become more sensitive to the effects of alcohol as alcohol gets broken down more slowly. If they do not change their drinking habits, then alcohol will affect them more and they will need to consider cutting back or stopping altogether. The usual standards for "safe" drinking norms have become too high for older people.

Care is needed when taking medications, especially if a new one is introduced. In the latter case, if a person has one or more of the signs of being extra sleepy, forgetful, confused or unfocused, unsteady or off-balance, dizzy or faint, queasy or nauseous, or less interested in eating they should talk their pharmacist or doctor, and check labels for any alcohol restrictions. A good idea is to try reducing the amount of alcohol they drink, even for just a little while, to see if it helps them feel better.

Sometimes medications can interact with each other so that a person's list of medications may need reviewing by their doctor. As noted above, alcohol can interact with many medications, and as people get older they tend to take more medications. Even paracetamol, some medicinal herbs (such as chamomile, valerian, lavender, St Johns wort, and kava), and some cough syrups that contain high amounts of alcohol can complicate the primary condition. Of course any effect will depend on a number of factors such as dosage and alcohol content. Stewart and McCambridge (2019) said that most people aged 65 or over have multiple medical conditions, and the proportion with multimorbidity (i.e. multiple conditions) can be expected to increase further as people live longer. Managing such conditions is made more difficult by alcohol consumption, even at low doses.

As already described above, alcohol can cause some health problems, and make existing problems worse, e.g., high blood sugar, high blood pressure, liver problems, stomach problems, insomnia and other sleep problems, weak bones (osteoporosis), and incontinence. For example, the bone density of even adolescent and young adult women can be affected by heavy episodic drinking (LaBrie, Boyle, et al., 2018). Some health conditions can also be harder to diagnose or treat if people drink alcohol. It is fairly obvious that drinking alcohol can increase people's chances of being injured, such as from falls and motor vehicle crashes, particularly with older people. As people get older they may tend to drink more because of loneliness, loss of friends or partners, more opportunities for drinking and socialising, or relief from boredom, trauma or pain. People should avoid alcohol if they are unwell, depressed, tired, or cold.

## 2.4 GENETIC INFLUENCE

In section 2.2.1 (*Acetaldehyde from alcohol*) we considered how genes can interact wth alcohol consumption,. Research (NIHAA, 2019) shows that genes are responsible for about half of the risk for alcohol use disorder (AUD) with brain neurotransmitter systems responsible for a substantial proportion of the genetic influence, though age is also a factor However, genes alone do not determine whether someone will develop AUD. Environmental factors (e.g., alcohol consumption and smoking) as well as gene and environment interactions account for the remainder of the risk. One way of assessing genetic factors independently of environmental factors is by examining twins. The genetic risk is specifically involved with genes that encode enzymes used in metabolizing (breaking down) alcohol (Druesne-Pecollo, Tehard et al., 2009). For example, one way the body metabolizes alcohol is through the activity of an enzyme called alcohol dehydrogenase, or ADH, that converts ethanol to toxic acetaldehyde. Subsequently, acetaldehyde is converted into acetate by aldehyde dehydrogenase (ALDH).

Many individuals of Chinese, Korean, and especially Japanese descent carry a version of the gene for ADH that codes for a "superactive" form of the enzyme that speeds up the conversion process with a consequent build up of acetaldehyde. Among people of Japanese descent, those who have this superactive ADH have a higher risk of pancreatic cancer than those with the more common form of ADH (Kanda, Matsuo et al., 2009).

Edenberg (2011) commented that accumulating evidence indicates that variations in numerous other genes have smaller but measurable effects. He also refers to the key roles of various alleles of ADH and ALDH as well as subunits of the neurotransmitter GABA.

Marshall and Chambers (2005) referred to studies that concluded the following:

(1) The sons of alcoholic parents were found to have significantly higher incidences of alcoholism than the sons of non-alcoholic parents, whether raised with their biological parents or by non-alcoholic foster parents. The highest levels of alcoholism were

found in the sons of alcoholic parents when raised by their biological parents.

(2) Adopted sons of alcoholics who become alcoholics do so at an earlier age than adopted sons of nonalcoholics.

(3) When the daughters of alcoholics are examined under similar conditions to those in (1) and (2), the same effects of parental alcoholism are not found.

(4) Susceptibility to non-alcohol related psychiatric disorders was the same in the sons of alcoholics and non-alcoholics raised by adoptive parents.

As already noted, there is not a single gene responsible for alcoholism, but there are hundreds of genes in a person's DNA that may amplify the risk of developing an AUD. There are also behavioural genes passed down that could influence a propensity for alcoholism. For example Gelernter, Sun, et al. (2019) in a genome-wide association study identified 5 new risk loci for harmful alcohol use that can be passed on from parents to children.

Epigenetics also plays a role. This relates to inherited switches that can be turned on and off and can genetically predispose a person to alcoholism (cf. Starkman, Sakharkar, and Pandey, 2011, for some background details). People with a mental illness have a higher risk of turning to substance abuse as a way of coping. Mental disorders can be hereditary, which partially illuminates the complex link between genetics and addiction.

### *Effect of mental illness*

Mental illness increases the likelihood of developing alcoholism by 20 percent. Family history is also important. Some statistics indicate that children of alcoholics are about four times more likely than the general population to develop alcohol problems. However, the genetic connection is more complex as more than one-half of all children of alcoholics do not become alcoholic (cf. https://www.addictioncenter.com/alcohol/genetics-of-alcoholism). It appears that different sets of genes seem to influence the level of alcohol consumption, as opposed to propensity for alcohol dependence. Although DNA can affect susceptibility to alcohol, the reverse is also true in that alcohol can affect our DNA, leading to long-term physiological changes.

People with harmful drinking habits will likely experience withdrawal symptoms such as nausea, headaches, agitation, tremors, hypertension, and in some particularly severe cases, even seizures once they remove alcohol from their diets. A study by Koehnke, Schick, et al. (2002) suggests that the intensity of these withdrawal symptoms may be due to certain genes. This is also supported by Smith, Ovesen, et al., (2018).

## 2.5   NO SAFE LEVEL

Just as there is no safe level of smoking, it has to been shown that there is no safe level of alcohol consumption, with negative effects outweighing any possible positive effects. Also, there is a linear risk (they increase together) between the number of drinks and the likelihood of cancer and other harms. These facts come from the 2018 Global Drug Survey (GDS), which looked at information from 130,000 people across 44 countries (including 3,200 New Zealanders) and came up with the following seven facts:

(1) Heart disease is a major cause of death among people with heavy alcohol use.

(2) Even people with heavy alcohol use can reduce their risk of liver disease by cutting down by even a small amount.

(3) Drinking less reduces your risk of seven different sorts of cancer.

(4) A bottle of wine or six bottles of beer contain as many calories as a burger and fries.

(5) Experts recommend having at least two alcohol free days per week. This can help a person reduce and control his or her drinking.

(6) Most people get little or no health benefit from alcohol use, even at low levels of drinking.

(7) Alcohol use increases the risk of violence and abuse.

## 2.6   ANY BENEFICIAL EFFECTS?

This has been a controversial topic for a long time (as we shall see below.)

### Possible protective effects

Before looking at some studies we note that scientists believe that there are two main mechanisms by which small amounts of alcohol may have a protective effect as one enters the age where heart disease commonly occurs. The first is that alcohol appears to affect the levels of cholesterol circulating in the blood, reducing the amount of fatty deposit (atheroma) which narrows our arteries and makes them more likely to block. Secondly, alcohol may help prevent the formation of blood clots which can close off the arteries, causing a heart attack. It can stop platelets from clumping together to form clots. A small amount of alcohol with a meal can also reduce the sudden rise of a protein (fibrinogen) produced by the liver, which may increase the likelihood of blood clots forming, leading to thrombosis. Moderate alcohol consumption may raise HDL (the "good") cholesterol in the bloodstream, lower the concentration of fibrinogen in the blood (a substance that contributes to blood clots), and reduce the risk of diabetes (but not with higher consumption). Bergmann, Rehm, et al. (2013) concluded that:

> Limiting alcohol use throughout life is associated with a lower risk of death, largely due to cardiovascular disease but also other causes. However, the potential health benefits of alcohol use are difficult to establish due to the possibility of selection bias and competing risks related to diseases occurring later in life.

Before looking look at some of these biases we mention a Guardian article (6 May 2019) entitled "Here's why moderate drinking is probably not good for you." A main message is that moderate drinking is not an isolated behaviour. The article states:

> You can't easily separate moderate drinking from the people who drink moderately, which means that you can't easily identify whether its actually the alcohol that's improving peoples health or something more complex.

We note that the word "moderate" is not defined. We discuss the whole question of moderate drinking below.

## Health of nondrinkers

There have been a number of studies looking at whether nondrinkers are less healthy than drinkers. These have tended to be flawed as they have not adequately taken into account the underlying health of each individual and the lifestyles of each individual, a so called "confounding" effect. They have only compared their alcohol consumption. However, any benefits are offset by occasional heavy drinking. For example, Roerecke and Rehm (2010) concluded from reviewing 14 studies that:

> Contrary to a cardioprotective effect of moderate regular alcohol consumption, accumulating evidence points to a detrimental effect of irregular heavy drinking occasions ($> 60$ gm of pure alcohol or $> 5$ drinks per occasion at least monthly) on ischaemic heart disease risk, even for drinkers whose average consumption is moderate.

This means that the cardioprotective effect of moderate alcohol consumption disappears when, on average, light to moderate drinking is mixed with irregular heavy drinking occasions. Naimi, Xuan et al. (2012) concluded that:

> Among those with low average alcohol consumption, infrequent drinkers drink more during drinking days and have unfavorable risk factors profiles compared with more frequent drinkers, suggesting that confounding may contribute to favorable associations with 'moderate' average alcohol consumption and increased drinking frequency observed in non-randomized studies.

Roerecke and Rehm (2012), in another investigation using 44 observational studies and 957,684 participants, endeavoured to quantify the dose-response relationship between average alcohol consumption and ischaemic heart disease (IHD). Although some form of a cardioprotective association was confirmed in general, substantial heterogeneity across studies remained unexplained. They concluded that a cardioprotective association between alcohol use and ischaemic heart disease cannot be assumed for all drinkers, even at low levels of intake.

### Beneficial effects controversial

The so-called putative beneficial effects of low and regular levels of consumption of alcohol for cardiovascular health are therefore controversial, and we now give further reasons why (Klatsky, 2015, gives a good summary of the issues; see also Caetano, 2017 and Sellman, Connor, et al., 2009). Firstly, as we saw above, it is likely that epidemiological studies have overestimated the apparent benefits of low to moderate consumption on the risk of ischaemic (coronary) heart disease because they were influenced by uncontrolled confounders which need to be built into the statistical method used (Chikritzhs, Fillmore et al., 2009). The relationship between the risk factor (alcohol) and a disease has been described by a J-shaped curve, which does not proceed as a rough straight line, but where at some point the graph of the relationship changes from a negative slope to a positive one (Kunzmann, Coleman, et al., 2018). This has been interpreted as a drink a day might make one less likely to die of heart disease than teetotaling peers, but drinking more might also make one more likely to get cancer than those who abstain.

For alcohol and all-cause mortality, the J-curve corresponds to a situation in which teetotallers fare worse than moderate drinkers, who in turn fare better than heavier drinkers. The problem with this is that people who only consume light to moderate amounts of alcohol also tend to have healthier lifestyles than heavy drinkers (Klatsky and Udaltsova, 2013). They tend to be wealthier, more educated, smoke less, live in more affluent areas, are less likely to have been in prison, less likely to be overweight, and in general are better off than both people who drink a lot and those who say that they never drink. Also many abstain from alcohol because they already have health problems, not so they can avoid them. For example, abstainers may have shorter lives because they were either ex-alcoholics, suffered from a medical condition, or took medication that restricted them from drinking. Also, alcohol consumption decreases with the development of disease (Shaper, 2011). Some also did not have healthy lifestyles. As Stockwell and Chikritzhs (2013) comment,

> moderate drinking may be more a sign of good health than a cause of it.

Ervasti, Kivimäki, et al., 2018) found from a study of 47,520 people from Finland, France, and the UK that abstainers and at-risk drinkers were at an increased risk of sickness absence compared with low-risk drinkers. Abstainers had a higher risk of sickness absence due to mental disorders, musculoskeletal disorders, diseases of the respiratory system, and diseases of the digestive system. They suggested that this could be partly due to the inclusion of former at-risk drinkers, and to health selection bias; people abstaining due to health reasons.

### Misclassification errors

Another source of error is the systematic misclassification of ex-drinkers and occasional drinkers as "abstainers" in longitudinal studies (followed through over time) resulting in negatively biasing the health status of the reference group of abstainers. All of the studies affected by misclassification error showed protective effects, and none of the few which were error-free displayed a protective effect.

This problem of biases was discussed by Naimi, Stockwell, et al. (2017). Zeisser, Stockwell, and Chikritzhs (2014) found that of 60 studies identified, only 6 were free of all misclassification errors. The abstainer reference group was biased by the inclusion of former drinkers in 49 studies, occasional drinkers (< 10 gm ethanol per week) in 22 studies, and by both these groups in 18 studies. Occasional drinkers were also mixed with light or hazardous-level drinkers in 22 studies. Only the misclassification of occasional drinkers was found to bias risk estimates significantly. We note, for example, that estimates based on error-free studies confirmed that low and harmful levels of alcohol use both significantly increase the risk of breast cancer. Liang and Chikritzhs (2013) found that:

> Excluding former drinkers from drinker groups exaggerates the difference in health status between abstainers and drinkers, especially for males.

They concluded that:

> In cohort study analyses, former drinkers should be assigned to a drinking category based on their previous alcohol consumption patterns and not treated as a discrete exposure group.

## Misreporting

There is also problem of the under-reporting or misreporting of drinking habits. Most epidemiological studies rely heavily on the ability of respondents to accurately report their own current and past alcohol consumption. Yet it is well-documented that most self-report drinking surveys under-report consumption, sometimes substantially (e.g., Dawson, 2000). For the majority of economically developed populations like the US and European countries with J-shaped curves, some people who abstain from drinking are in themselves atypical, as already noted above. For example, it was found that abstainers may be typically older, poorer, less educated, in worse health, and have lower levels of medical well-being and access to health care or prevention health services than moderate drinkers (Naimi, Brown et al., 2005).

A review by Zhao, Stockwell, et al. (2016) found that after making an adjustment for abstainer biases and quality-related study characteristics, no significant reduction in mortality risk was observed for low-volume drinkers. In addition, higher-quality bias-free studies also failed to find reduced mortality risk for low-volume alcohol drinkers. Under-reporting can affect studies on the effect of alcohol on other diseases like cancer (e,g., Klatsky, Udaltsova, et al., 2014)

## Coronary risk

Alcohol consumption, carotid IMT (intima-media thickness) and conventional cardiovascular risk factors were investigated in 2074 subjects, aged 24–39 years in Finland. The authors Juonala, Viikari, et al. (2009) studied the effect of alcohol on atherosclerosis, in particular whether alcohol consumption is associated with carotid IMT, a marker for subclinical atherosclerosis, in young, healthy adults. Their conclusion was:

> We found a direct relationship between alcohol consumption and carotid IMT in young adults. This association was independent of cardiovascular risk factors suggesting that in young healthy adults alcohol consumption may have pro-atherogenic effects. These population-based data do not encourage recommendations to consume alcoholic beverages for atherosclerosis prevention.

Another study, by Karády, Szilveszter, et al. (2016), used coronary computed tomography angiography to look for the presence of coronary plaques in drinkers and nondrinkers of alcohol and found no association between light to moderate alcohol consumption and coronary artery disease. They studied 1,925 consecutive patients and considered different types of alcohol (beer, wine and hard liquor). Comparing the consumption between patients who had coronary artery plaques and those who had none, no difference was detected. Also, while no protective effect was detected among light drinkers, as previously thought, no harmful effects were detected either.

One American study found that while alcohol consumption reduced the risk of coronary heart disease in white men, it increased in black men, thus suggesting that the cardio-protective effect could be explained by consistent confounding of lifestyle characteristics of drinkers (Fuchs, Chambless, et al., 2004). An Australian study (Rodgers, Korten, et al., 2000) found that nondrinkers had a range of characteristics known to be associated with anxiety, depression, and other facets of ill health, such as low status occupations, poor education, current financial hardships, poor social support, and recent stressful life events, as well as increased risk of depression. All of these factors could explain an increased risk of heart disease amongst nondrinkers compared with light drinkers. The authors found that both non-drinkers and heavy drinkers reported more symptoms of depression and anxiety than those drinking at moderate levels. Greenfield, Rehm, and Rogers (2002) found that depression was associated with heavy male drinkers and heavy female ex-drinkers.

## Possible genetic factors

In section 2.2.1 we briefly considered how genes can interact wth alcohol consumption, and we look at this topic further. A large Chinese study following over 500,000 people for ten years by Millwood, Walters, et al. (2019) considered the effect of two variant genes ALDH2-rs671 and ADH1B-rs1229984 that are common in China and greatly effect alcohol drinking patterns especially with regard to cardiovascular disease (including ischaemic stroke, intracerebral haemorrhage, and myocardial infarction). The study showed that the apparently protective effects of moderate alcohol intake against stroke were largely non-causal, suggesting the key factor was genetic. Also alcohol consumption uniformly increases blood pressure and stroke risk, and appears in this one study to have little net effect on the risk of myocardial infarction. The researchers found no protective effects for moderate drinking.

A study by Christensen, Nordestgaard, and Tolstrup (2018) also demonstrated the role of genetic factors in assessing observational effects, as did a large international study by Holmes, Dale, et al. (2014). They concluded that individuals with a genetic predisposition to consume less alcohol had lower, not higher, odds of developing coronary heart disease regardless of whether they were light, moderate, or heavy drinkers.

In addition to genetic factors, we see then, as emphasised by Jarl, Gerdtham, and Selin (2009), that we need to take into account all epidemiological factors. With the inclusion of all alcohol-related diseases, it turns out that low alcohol consumption has a net detrimental effect. They stated that

> The only age group, for both genders, that show a protective effect of low alcohol consumption on medical care costs are 80+.

While it may be true that some older men may gain a small benefit of reduced cardiovascular risk from a very small amount of wine, they could die prematurely from something else. Rehm, Mathers, et al. (2009) also noted that any potential benefit of low to moderate consumption of alcohol seems to be restricted to middle aged and older people; yet even in these population groups, the overall effect of alcohol on the burden of disease is detrimental. However, low to moderate levels of consumption do not seem to confer any cardio-protective association when combined with heavy drinking episodes. At least in men, heavy drinking episodes appear to increase deaths from coronary heart disease. Former drinkers also have a significantly higher risk of death from coronary heart disease than abstainers (Roerecke, Greenfield, et al., 2011).

Wannamethee, Whincup, et al. (2015) found that there was no evidence that light-to-moderate drinking is beneficial for the prevention of heart failure in older men without a history of myocardial ischaemia. However, a large study of over 48,000 women in Sweden for women aged 30–49 found that for the cohort of young women, light alcohol consumption was protective for cardiovascular and ischaemic heart disease mortality but not for cancer and overall mortality. It is clear that although there is some disagreement among studies about any protective effects of alcohol, there is agreement that the net affect of alcohol is harmful.

Braillon (2018) proposed that although "moderate alcohol use" is a usual term it should be avoided in medical literature. Public health advocates use the term "drinking at low risk" as there is no level of alcohol use that is risk free. Braillon suggested that "Moderate alcohol use" is a

> marketing tool of the industry to promote sales as shown by the flawed French and UK Responsibility Deal.

(cf. Braillon, 2017). Part of the problem arises from misconceptions about moderate drinking. For example, the SBS (Special Broadcasting Service) news in Australia (8 May, 2019) referred to a report of a poll of 1820 people released by FARE (Foundation for Alcohol Research and Education). It found that a majority of Australians who consumed alcohol to get drunk at least twice a week believed that they were responsible drinkers. The report said:

> These findings demonstrate that there is no clear, single definition of a
> 'responsible drinker', something the alcohol industry continues to exploit
> to its full advantage.

When it comes to considering who is a responsible drinker some people refer to what happens in France with the belief that the French are healthier than most everyone else because they drink wine.

### The French connection

Unfortunately the French suffer from serious problems with alcohol, as well as not being able to control their drinking habits. For example, France's death rate for cirrhosis of the liver is about four times higher than that in New Zealand (Kaner, Newbury-Birch, et al. 2007). According to the newspaper The Local (19 February, 2019), alcohol in France kills tens of thousands each year. According to an earlier report in 2017, 41,000 people died from alcohol-related causes, which is 7% of the total number of people over 15 who die in France every year. More than one in ten men (11%) in France die every year from alcohol-related causes, which is more than twice as much as for women (4%). Over a decade ago it was suggested that many more French men might die early from alcohol-related causes before they have the opportunity to die of heart disease. Fenoglio, Parel, and Kopp (2003) concluded that:

> Alcohol is the drug that gives rise to the greatest cost in France ... alcohol represents more than half of the social cost of drugs to society. The greatest share of the social cost comes from the loss productivity due to premature death, morbidity, and imprisonment.

Also:

> There is a collective misunderstanding of the dangers of alcohol in a country where a regular intake is claimed as a protection against heart problems.

Generally, there is still some controversy about any cardiovascular benefits as a meta-analysis of 45 studies by Zhao, Stockwell, et al. (2017) found that low volume drinkers had a reduced risk of coronary heart disease except for those under 55 years in higher quality studies, or in studies that controlled for heart health. They suggested that:

> The appearance of cardio-protection among older people may reflect systematic selection biases that accumulate over the life course.

Bell, Daskalopoulou, et al. (2017) investigated the association between alcohol consumption and cardiovascular disease at higher resolution by examining the initial lifetime presentation of 12 cardiac, cerebrovascular, abdominal, or peripheral vascular diseases among five categories of consumption. Linked electronic health records covering primary care, hospital admissions, and mortality in 1997-2010 (median follow-up six years) were considered for a population of 1,937,360 adults (51% women) who were aged 30 or older and free from cardiovascular disease at baseline. They concluded that moderate alcohol consumption is associated with a lower risk of initially presenting with several, but not all, cardiovascular diseases. They made the comment that:

> Finally, from a public health perspective, our finding that moderate drinking is not universally associated with a lower risk of all cardiovascular conditions also supports the decision not to incorporate the apparent protective effects of drinking for cardiovascular disease in the recent UK chief medical officers' alcohol guidelines review.

Although there are a great many factors that can affect how alcohol impacts the cardiovascular (CV) system, Piano (2017) sums up the situation with the words:

> Low-to-moderate alcohol use may mitigate certain mechanisms such as risk and hemostatic factors affecting atherosclerosis and inflammation, pathophysiologic processes integral to most CV disease. But any positive aspects of drinking must be weighed against serious physiological effects, including mitochondrial dysfunction and changes in circulation, inflammatory response, oxidative stress, and programmed cell death, as well as anatomical damage to the CV system, especially the heart itself.

In the end, any problem association with alcohol comes back to the dose and pattern of alcohol consumption. Piano notes that comparing studies is made difficult by variations in what constitutes both a "drink", a standard drink, and binge drinking, along with the underreporting of alcohol consumption, study design problems (cf. Appendix A.3), and unaccounted confounding variables such as life-style characteristics mentioned above. Reliable biomarkers (e.g., phosphatidylethanol or PEth that forms phospholipid only in the presence of ethanol) can be used to corroborate the accuracy of self-reporting of alcohol consumption and distinguish among low, moderate, and heavy alcohol consumption. Piano provides a detailed review along with data and a large bibliography. Bergmann, Rehm, et al. (2013) made the statement:

> The apparent health benefit of low to moderate alcohol use found in observational studies could therefore in large part be due to various selection biases and competing risks.

Stockwell and Chikritzhs (2103) highlighted their thinking underlying this conclusion, backed up by some references, as follows:

(1) If individuals are recruited across the age spectrum (say between 25 and 70 years of age) this is in effect selecting survivors who were well enough to participate. This bias increases with age.

(2) Selection biases occur during the teenage and young adult years because those who elect to be total abstainers also tend to have lower income and poorer health. This means that right from the beginning all drinkers are biased towards looking good compared with people in the abstainer comparison group.

(3) The common practice of removing former drinkers from the abstainer reference group reduces one form of bias because they tend to have poor health profiles even if previously only light drinkers. However, there is still bias because of systematically removing less healthy drinkers.

(4) Removing individuals with compromised health at baseline only adds to the effectiveness of the above selection biases. The significant protection of drinking against coronary heart disease was found in the study only after performing this removal.

(5) The mean age of death from coronary heart disease tends to be several years later than from cancer and many years after deaths from acute causes. The appearance of protection against heart disease may be caused by drinkers being more likely to die of other causes before heart disease gets them, especially for heavier drinkers.

Clearly these issues need to be resolved in assessing the hypothesis that light/moderate alcohol consumption is beneficial to health.


## 2.7 CONCLUSION

The physical and mental effects of alcohol on the body are extensive and well documented. Using alcohol is fraught with risks. The less a person drinks the healthier they will be, with a reduction in the relative risks of such things as heart disease, cancer, hypertension, diabetes, and mental disease.

There are many mistaken beliefs about drinking alcohol with often an emphasis on the so-called protective effects. However these are commonly cancelled out by the negative effects of other health disorders such as cancer.

The clear message is that drinking alcohol is not a safe activity and despite the temporary pleasure it may give, the wise person might be well advised to avoid it completely.

# CHAPTER 3

# SOCIAL EFFECTS OF ALCOHOL

## 3.1 OTHER'S DRINKING

The consumption of alcohol has a range of harms to people other than the individual drinker. The flow-on effects of alcohol are considerable.

### Second-hand effect of alcohol

Nayak, Patterson, et al. (2019), in a study of 8,750 adults concluded that secondhand effects of alcohol in the United States are substantial with one in five adults experiencing at least one of ten 12-month harms because of someone else's drinking (described below). In a large New Zealand national survey, one in four respondents indicated they had at least one heavy drinker in their life, with most of these respondents experiencing a range of harms because of this person's drinking (see Casswell, Harding et al., 2011; Casswell, You, Huckle, 2011). According to Florenzano, Huepe, and Barr (2016), there has been a change in alcohol research from a traditional individual focus on individual bodily

*Alcohol: A dangerous love affair.*
By George A. F. Seber and D. Graeme Woodfield Copyright © 2019

and mental effects to a broader focus on harm to others. They found that in Chile a sample of 1500 showed that about a third were negatively affected by the drinking of others, with women being more affected than men.

Nayak, Patterson,et al. (2019) inquired about 10 harms that might have resulted from the drinking habits of another person. The harms were:

(a) being harassed, bothered, called names, or otherwise insulted; (b) feeling threatened or afraid; (c) having clothing or belongings ruined; (d) having house, car, or other property vandalised; (e) being pushed, hit, or assaulted; (f) being physically harmed; (g) being in a traffic accident; (h) being a passenger in a vehicle with a drunk driver; (i) having family problems or marriage difficulties; and (j) having financial trouble.

The effect of other people's drinking can be seen with regard to public spaces and public amenities. With regard to amenities, the pleasantness or attractiveness of a place can be affected, while the inclusivity of public spaces, the extent to which people are willing to enter, use or live in a locality, can also be affected by alcohol (Randerson, Casswell, and Rychert, 2019).

### International project

What is really helpful is that an international project called the International Alcohol Control (IAC) study has been set up initially involving nine countries, with the goal of adding other countries to measure the range and magnitude of alcohols harm to others (Callinan, Laslett, et al., 2016). Two comparable face-to-face questionnaires were developed for collecting data for an international data base. A survey and an Alcohol Environment Protocol were also developed that could be readily adapted to each country (Huckle, Casswell, et al., 2018). Further models have been developed such as using a longitudinal design to examine the affect of implementing an alcohol policy (Casswell, Meier, et al., 2014). The IAC methodology has provided cross-country survey data on key measures of alcohol consumption (quantity, frequency, and volume), aspects of policy relevant behaviour, and policy implementation: availability (outlet density, trading hours), price, purchasing (minimum purchase age), marketing, and drink driving. A country comparison is given by Casswell, Morojele, et al. (2018). Below we consider some of the harms relating to alcohol from a social viewpoint, which complements the previous chapter that focused more on individual harms.

### 3.1.1 Tertiary Students and Alcohol

Tertiary students are sometimes pressured by their peers to engage in binge drinking. For example, Robertson and Tusin (2018) found that students who drink heavily are labeled positively and viewed as sociable in New Zealand. However, those who limit drinking were viewed similar to those who abstain, and being hurtfully labeled using explicit, emotive, and derogative terminology. They were excluded, ostracised, or the subject of peer pressure, and expected to provide a justification for moderating their drinking (e.g., being an athlete or broke).

Alcohol is sometimes used by students as an initiation or at a birthday party, where it is drunk rapidly ("sculled"). For example, there was a news item in April 2011 that said that Coroner Gordon Matenga ruled on the death of 16-year-old Auckland high school pupil James Webster, who died in 2010 after sculling Jagermeister and vodka at a birthday party. The ruling said Webster's blood-alcohol level was nearly five times the legal driving limit. It said the King's College pupil sculled vodka "like it was nothing . . . in a matter of seconds", while being encouraged by a friend. Later, after being put to bed in someone else's home, he died. Matenga said

> Teenagers should be aware that drinking 250ml or more of spirits over a short period of time —30 to 60 minutes— will cause you to become drunk very quickly to the point of unconsciousness. ... This will endanger your life.

Langley, Kypri, and Stephenson (2003) found in a random sample of 1910 university students (aged 16–29 years) at the University of Otago, New Zealand, that 84% of the students experienced at least one type of harm during the previous month because of another student's drinking. The authors said:

> Our findings reveal that limiting consumption, even occasionally, threatens students' social identity and inclusion in the student drinking culture.

A study by Kypri, Maclennan, et al. (2018) looked at changes in hazardous drinking among students over a decade at Otago university, New Zealand, and 12 residential colleges in North Dunedin using three New Zealand universities as controls. The surveys were done before and after an Otago university policy change. High levels of alcohol-related harm among students led to Otago university deploying a security and liaison service, strengthening the Student Code of Conduct, banning alcohol advertising on campus, increasing the university's input on the operation of alcohol outlets near campus, and being involved in objecting to license renewals. This may have created a tipping point for businesses that had survived by breaching server laws, and the banning alcohol advertising on campus would have had an affect. The authors concluded that in this period of alcohol policy reform, drinking to intoxication decreased substantially in the targeted student population. It seems likely that the actions of the university along with the reduction in pubs surrounding the campus had helped to reduce hazardous drinking in the Otago student population. The study suggested that with a concerted effort, it is possible to change a drinking culture.

### 3.1.2   Pre-Loading

Heavy drinking prior to going out has emerged as a common and celebrated practice among young adults around the world. Some reasons for doing it are: (i) to avoid paying for high priced drinks at commercial drinking establishments; (ii) to achieve drunkenness and enhance and extend the night out; and (iii) to socialise with friends, reduce social anxiety, or enhance male group bonding before going out (Wells, Graham, and Purcell, 2009). The authors argued that policies focused upon reducing drinking in licensed premises may have the unintended consequence of displacing drinking to predrinking environments, possibly resulting in greater harms.

Also early closing times may result in drinking events occurring in private settings after bars close, while late closing times may encourage private drinking to precede rather than to follow public drinking. Effective policy needs to take into account the entire drinking occasion (not just drinking that occurs in the licensed environment), as well as the "determined drunkenness" goal of some young people. One of the problems with pre-drinking is that it occurs in locations that do not have serving restraints and other social controls, thus allowing for the rapid consumption of large quantities of alcohol.

Some research suggests that pre-drinking may increase the overall level of alcohol consumption among young people. Also predrinking means that young adults require transportation both on their way to and from licensed premises. They end up navigating public places and using various modes of transportation with impaired judgement and reduced perception of risk on their way to licensed premises. They may drink and drive, or may experience other problems such as violence or victimisation. Unlike downtown areas in which licensed premises are located, these problems may occur in out-of-the-way locations where there is little police surveillance.

## Australian teenagers

Wilson, Ogeil, et al. (2018) considered a sample of 351 Australian teenagers from 16–19 years, and found that just under half ($n = 149$) reported pre-drinking on their most recent session when 7+ standard drinks were consumed. They considered

> pre-drinking to be a normative, regular and collective drinking practice, generally occurring in private settings prior to organised events or going to town, with cost reported as the primary motivation for pre-drinking, as it enabled one to save money.

They came up with the following additional reasons for pre-loading: (i) to achieve a relaxed state ideal for socialising; (ii) opportunism arising from boredom, and the availability of alcohol also enabled some participants to fill idle time; and (iii) the need to capitalise on these often unique and rare circumstances (e.g., obtaining a free bottle of vodka). Pre-drinking also required locating private space, most often homes with absent parents. Several participants asserted that using one's own family home for private drinking sessions was undesirable, given the increased potential for damaging property or getting in trouble. The authors noted:

> The presence of parents, or the degree to which parents permitted alcohol use at parties, was identified as one of the most significant factors shaping pre-drinking.

A recent study from Australia's Queensland University (Ferris, Puljević, et al., 2018) explored the pre-drinking habits of people in 27 countries. It found that pre-drinking usually declines in most countries after the age of 21, but the trend continued, or increased in people aged over 30 in Brazil, Canada, England, Ireland, New Zealand and the United States, with Greece the lowest and Ireland the highest overall.

## 3.2   ALCOHOL AND EMERGENCY HOSPITAL ADMISSIONS

A press release by the Australasian College for Emergency Medicine (ACEM) Tuesday, 20 December 2016, 2:59 pm (Scoop news, health) stated that 1 in 4 patients in NZ emergency departments (EDs) are affected by a harmful use of alcohol. It was a big study with all New Zealand EDs participating. Dr John Bonning, Clinical Director of the Waikato Hospital Emergency Department, said that:

> The level of harm these people cause to their own health is bad enough but they also divert time and resources from other patients, including older people and young children ... They put an undue strain on our emergency departments and can be rude, aggressive, or—in the worst circumstances—even violent towards doctors and nurses.

Some drunk patients can be very difficult and can affect hospital staff in terms of abusive behaviour, which led to an online NZ Herald article (December 21, 2016) entitled "We are over drunk patients: Top emergency department doctors" followed by "New Zealand hospital staff abused daily: It's time to talk." There has been an increasing number of "extremely violent" incidents by patients and their family members towards staff.

Professor Anthony Lawler, ACEM President, said that:

> Examples from overseas —as well as the considerable research that ACEM and other organisations have undertaken in Australia and New Zealand—indicate that there is a range of measures that can be pursued to curb the level of harm caused by excessive drinking. These include reducing the availability of alcohol, taxation policy, and limiting exposure to advertising.

He also noted:

> There had been a considerable reduction in the levels of violent assault in New South Wales after policy-makers addressed the issue of the late night availability of alcohol.

### Innocent bystanders

Connor and Casswell (2009) found that for the period 2003-2007 in New Zealand more than 40% of alcohol-related crash injuries in New Zealand are suffered by people who have not themselves been drinking. While the rate of road traffic injuries and the involvement of alcohol is the highest amongst young adults, so too does the proportion of all road traffic crash injuries that are due to other people's drinking, reaching one in five in the 15–19-year age group. What is sad is that most of the innocent victims are car passengers, and this includes many children who are injured by drink driving. For most of the children injured, the driver affected by alcohol is the driver of their own car. From official cost figures, they found that alcohol-related injuries to innocent victims cost the country more than half a billion dollars per year, or about 0.4% of current GDP in New Zealand. More recently, the estimated social cost of all crashes in 2017 was $5.6 billion, $0.6 billion more than the previous year (NZ Herald, April 17, 2019). Since 30-40 per cent involve alcohol, it is causing a huge cost to the country particularly at the time of writing when the government is trying to decide priorities for government spending.

### 3.3   ALCOHOL AND CRIME

Alcohol is a factor in a large proportion of criminal offending across New Zealand. Police data revealed that 31–46% of all offences are committed by persons affected by alcohol, as reported by Connor and Casswell (2012). They also reported that alcohol was involved in one in three cases of violent offending and in nearly half of all homicides. We refer again to data in chapter 2 where it was stated that over 62,000 physical assaults (54% of all physical assaults) and 10,000 sexual assaults (57% of all sexual assaults) occur in New Zealand every year, where the perpetrator has been drinking. Increasing evidence showed that violence is a major alcohol-related harm experienced by women and children as a consequence of the drinking of others, overwhelmingly men. In a later survey of 3,068 people (Huckle, Wong et al., 2017) aged 12–80 it was stated that:

> Ten percent of New Zealanders reported having called the police at least once in the past 12 months because of someone else's drinking—corresponding to 378,843 New Zealanders making at least one call to police. Almost 7% of the sample, representing 257,613 New Zealanders, reported requiring health-related services at least once for the same reason.

Alcohol-related presentations also had a significant impact on emergency departments in hospitals, especially on weekends (Huckle, Casswell, and Greenaway, 2011; Stewart, Das et al., 2014), and such incidents tend to be under-reported (Richardson, Grainger et al., 2018).

A Ministry of Health (2007) report gave figures of 5.7% and 5.3% of people aged between 12 and 65 years reported being physically assaulted and sexually harassed, respectively, by someone who had been drinking.

### 3.4   ALCOHOL AND THE NZ ECONOMY

Alcohol is associated with considerable economic costs to society that are borne largely by the taxpayer. These include the burden on the police, the judicial system, the penal system, healthcare resources, and the traffic safety agencies. A study by the Business and Economic Research Limited (BERL) applying a methodology endorsed by the World Health Organisation (Slack, Nana, et al., 2009) estimated that harmful alcohol use in 2005/06 cost New Zealand an estimated 4.4 billion of diverted resources and lost welfare. To put this figure in perspective, this was equivalent to almost two fifths of Vote Health at the time. A recent update (2018) by BERL, however, puts the figure at $7.85 billion (3% of GDP). Alcohol corporates attempted to discredit this figure pointing out that the benefits of alcohol had not been factored in. There was also some local university criticism (Crampton and Burgess, 2009), with a reply in a local newspaper New Zealand Herald (9 July, 2009) by BERL who rejected the criticisms and added that they did not write "reports to order". With such a large sum involved, this raises the question of who should pay for alcohol-related admissions to emergency hospital departments, as those who drink safely or not at all end up paying for other people's harm via income taxes going towards public health; not a fair system.

Dr Martin Than of the Christchurch Hospital, in a news item, said in January 2018 that there should be a discussion about whether bars with late-night opening hours should contribute in some way to the cost to emergency services. In response, Casswell (2018a) mentioned that license fees are paid to local authorities, but questioned whether this was enough to cover costs. To follow Dr Than's suggestions, any compensatory funds needed to end up in the government coffers. She made two further general suggestions: increase the alcohol excise tax, and make sure that transnational corporations selling and marketing alcohol in New Zealand pay tax. She referred to a New Zealand Herald investigative journalist who revealed the 20 corporations most likely to be profit shifting to avoid paying tax in New Zealand—three of which were transnational alcohol corporations (Nippert, 2018). Both of her suggestions are discussed later. There are also similar problems in Australia (Lanis, McClure, and Zirnsak, 2017).

## 3.5    YOUTH, MEDIA, AND ALCOHOL PROMOTION

Social media are used extensively by everyone and not just by young people. For example, in New Zealand about 88% visit social media across a month, with Facebook and YouTube being the most popular (Nielsen, 2016), along with mobile camera/video phones. Alcohol marketing in recent years has greatly increased in complexity, innovation and diversification over a range of media and new technology. Even back in 1999, the Federal Trade Commission figures showed that alcohol producers in the US spent two to three times their measured media expenditure on unmeasured promotions such as sponsorships, internet advertising materials, point of sale materials, product placement, and other means (Casswell and Maxwell, 2005b).

With young people, much of their drinking is socially related, and social media have helped boost the culture of intoxication in many Western countries (Lyons, McCreanor, et al. 2017). Young people routinely tell and re-tell drinking stories online, share images depicting drinking, and are often exposed to intensive and novel forms of alcohol marketing. The stories told can be quite devastating such as " riding a bike, drunk as, down a flight of stairs blindfolded" and "I shared a bottle with a friend and ended up in bed with him. I got pregnant!" One post promoting a brand was:"I usually turn to God for guidance. But today I'm turning to Mr Smirnoff for guidance. Same difference, really life is still being guided by a spirit".

In the UK and the Netherlands, children and adolescents were significantly more exposed to alcohol advertising on television than adults, given what would be expected from their patterns of television viewing. (Patil, Winpenny, et al., 2014). Lyons, McNeill, and Britton (2014) concluded that exposure to alcohol consumption and product imagery in films in the UK is associated with increased alcohol consumption among young people. In the US, Stoolmiller, Wills, et al. (2012) found that young teenagers who watched a lot of movies were twice as likely to start drinking, compared to peers who watched relatively few such films. Drinking alcohol by actor and actresses in movies is very common, leading to a normalisation of the practice. For example, the Guardian (18 June 2019), in an article entitled "Reality TV encourages children to drink and smoke" said that public health experts warn that:

> Reality TV shows such as Love Island are encouraging children and young people to smoke or drink under age by showing contestants regularly engaging in both pursuits, public health experts warn.

Through protest, there was no tobacco content in the 2018 series of Love Island.

When a mobile device is used such as a smart phone, tracking 24/7 commences enabling social marketeers seeing us as the active marketeer rather than a passive consumer. We do the job for them! We can use images not allowed by marketing regulations. Images that are hashtag (#) with brand tags become promotional material on websites and in-store. Also, marketers know when a person is out drinking because they can track the person using geolocation. This information can then be used to send a person drink offers in bars that the person is visiting based on where they are and what is popular with them, their friends, and their demographic. Brands explicitly craft their posts to mimic friends' posts. Also there exist so-called "nightlife photographers" who create what are essentially marketing images, which are paid for by alcohol companies and the venues that sell their products.

Marketers use the term "Brand Activation" to describe the ways in which they embed brands within cultural events and practices such as music festivals, gigs and club nights. Carah and Shaul (2015) stated that so-called "activations" are used to organise consumers, and "cultural intermediaries", who are essentially trendsetters (e.g., bloggers). The latter produce image sequences that link the brand to scenes, people, and objects highly sought after by young people groups. The authors described the Instagram as an "image machine that captures and calibrates attention." The Guardian (9 April, 2019) stated that:

> Most of Australia's top 70 Instagram personalities are under the influence of the alcohol industry, with almost three-quarters featuring alcoholic drinks in their accounts in the past year.

Only a quarter of the personalties fully revealed they had been paid to do so. A recent NZ Herald article (7 April, 2019) referred to Instagram photos showing two All Blacks pouring Champagne at the January ASB Classic, which were found to be in breach of alcohol advertising rules.

When comments are placed about alcohol on Facebook, the marketeers are interested not only in individual comments, but also in the responses by others. We also have Global Positioning Systems (GPSs) built into mobile devices that show where the device and its user are located. This location data is accessed through apps, and users grant their apps permission to use it. All this information enables organisations to get beyond the scope of many current marketing restrictions. For example, as noted by Noel and Babor (2018), 50 Facebook advertisements published by Bud Light and Budweiser were compared to the alcohol industry's content guidelines by a panel of public health experts, and 82% of the advertisements were deemed noncompliant. Clearly self- regulation is not working here.

David Hookway in a regular newsletter summarised some useful information about Facebook described below. For example,

> Facebook earns an average of NZ$5.31 quarterly from each of its 1.65 billion regular users by sharing their information with third parties, particularly alcohol companies,

which, in turn,

> make millions of dollars of profit by targeting young adults on social media sites.

This has led to exponential growth in alcohol brands advertising on digital platforms with, for example, Heineken spending 25% of its marketing on this method. David said:

> Messages that go viral are an alcohol company's dream because they provide detailed information about social groups and people's tastes, values and preferences.

Diageo (an alcohol multinational that owns brands such as Smirnoff and Johnny Walker) is another company using Facebook, with individual pages for each of its 30 brands. Intense marketing via social media has helped net Diageo billions of dollars in sales with NZ$24 billion in 2018 (see amigobulls.com/stocks/DEO/income-statement/annual). Andy Fennell, who was Diageo's outgoing chief marketing officer said "Facebook is now just a central part of all our campaigns." He mentioned a recent YouTube ad by Johnnie Walker that had 250,000 views on Facebook before it was even launched on TV.

We see then that the alcohol industry clearly likes social media, as it opens the way to obtaining extensive data on consumers that can be used for highly targeted marketing. As previously mentioned, it encourages social media users to like and share their brands. This sharing becomes the norm within peer groups so that the sharers are unknowingly doing the marketing for the industry. Being visible online is very important for many young adults for their identity, so that they put lot of effort into maintaining Facebook pages, especially with regard to drinking practices and events (Lyons, McCreanor, et al., 2014).

The small study by Noel and Babor (2018) found that advertisements had a significant effect on consumption, as with other studies. For example, the desire to drink was 3.5 times higher in the pro-drinking group than in an anti-drinking group after participants saw an ad with pro-drinking comments. It is the cues from the ads that increases the desire to drink, and can, for example, cause a relapse after treatment for alcoholism. Social media users viewing alcohol ads were more than twice as likely to "Like" or "Share" an ad when it had pro-drinking comments attached. The authors concluded that:

> Pro-drinking comments may increase the desire to drink and ad engagement, both of which may be predictive of future drinking behavior. Regulations are needed to limit the ability of SNS (Social Network Site) users to engage with alcohol ads.

McCreanor, Lyons, et al. (2013) noted that UK alcohol brands employed a range of strategies, including competitions, interactive games, and real-world events. The brands also blurred user-generated material and brand promotion such as mixing fan photos with official images. Also real-world and online activity were combined along with encouragement to drink on particular occasions. The authors indicated how social networking sites with all their attractions, have played a role in the US, Australia, and New Zealand "in normalising drinking within young peoples lives and cultural worlds, contributing to intoxigenic environments." For example, in New Zealand, Bebo profiles of 16–18-year olds revealed high levels of content about drinking with photos and comments representing intoxicated behaviour and heavy alcohol consumption, creating an online "intoxigenic social identity."

Young New Zealand adults tend to see heavy drinking as part of a national identity. Massey University in New Zealand have a website where they describe "five ways alcohol brands are ripping you off on social media." It is worth a read at www.psychologytoday. com/us/blog/freedom-learn/201402/five-myths-about-young-people-and-social-media.

The New Zealand government received a report from the Ministerial Forum on Alcohol Advertising and Sponsorship in 2014 that was organised by the government cabinet to see whether further restrictions on alcohol advertising and sponsorship would help reduce alcohol-related harm in society. The report, which included recommending the banning of alcohol advertising in sport, met with silence from the government at the time. The 14 major recommendations of the report addressed the areas of reducing youth exposure through sponsorship, reducing youth exposure through advertising, and strengthening the current system of co-regulation.

In a US study, Alhabash, McAlister, et al. (2015) found that young adults' intentions to consume alcohol is higher when their attitude toward alcohol's social media communications, and their intention to "like" or "share" those messages, is more positive. Also alcohol marketing on social media reflected a social norm of alcohol consumption, which leads users to consume more alcoholic drinks. An Australian study (Jones, Robinson, et al., 2016) investigated a group of young Australian Facebook users (aged 16–24 years) and found that more than half of the respondents reported using Facebook for more than an hour daily. While only 20% had actively interacted with an alcohol brand on Facebook, they found (controlling for a number of possible confounding variables)

> a significant association between this active interaction and alcohol consumption, and a strong association between engagement with alcohol brands on Facebook and problematic drinking.

### 3.5.1 Sport and Alcohol

It has been reported that non-elite football players consume between four and nine times the recommended level of alcohol per drinking session within Australia. These findings are similar among individuals involved in football in other countries. In the US, up to three times the number of alcohol-related arrests are reported to occur on college football game days compared to equivalent non-game days and public holidays. O'Brien, Ferris, et al. (2014) concluded that:

> University students in the United Kingdom who play sport and who personally receive alcohol industry sponsorship or whose club or team receives alcohol industry sponsorship appear to have more problematic drinking behaviour than UK university students who play sport and receive no alcohol industry sponsorship.

There is also a major concern in Ireland that alcohol abuse is encouraged by the sponsorship of sporting events by alcohol companies (DeBruijn, 2014).

The Department of Health in Ireland recommended that a ban on alcohol sponsorship of big sporting events should be in force by 2020. This met a great deal of resistance, with some arguing that Ireland will fall behind its European neighbours if strict alcohol-related provisions are implemented. In this case the question, which is often raised in other countries as well, is whether sport could recover from the loss of income from alcohol companies. This problem arose with tobacco sponsorship, but was overcome with other sectors becoming sponsors to fund sports teams, concerts, and other events. In particular, the European Union pushed the drive to eliminate tobacco sponsorship from sport. What is interesting is that four years after banning tobacco sponsorship in Australia, sport sponsorships increased by 45% (De Bruijn, 2014).

O'Brien, Lynott, and Miller (2013) considered a further question of whether there is an association between the receipt of alcohol industry sponsorship and attendance at alcohol sponsor's drinking establishments (e.g., bars), and alcohol-related aggression and antisocial behaviour in 652 university students who played sport in Australia. Using Alcohol Use Disorders Identification Test and alcohol consumption (AUDIT-C) scores (cf. Appendix ), they concluded that:

> Higher AUDIT-C scores, gender and receipt of alcohol industry sponsorship were associated with alcohol-related aggression/antisocial behaviours in university sportspeople.

In the UK, the sponsorship of sport has enabled alcohol marketers to bypass regulations that tend to focus on traditional forms of advertising (Adams, Coleman, and White, 2014).

### Sport advertising and children

Chambers, Signal, et al. (2017) mentioned several studies in which alcohol sponsorship of televised sport had an affect on children. For example, 71% of Thai youth watching the 2006 World Cup appreciated the broadcast sponsorship of the ThaiBev alcohol company and wanted to repay the sponsor by purchasing their product. In another study in the West of Scotland, a longitudinal investigation of 552 12–13 year-old children showed 61% recalled alcohol sponsorship of televised sport, with a further 66% recalling the logos on sports clothing. They also found that such awareness increases the odds of children drinking alcohol by 35%. A US a study found that children who owned alcohol-branded merchandise were both more likely to initiate drinking as well as binge drinking. Also in the US, Budweiser, an American beer brand, sponsored New Zealand versus the US in football, thus providing the brand promotion to New Zealand, United States, and other global consumers. Australian Open tennis was sponsored by an Australian wine brand with the event broadcast to 40 countries.

### Advertising partnerships

A study by the Foundation for Alcohol Research and Education (FARE, April 2019) in Australia highlighted how the alcohol industry forms advertising partnerships with the sports teams in the AFL and NRL. (For further information and pictures look up "alcohol industry forms advertising partnerships" on the internet.) It was found that 17 of 18 men's AFL clubs and 15 of 16 official NRL clubs accepted money from the alcohol industry for advertising deals. The deals are with a small group of foreign-owned multinationals. According to Stuff news in New Zealand (February 26, 2019), Baseball Australia urged other sports to follow its lead after it became the first national sporting organisation to ban alcohol sponsorship.

The alcohol advertising occurs through multiple channels, including the following:

- partnering with the league itself

- partnering with individual teams (often in a hierarchy reflecting the value of the deal, e.g., "premier partner", "major partner", "platinum partner", "premier partner" and "associate partner")

- branding the playing jerseys, training kit or merchandise of individual teams or the league

- becoming an official supplier of alcohol to a club e.g., Carlton and United Breweries as the official 'Beer Partner' of the Parramatta Eels

- commercial partnerships with alcohol industry organisations listed on the club's official website, as well as on-kit advertising and merchandise

- commercial partnerships with alcohol industry organisations publicised on official club social media channels (Facebook, Twitter, LinkedIn and Instagram).

- using rugby goal protectors and flags sponsored by various alcohol firms

According to FARE's director Trish Hepworth, "the teams are paid to promote various harmful alcohol products to sports' youngest fans." For example, research has identified jersey sponsorship as a particularly pervasive form of alcohol advertising to young children.

In Australia, a number of sporting greats came together very recently to help launch the End Alcohol Advertising in Sport campaign in Melbourne, calling for a lifetime ban on alcohol advertising in sport (Foundation for Alcohol Research and Education, fare.org.au). This happened after a new report revealed that children were exposed to more than three instances of alcohol advertising every minute of the 2018 National Rugby League Grand Final (http://www.endalcoholadvertisinginsport.org.au). What happens with children, adults, and alcohol advertising is very subtle and subliminal. According to a study by Zerhouni, Bégue, and O'Brien (2019) in France,

> Incidental exposure to alcohol marketing messages appear to impact indirect measures of attitudes toward the brand and alcohol in general, and seems to rely on non-conscious automatic processes.

Westerberg, Stavros, et al. (2018) examined how alcohol brands use sport in their communication activities on social media in Australia. They concluded that:

> Sport-linked social media strategies utilised by alcohol brands extend beyond just promoting their product. They seek higher levels of engagement with the consumer to amplify and augment the connection between alcohol and the sport spectator experience.

Also:

> These strategies allow alcohol brands to extend their marketing efforts in a manner which can elude alcohol codes and prove difficult for regulators to identify and control.

The authors identified four communications strategies used on Twitter and Facebook: (i) Call to collaborate; (2) Call to compete; (3) Call to celebrate, and (4) Call to consume. Rather than just consumers taking in the brands, there is a call to action. The focus was to target identity (e.g., sport identity, male identity, and national identity) and camaraderie (e.g., a shared sporting passion bringing alcohol brand and consumer together as part of a community).

A study was carried out in Australia by McFadyen, Tindall, et al. (2018) to determine the validity of online self-report of alcohol-management practices by community football clubs via comparison with observational methods. It has been found that the implementation of alcohol management practices can reduce risks of harm. However, such approaches are expensive and present considerable logistical challenges when applied at a population level.

Similar problems exist in New Zealand with sport and alcohol, especially with clubs. For example, O'Brien and Kypri (2008)

carried out a purposive sample of 1279 people from various sporting codes in New Zealand and asked them whether they person-
ally, their team, or club received free and/or discounted alcohol
or funding from an alcohol industry body (e.g., a pub, brewery,
or wholesaler); how much they received; and whether they felt
they should drink their sponsors product and/or at the sponsor's
premises. They found that alcohol industry sponsorship was reported by 47.8% of the sample, and of these 47% reported receiving free and/or discounted alcohol products. Using the AUDIT
questionnaire test, the authors concluded that:

> Alcohol industry sponsorship of sports people, and in particular the provi-
> sion of free or discounted alcoholic beverages, is associated with hazardous
> drinking after adjustment for a range of potential confounders.

### Sport sponsorship in New Zealand

Chambers, Signal, et al. (2017) carried out a study of alcohol
marketing during some major sports events on New Zealand television in the summer of 2014–2015. They noted that with the
growing of restrictions on traditional forms of alcohol marketing,
the alcohol industry is able to bypass some of the traditional restrictions and continues to increase its sponsorship of many major
sports and cultural events globally. Such sponsorship is effective
in getting the industry's message across to audiences, including
young people, which is contrary to the industry's own New Zealand
self-regulatory codes on advertising (Advertising Standards Authority, ASA, 2016). The authors commented that New Zealand
sport administrators justify seeking sponsorship income as necessary to cover expenses, arguing that reducing sponsorship would
impact participation in the sport, especially with children playing club sport. However, they pointed out that only a few sports
receive the majority of their income from alcohol sponsorship.

Other non-alcohol sponsors can be found, which is happening
and has happened with tobacco in New Zealand. We note that
Steinlager, the beer brand owned by drinks company Lion, has
been named the official sponsor of Emirates Team New Zealand
for the America's Cup in 2021, their 35th year of support (NZ
Herald, 21 February, 2019).

Referring again to Chambers, Signal, et al. (2017), they looked
at five major sporting events popular with men, women and children, Māori and Pacific audiences, and watched by very large audiences. Each broadcast was analysed for alcohol brands screened
during the game, including those on advertising hoardings, players' uniforms, on-field sign writing, goal posts, corner flags, and
commercial graphics. Most brands were observed on advertising
hoardings on the sideline. All advertisements in pre- and post-

match interviews and half-time shows were excluded. Researchers recorded the length and number of times a brand was observed. Audiences were exposed to between 1.6 and 3.8 alcohol brand exposures per minute. Sports that are played over a long duration tended to have a higher frequency of exposure. For three out of the five events, alcohol brands were visible for almost half of the game, most frequently on side-line hoardings. Interestingly, the duration of exposure in sports played by female athletes was just as high as (and higher in some cases than) the sports played by male athletes. Sports merchandise including player's uniforms, complete with sponsor's branding are popular with fans (particularly children), and is sometimes free.

The association of alcohol with sporting heroes means that role models for children are used to promote an unhealthy and harmful product, also contravening the ASA self regulatory code. The authors concluded that:

> Given the popularity of broadcast sport, especially with children, there is an urgent need for regulation that addresses alcohol marketing though sport.

In particular, many people now believe that alcohol advertising should be phased right out of sport, or if that is not possible, a least replace self-regulation (which we know does not work) by legislation.

Innovative camera research has revealed that New Zealand children are exposed to alcohol marketing on average 4.5 times per day (Chambers, 2018). What was disturbing was that Māori and Pacific children had five and three times higher rates of exposure to alcohol marketing than New Zealand European children, respectively. Disparities are mainly attributed to higher rates of exposure via off-licence outlets and sports sponsorship for Māori children. Chambers also noted that:

> There is now a large evidence base that shows exposure to alcohol marketing is associated with increased childhood alcohol consumption and alcohol-related harm

and

> research has shown exposure to alcohol marketing via sports sponsorship and at alcohol outlets is associated with children's alcohol consumption, including starting to drink at earlier ages.

Although alcohol is now less visible on TV sporting events, all of New Zealand's main professional sporting teams, except for the Breakers (indoor basketball), have alcohol sponsors or partners (Newshub, 21 April, 2018). The All Blacks have had a commercial relationship with Steinlager for more than three decades, and every NZ Super Rugby team has a beer partner. The Warriors ( a league club) are currently sponsored by Woodstock Bourbon, and have had alcohol sponsorship since the club formed in 1995. The Blackcaps enjoy the investment of Dominion Breweries, who call Tui the official beer of New Zealand Cricket. The Silver Ferns take to the court in partnership with champagne Veuve du Vernay.

Alcohol has had a big effect on rugby and on the New Zealand Rugby Players' Association (NZR), and there is a strong drinking culture in New Zealand associated with rugby. However, a recent newspaper article in the New Zealand Herald (April 21, 2019) highlighted the fact that "NZR has stepped up when it comes to rugby's relationship with alcohol." It plays a leading role in protecting the wellbeing of professional players, particularly with alcohol problems. In the same newspaper there is an extensive article about an All Black captain and his successful recovery from descent into alcoholism. This sounds like an ambulance at the bottom of the cliff rather than a fence at the top. Chambers (2018) suggested that by raising the tax 5 cents on beer, you could completely remove alcohol sponsorship and fund sports with the replacement revenue.

Finally there is the problem of unruly behaviour on the sideline. Stuff news (April 3, 2019) in New Zealand has the line:

> The days of having a beer on the sideline during rugby league games in Christchurch are nearly over.

The Christchurch City Council is considering banning alcohol at 17 parks across the city during rugby league games and training to try and control control "volatile and unsafe" sideline behaviour. After last year, Canterbury Rugby League first called for the ban when 70% of clubs said they were dealing with alcohol-related behaviour issues on a weekly basis. Spectators had been consuming alcohol even at junior games, and causing problems.


### 3.6  CONCLUSION

In the previous two chapters we have looked at the effect of alcohol on the individual. However, alcohol has a much wider effect, extending into all aspects of society. It features heavily in accident and emergency hospital statistics, and is frequently involved with crime. All of this poses a big burden on a country's economy, as is seen in New Zealand today.

Social effects of alcohol play a major role with youth where, for example, pre-loading has become an increasing activity. We have seen how alcohol is advertised and promoted in various TV and social media, where subtle methods of advertising are used under the radar.

Sport, in particular, has been the focus of the alcohol industry, where there are a considerable number of partnerships with sporting organisations using multiple channels. With some sports there is a drinking culture that needs to be brought under control. Binge drinking is all too common and there needs to be a change in societal attitudes towards it.

# CHAPTER 4

# ALCOHOL INDUSTRY

---

## 4.1 AN EXTENSIVE INDUSTRY

The alcohol industry is a multinational business complex that includes not only the producers of alcohol, but also a large network of distributors, wholesalers, and related industries, such as hotels, restaurants, bars, and advertisers. The industry has become increasing globalised and is promoted by trade associations representing the interests of brewers, distillers, winemakers, bartenders, importers, wholesalers, and the hospitality industry. There are three international confederations and more than 36 national trade associations devoted solely to beer (Worldwide Brewing Alliance, 2007). Some alcohol corporations have a combined wealth that is greater than the gross national product of many non-industrialised nations (Babor, Caetano, et al., 2010). With such financial power they are able to scale up up their influence on governments and public opinion. In 2014 the top five biggest liquor distributors were Diageo (London), United Spirits Ltd. (India), Pernod Ricard (Paris), Suntory/Beam (Osaka) and Bacardi (Hamilton, Bermuda), showing the diversity of the distributors.

Alcohol is an excellent product for making money, and yields huge profits for the alcohol industry. Exactly how much profit is derived seems to be unavailable for public scrutiny. However, the enormity of alcohol industry profit in New Zealand, for example, can be appreciated by considering that the industry pays around $1 billion to the government annually as excise tax (NZ treasury, 2017), and apparently spends about $150 million on advertising.

## 4.2 MARKETING TACTICS

There have been four key tactics used in marketing alcohol by the industry according to Wallack (1992) in an editorial:

(1) It markets alcohol as part of the "good life", especially to young people. It associates alcohol use with a range of human needs such as having fun, having a good social life, being accepted, and being independent.

(2) It attempts to downplay the extent of heavy drinking by linking alcohol problems with an "irresponsible" minority who can't handle alcohol, or to those who have a genetic predisposition to experiencing alcohol-related problems.

(3) It works strategically to be seen as part of the solution rather than being central to the problem. Also, it advocates personal responsibility for users and saying that it is simply helping people fulfil lifestyle choices.

(4) It attacks people who throw light on its questionable commercial activities by trying to marginalise them and portraying them in denigrating terms.

Wallack's editorial stirred up a large number of responses (Addiction, 1993, 9–24). One commentator from the industry essentially praised all the good things the industry was doing. Another suggested that there should be collaboration with the industry to find common ground. Two commentators endeavoured to establish a difference between the alcohol and tobacco industries. Unfortunately many of the comments made will not stand up today. Wallack (1993) replied to the commentators and quoted a comment that the industry's chief aim "is to protect the industry's long-term commercial interests." He added, "The goal is not to promote public health or even prevent alcohol-related harm." He put forward the following four proposals for the industry:

(1) It could show its commitment and concern for preventing alcohol problems by agreeing in principle with the World Health Organization's European Health for All target of reducing alcohol consumption by 25%.

(2) They could simply stop the rhetoric that advertising does not work to attract new consumers and increase consumption, but does work to prevent alcohol problems.

(3) It could accept responsibility for paying its fair share of the enormous social and economic cost of alcohol problems.

(4) It could gain public support by backing up its oft-stated claim that it does not want underage people to use its product by agreeing to donate the unwanted profits from underage sales to an independent foundation. This foundation would, in turn, disburse these funds to youth programmes.

## 4.3  SOME KEY INDUSTRY MESSAGES

EUCAM (2011), that covers many European organisations, outlined the following seven key messages of the alcohol industry, illuminated through examples from various countries.

(1) Consuming alcohol is normal, common, healthy and very responsible. (We note that Alcohol advertisements nearly always associate alcohol consumption with health, sportsmanship, physical beauty, romanticism, having friends and leisure activities. Also humour is used.)

(2) The damage done by alcohol is caused by a small group of deviants who cannot handle alcohol. The image communicated by the industry is that this group are the cause of any and all problems associated with high alcohol consumption such as crime, the spread of diseases, staff absenteeism, violence, sexual abuse, and poverty. (The industry shifts the focus away from the majority of drinkers to the "minority" of heavy alcohol users. Also, any restrictive measures would penalise the majority of individuals who are responsible consumers of alcohol.)

(3) Normal adult non-drinkers do not, in fact, exist. Non-drinkers do not genuinely matter and are not a part of contemporary

culture and tradition. Only children under 16 years of age, pregnant women, and motorists are recognised by the industry as the need to be non-drinkers. (Contrary to this we know that worldwide 45% of men and 66% of women do not drink alcohol so that on a global level more than half of the population (55%) does not consume alcoholic beverages (World Health Organisation, 2007).

(4) We should ignore the fact that alcohol is a harmful and addictive chemical substance (ethanol), for the body. The industry advocates that alcohol is a tasty drink that is prepared with craftsmanship; the "natural origin" of beer counts, wine is particularly beneficial for body and spirit, and with liquor, the age-long tradition guarantees the quality.

(5) Alcohol problems can only be solved when all parties work together. The image communicated by the industry is that we can only solve alcohol problems together. (This has been found not to work as the industry has often opposed legislation that will help to reduce alcohol-related harm. Examples of this are given elsewhere. Also this question of cooperation with the alcohol industry is is commented on below in section 4.3.1.)

(6) Alcohol marketing is not harmful. It is simply intended to assist the consumer in selecting a certain product or brand. The industry would say that advertisements do not make people drink more, and advertisements simply assist the consumer in choosing the best brand. The system of self-regulation works globally and has excellent results. (The latter is not true since self-regulation does not work, as mentioned elsewhere in this book.)

(7) Education about responsible use is the best method to protect society from alcohol problems. (However, based on scientific research, professionals are convinced that education alone will not change individuals' drinking habits. Again this is discussed elsewhere. Of course some education is helpful such as with regard to alcohol and pregnancy.)

Current tactics by the alcohol industry in New Zealand were discussed by Casswell (2018c) beginning with the setting up of a new body, the Alcohol Beverages Council, representing alcohol industry interests in New Zealand. She said:

> The Council's messages are the usual ones offered by the alcohol industry: a focus on the drinker, not the product; protection of the rights of the moderate drinker; arguments for education; and erroneous statements about evidence-based policies.

She indicated that some of the statements made by the new Chief Executive (CEO) are not supported by the evidence. For example, she wrote:

> Education, promoted as the only strategy by the industry, is not a cost effective, or even effective, solution.

The CEO also said on TV that having a drink is "a Kiwi right of passage", and "When we go out to a restaurant or a pub, alcohol should be part of that experience." His statement:

> Alcohol is one of those things that really allows people to come together, it's just like food, and if we're doing it in moderation it can be part of a healthy lifestyle.

has been disputed with regard to health in this book. In fact 46% of alcohol consumed in New Zealand is consumed in very heavy drinking occasions (Viet Cuong, Casswell, et al., 2018).

Casswell emphasised the growing awareness of the costs associated with alcohol harm, and internationally there is a growth in focus on alcohol as one of four risk factors addressed in the prevention of non-communicable diseases by the UN and WHO. She said that that the industry response was to employ lobbyists who build long-term relationships with key policy makers, promote self regulation, oppose effective policies, and engage in corporate social responsibility activities, using their considerable resources.

### 4.3.1 Corporate Social Responsibility

Yoon and Lam (2013) point out that corporate social responsibility (CSR) has become an integral element of how the alcohol industry promotes itself. The existing analyses of CSR in the alcohol industry point to the misleading nature of these CSR practices, though the literature on the subject and its impact on public health has been sparse. The authors identified three tactics used by the alcohol industry using CSR: (1) deflect and shift the blame from those who manufacture and promote alcoholic products to those who consume them, (2) promote CSR initiatives on voluntary regulation in order to delay and offset alcohol control legislation, and (3) undertake philanthropic sponsorships as a means of indirect brand marketing as well as gaining preferential access to emerging alcohol markets.

An article entitled "Beware of the alcohol industry bearing gifts" (Rutherford, 2013) referred to a quote from Global Alcohol Producers Group (GAPG) that its

> companies are deeply committed to continuing to work with WHO, Member States and other stakeholders to combat the harmful use of alcohol and the growing problem of noncommunicable diseases.

He notes that such a comment is surprising when GAPG companies have consistently opposed three of the more effective recommended strategies for reducing alcohol-related harm: availability, marketing, and pricing policy. He refers, in particular, to opposition from the alcohol industry with respect to Scottish proposals: (1) to raise the minimum age for buying off-licences from 18 to 21; (2) to introduce alcohol-only checkouts in supermarkets; (3) to set minimum prices, and (4) to end two for one deals. It should be noted that (Torjesen, 2019):

> WHO will not engage with the alcohol industry when developing alcohol policy or implementing public health measures, its staff have been told, and any government seeking advice from a collaboration with industry should be warned of the dangers.

Such an approach makes good sense, and this was seen for example by some 332 leading academics threatening to stop cooperating with Public Health England unless it abandoned plans to work with Drinkaware because that charity is funded by the alcohol industry (Daily Mail, 11 October, 2018, from the Times, 10 October).

We see another reaction in an open letter to the Global Fund to Fight Aids, Tuberculosis and Malaria. An alliance of more than 2,000 health organisations voiced misgivings about the alliance of the global health fund with Heineken and called for its immediate end (Guardian, 2 Februrary, 2018). The campaigners warned that such a move would "undermine and subvert" alcohol policy implementation in Africa. As noted in chapter 2, there is evidence that harmful use of alcohol increases the risk factor of both HIV and tuberculosis.

Rutherford (2013) referred to a South African report on the activities of the liquor industry that came to the following conclusions:

(1) Industry spending priorities were out of keeping with the burden or alcohol-related harm.

(2) Major alcohol-related harms such as violence, HIV/AIDS, and tuberculosis received disproportionate and little attention.

(3) The majority of programmes were not evidence-based nor were they evaluated.

(3) Money was spent on interventions that have been shown to be ineffective.

(4) Groups at risk were not targeted.

(5) Programmes data was denied to a regulator and therefore lacked accountability.

(6) There is an inherent conflict of interest between the commercial objectives of profit maximisation, reducing the volume of harmful drinking, and decreasing how much people drink.

Rutherford (2013) referred to a list of threats to the alcohol industry in the 1980s that the industry proposed to deal with such as:

(1) Duties to be raised faster than inflation.

(2) More rigorous measures to be taken to reduce drunken driving.

(3) Funding for rehabilitation.

(4) Advertising promotion and other marketing restrictions.

(5) Warning labels on alcoholic drinks.

(6) Ingredient labelling.

Babor and Robaina (2013) pointed out that among the most prominent and contentious health issues that apply to the alcohol industry are

> the burden of disease attributable to alcohol, the amount of alcohol consumed by populations at risk, the health benefits of moderate alcohol use, and the effectiveness of different alcohol control policies.

They were interested in how much the alcohol industry promoted corporate social responsibility (CSR) initiatives that many large corporations practiced. In recent years the industry has become more involved with scientific research, alcohol education, prevention programs, and alcohol control policies, mainly to further their economic interests. Also, the authors discussed the problems associated with alcohol industry funded research, and were critical of it on a number of counts because of conflict of interest (for example, its "focus on industry-favourable positions, such as the health benefits of alcohol and the value of alcohol education programs"). We have seen the use of CSR activities in other unhealthy industries like smoking, tobacco, and gambling as one of the few remaining strategies available. Humour is also used in advertising with considerable effect.

The industry's corporate social responsibility programme includes such things as alcohol information websites and social marketing of ineffective harm-reduction campaigns, partnerships with government related to drink-driving, and funding scientific research. Rather than focusing on public health, their activities provide cover for maintaining a heavy drinking culture that yields enormous profits for private shareholders.

In a world-wide study using six global geographic regions, Babor, Robaina et al. (2018) asked the question of whether the alcohol industry was doing well by "doing good." They took a sample of 1046 CSR actions from a compendium of 3551 actions issued in 2012 representing the efforts of the alcohol industry to reduce harmful alcohol use. Nineteen public health professionals rated the actions using a reliable content rating procedure. They concluded that only 27% conformed to recommended WHO target areas for global action to reduce the harmful use of alcohol, 96.8% lacked scientific support, and 11.0% had the potential for doing harm. They concluded that:

> Alcohol industry CSR activities are unlikely to reduce harmful alcohol use but they do provide commercial strategic advantage while at the same time appearing to have a public health purpose.

### 4.3.2  Underage Drinkers

Alcohol epidemiologists have long been interested in the health effects of alcohol consumption and, more recently, in estimating the extent to which the industry profits from selling alcohol to underage drinkers and to those with alcohol use disorders. In the United States underage drinkers consume 20% of the alcohol, representing an estimated $22.5 billion in consumer expenditures. The combined value of illegal underage drinking and adult pathological drinking to the alcohol industry was estimated at $48.3 billion in 2001 dollars (Foster, Vaughan, et al., 2006). Recent research has focussed on the most effective policy approaches to reducing alcohol-related harm, either through regulatory measures that target per capita alcohol consumption or through interventions targeted at high-risk drinkers.

Babor and Robaina (2013) commented that the most effective approaches have found to be pricing and taxation policies, availability controls, drunk driving countermeasures, restrictions on alcohol marketing, specialised treatment of alcohol dependence, and brief interventions for hazardous drinking. As many of the strategies are universal measures that restrict the affordability, availability, and accessibility of alcohol, they come into conflict with industry interests. Voluntary practice codes have been promoted as an alternative to advertising bans designed to protect vulnerable populations from exposure to alcohol marketing. However, they found significant violations of industry self-regulation codes in sub-Saharan Africa, Australia, Brazil, United States, Canada, United Kingdom, and the European Union. Voluntary self-regulation does not work.

### 4.3.3 Alcohol Industry and Cancer

Petticrew, Maani Hessari, et al. (2018) considered how the alcohol industry (AI) organisations mislead the public about alcohol and cancer. They studied the accuracy of industry's information disseminated from 27 AI organisations through its "social aspects and public relations organizations and related bodies." Most of the organisations were found to disseminate misrepresentations of the evidence about the association between alcohol and cancer using three main strategies: (i) denial/omission: denying, omitting or disputing the evidence that alcohol consumption increases cancer risk; (ii) distortion: mentioning cancer, but misrepresenting the risk; and (iii) distraction: focussing discussion away from the independent effects of alcohol on common cancers. Breast cancer and colorectal cancer appeared to be a particular focus for this misrepresentation.

Casswell, Callinan, et al. (2016) state that:

> The alcohol industry have attempted to position themselves as collaborators in alcohol policy making as a way of influencing policies away from a focus on the drivers of the harmful use of alcohol (marketing, over availability and affordability). Their framings of alcohol consumption and harms allow them to argue for ineffective measures, largely targeting heavier consumers, and against population wide measures as the latter will affect moderate drinkers.

Although the alcohol industry says it promotes responsible drinking, we noted above that it relies on heavier drinking occasions for about 50% of sales in higher income countries (46% in New Zealand), and in middle income countries it is closer to two-thirds (Viet Cuon, Casswell, et al., 2018).

Given the large number of deaths related to alcohol, a responsible industry of any product that causes so many cancer deaths in a year would quickly warn its customers about the risk. However, the alcohol industry is actively engaged in the opposite approach, and has endeavoured to muddy the waters about the findings of medical science. It is attempting to confuse the public about the strong linkage between alcohol and cancer, to bring as much doubt to the public discussion as possible, and to denigrate those who present this information to the public.

Following a highly successful national conference on Alcohol and Cancer co-hosted by the Cancer Society of New Zealand and Alcohol Action NZ in 2015, Professor Doug Sellman of Otago university, New Zealand, in 2016 wrote a news article (tinyurl.com/zjo7b9j) referring to the University of Otago's Professor Jennie Connor who had two prestigious publications highlighting the fact that alcohol causes cancer in moderate drinkers in New Zealand. He said:

> A responsible industry of any product that is causing 250 cancer deaths
> each year would quickly warn its customers about the risk.

Sellman referred to an opinion editorial written by an American biomedical scientist, Dr Samir Zakhari, who works for the Distilled Spirits Council of the United States. Zakhari claimed that "attributing cancer to social moderate drinking is simply incorrect and is not supported by the body of scientific literature" and referred to the conference speakers as "well-intentioned" but mistaken.

Sellman also mentioned that the chief executive of Spirits New Zealand, Robert Brewer, made comments after the latest publications by Connor suggesting her latest paper was just "an opinion piece", likening her work to that of an amateur who on finding a study that shows people who wear blue jeans drive fast then concludes that blue jeans must cause road fatalities. Zakhari is a little more circumspect about his words compared with the previous year's flat denial of an association between moderate drinking and cancer, resorting now to terminology aimed at hiding alcohol as a direct causative agent in cancer such as "complex interactions between lifestyle, sociocultural and genetic issues" and referring to "light to moderate drinking" rather than "moderate drinking". However, he is just as forthright in accusing Connor of "lacking scientific credibility" and basing her conclusions on "cherry-picking epidemiological articles".

Michaels (2008) summed up the situation of doubt promoted by some large corporations. Quoting from his book jacket:

> "Doubt is our product," a cigarette executive once observed, "since it is the
> best means of competing with the 'body of fact' that exists in the minds
> of the general public. It is also the means of establishing a controversy.

In this exposé, David Michaels reveals just how prevalent — and how effective—such strategies have become. He argues that to keep the public confused about the hazards posed by global warming, secondhand smoke, asbestos, lead, plastics, and many other toxic materials, industry executives have hired unscrupulous scientists and lobbyists to dispute the scientific evidence that would alert the public to these dangers. Their goal is the manufacture of doubt.

In the tobacco industry we saw how they denied any cancer link, especially lung cancer, for decades. They hid the facts and attempted to discredit the growing body of medical and scientific evidence by treating it as "junk science." In the case of alcohol, there is a difference as there have been studies referred to in section 2.6 that suggested that alcohol in some forms might be good for you. An editorial in the New Zealand Listener (Sept. 1, 2018) said:

> What's needed is a balanced debate that takes into account the social and
> economic benefits of alcohol.

On the surface, it sounds a good idea, and dialogue is always useful provided the alcohol industry is prepared to look at health issues. Also it would be interesting to know what are the social and economic benefits of alcohol, given the huge cost of the individual and social harm it causes. It is now up to the industry to come to the party and show that they care for more than just profits!

## 4.4   LOW AND ZERO ALCOHOL DRINKS

One innovation by the alcohol industry is the introduction of low and zero alcohol drinks, and even gluten-free alcohol-free beer. The question is: "How much will these reduce the amount of alcohol consumed and the consequent harm from alcohol?" In many cases, bottles with "zero" alcohol state that they contain no more than 0.5% alcohol per bottle (about the amount that can naturally occurs in fruit juice). Low calorific alcoholic drinks are also available, since sugar in drinks can be problem. If one is cynical about this new development, a question that might be asked is what is in it for the alcohol industry. Possibilities might be:

- to break into the abstainers market (e.g., pregnant women, children, young drinkers, drivers)

- to provide a more sophisticated soft drink

- to take over the soft drink market

- to reinforce a brand name and provide more options under that name

- to encourage people to drink more of low alcoholic drinks to achieve the same "buzz" as for normal alcoholic drinks

- to normalise alcohol brands as the go-to drinks for all occasions (e.g., weekday lunchtimes, family occasions)

- to produce products that may be perceived as extensions to regular strength alcoholic drinks rather than as substitutes for them

- to offset a long-term downturn in global alcohol consumption

It will be of interest to see how this new market flourishes, as the alcohol industry tends to make much of its money from heavy drinkers. If it does lead to the consumption of less alcohol, it will be a good thing. The world's first non-alcoholic spirit (Seedlip) arrived in New Zealand after a two-year wait, and sold out within a week (Stuff news, 5 March, 2018). However, one of the problems is the branding of non-alcoholic beer and other similar drinks to look like alcoholic products. Habib Kadiri from the the Institute of Alcohol Studies wrote an interesting blog (http://www.ias.org.uk/Blog/Alcohol-free-alcohol-A-00-sum-endgame.aspx) that looked at this and related issues. He stated that with respect to the downturn in consumption:

> Some major alcohol producers have responded to this trend by premiumising product ranges—meaning customers spend more on the same amount of alcohol in a product of a higher quality —while relying on heavy drinkers consuming lower quality products to maintain healthy profit margins for their shareholders.

The identical branding of both alcoholic alcohol-free beers raises concerns that such exposure to children would lead to a progression from soft drinks to an earlier onset of drinking alcohol and heavier drinking in young people.

The Sun newspaper (28 Apr 2019) said that alcohol-free beer is being rolled out across the UK for the first time and Heineken put its alcohol-free brand "0.0" on tap at 1,500 pubs. City Pub Group, which has 44 pubs across the south of England and Wales, is also stocking a range of alcohol-free craft beer on draught at its locations. Also new brewing technology means that low-or-no alcohol beers are becoming tastier, helping them to become one of the fastest growing drinks sectors on the market (2018 Global Data report). In 2018, Anheuser-Busch InBev, Budweiser's parent company, launched 12 new no- and low-alcohol beers with 8% of the company's global beer sales by volume being from beers with lower or no alcohol, with plans to grow that figure to 20% by 2025. As overall beer sales stagnate, nonalcoholic-beer sales have grown by 3.9% on average for the past five years, according to The Wall Street Journal (Business Insider, February 8, 2019).

A news item (7 May 2019) from the National Business Review (NBR) in New Zealand stated that, from the sales figures, big New Zealand breweries are experiencing rocketing value and sales growth in their "better for me" categories, boosted by younger Kiwis wanting to live more healthily and avoid hangovers. The "better for me" category includes low/zero alcohol, carbohydrate and sugar beers, and adult non-alcoholic beverages, such as kombucha– a fermented tea. For example,

> in New Zealand, DB has sold 2.2 million bottles of Heineken 0.0 since the beer's launch in August last year, a demand which is 'absolutely' driven by younger generations wanting to moderate their alcohol consumption.

The Lion brewery had a good response to the February (2019) launch of its 2.5% low alcohol beer, Steinlager Pure Light. Sales over a four-week period in April grew from $40,500 to $101,500. What is encouraging is that here has also been an increase in sales of the low carb category for the alcohol companies.

On the other side of the coin, NBR comments that:

> Alcohol Healthwatch director Nicki Jackson says younger people are seeking healthier diets but there are 'certainly' people who are adding, instead of substituting 'better for me' drinks to their normal consumption of alcohol.

She says "They increase the number of drinking occasions." A study in the UK (Vasiljevic, Coulter, et al., 2018) concluded that:

> Low/er strength wines and beers appear to be marketed not as substitutes for higher strength products but as ones that can be consumed on additional occasions with an added implication of healthiness.

There is also another angle in New Zealand and probably elsewhere. It appears that some young people are favouring marijuana over alcohol, which may become a bigger factor if alcohol becomes more expensive. No doubt such issues will become avenues for further research.

We note that according to Statistics New Zealand (26 February, 2019, https://www.stats.govt.nz/news/more-high-strength-beer-available-in-2018), the volume of high-strength beer (above 5% alcohol) available for consumption has almost trebled in five years, rising 21% in 2018 alone, and reflecting the rising popularity of craft beers. The rise was partly offset by a fall in lower-strength beers available to the domestic market in 2018. Consequently, the overall amount of beer available in 2018 was only up 1.4 percent, recovering from a 1.2 percent fall the previous year, suggesting a near-flat market over two years. In 2010, the average adult would have had about 800 standard drinks available to consume. By 2018, that was down to about 730 a year. In 2018, there was enough alcohol for each adult New Zealander to drink the equivalent of 2.0 standard drinks a day, down from a recent peak of 2.2 in 2010. Spirits and spirit-based drinks (such as ready-to-drink (RTD) beverages) are among the fastest growing sectors in the alcoholic drinks market. The total volume of spirits (including spirit-based drinks such as RTDs ) rose 4.9 percent, following similar rises in each of the previous three years followed up.

An Australian study (Keric and Stafford, 2018) looked at some of the so-called "healthy" alcoholic products labels and concluded that the alcohol industry was using misleading health "halos" to sell alcohol like "pure", "fresh"," low-carb" and "low-calorie" to lure in health-conscious consumers. At least some of alcohol's health halos seem to be working: research suggests low-carb beer is perceived by some drinkers as a healthier alternative to regular beer, even though the alcohol content is similar and the absolute difference in carbs is small. Low carb beer is not low alcohol. The authors concluded that:

> Existing regulations do not appear to be sufficient to effectively restrict health-related claims from being made by alcohol producers and marketers, or the use of health imagery in alcohol advertising, despite implications for the way consumers perceive these products.

Once again we see the limitations of industry self-regulation.


## 4.5 CONCLUSION

The alcohol industry has endeavoured to develop some strategies to deal with some downward trends in incomes because of health issues and some regulation changes. Also younger people are drinking less alcohol. Generally the industry prefers to concentrate on those strategies dealing with individuals like self-regulation and education that have however shown not to work. Also blaming a "minority" group for alcohol problems.

Population statistics tend to be seen as a threat as they lead to restrictive regulation changes, in particular universal measures that restrict the affordability, availability, and accessibility of alcohol. One strategy is the introduction of low or zero alcohol drinks which, in the latter case, means a move into the soft drink industry. However, one of the problems with this is the branding of non-alcoholic beer and other similar drinks to look like alcoholic products, which could be a problem with young people.

# CHAPTER 5

# ALCOHOL, HISTORY AND THE NZ LAW

## 5.1 SOME HISTORY

Sugars suitable for the fermentation by yeast of plant sugars occur naturally within ripe fruit pulp. As fruit-eating has been around for a long time it is not surprising that ethanol arrived on the scene through very ripe fruit. In the history of life, the human production of alcohol is comparatively quite recent. Tartaric acid residue of grapes characterising Iranian pottery from 5400 to 5000 BC is one of the earliest indications of intentional fermentation by humans. McGovern, Zhang, et al. (2004) mentioned that:

> Chemical analyses of ancient organics absorbed into pottery jars from the early Neolithic village of Jiahu in Henan province in China have revealed that a mixed fermented beverage of rice, honey, and fruit (hawthorn fruit and/or grape) was being produced as early as the seventh millennium before Christ (B.C.).

This led the way for unique cereal beverages as early as 2000 BCE preserved as liquids inside sealed bronze vessels of the Shang and Western Zhou Dynasties. This nearly universal phenomenon of

*Alcohol: A dangerous love affair.*
By George A. F. Seber and D. Graeme Woodfield Copyright © 2019

fermented beverage production can be explained by ethanol's analgesic, disinfectant, and profound effects on the mind. It has been used on cultural, religious, and major historical events. Ancient biblical references to alcohol are given in the appendix. Some history since then, based on Caughey and Ney (1987), is now described.

In Roman times alcohol was a feature of orgies. Seneca (4BC–63AD) described the difference between a man who is drunk and a drunkard. The former is "maybe in that state for the first time, and may not have that habit", while a drunkard is "a slave to the habit". Distillation was apparently developed by the Arabs in the Middle Ages so that fortified wines and spirits could be produced. Given the problems it caused it is perhaps not surprising that Mohammad forbad his followers from drinking alcohol.

Alcohol was certainly a significant factor in the 18th century in Britain with lesser intoxicating drinks such as beer and cider being replaced by cheap gin. In 1727 the consumption of spirits in Britain was 3.5 million gallons, but by 1757 it had risen to 11 million gallons. This was the position when key figures such as Wesley, Wilberforce, and Shaftsbury spoke out about key issues such as slavery, child labour, and alcoholism. Alcoholism was a major problem with the miners in the West of England and elsewhere. In North America, the young American colony was fighting for its independence, with the civil war between the North and the South. Abraham Lincoln said,

> Alcohol is a stronger bond, a viler slavery, a greater tyranny than the slave traffic.

In 1840 a temperance movement was begun by recovered alcohols and other heavy drinkers, who encouraged people to join them and to sign a pledge, accepting abstinence. There was also a very successful Washington movement that led to the establishment of over 10,000 Washington societies across America. Dr. Franklin Buchman, Lutheran minister, founded a movement which became known as the Oxford Group in England in 1931. This eventually led to the founding of Alcoholics Anonymous (AA) in 1935 by Bill Wilson and Dr. Robert Smith in the US. It is a fascinating story.

### New Zealand

The love affair New Zealand has had with alcohol commenced in the early days of its history. Traditionally, Māoris did not drink alcohol, and initially described it as spirits waipiro (foul water). Up to the 1850s, Māoris did not use much alcohol, but with increasing availability their consumption soon increased. In 1847, 1870, and 1878 measures were introduced to restrict the sale of alcohol in Māori areas. Many leading Māoris presented petitions supporting such restrictions, and in 1884 liquor licenses were banned from, for instance, in the King country in the Waikato. Māoris quickly adapted to these new ways of living, and alcohol eventually became a major problem. Binge drinking amongst both Europeans and Māoris was frequent.

For early immigrants from Britain and Europe, beer was a normal part of their diet. As the colonial settlers came to New Zealand they brought with them the same attitude to alcohol. Perhaps this made life more pleasant for the hard-working settlers, mainly unmarried males. In 1879, there was one hotel for every 287 Europeans, and convictions for alcohol offences were very frequent.

By 1870 the consumption of alcohol per head was about the same as that of the UK, but became lower after that date. Colonial drinkers did not drink much beer, but usually drank spirits and fortified wines as beer was expensive to transport. Brandy and rum were the main drinks, and until the mid-1860s per capita consumption of spirits and wines were about 3 to 4 times the UK level. The stage was thus set for a high alcohol intake, which has continued since that time.

Local production of alcohol did not commence until the 1840s. Up to that time illegal stills were common, but the Distillation Act of 1868 legalised alcohol production. By 1867 the number of breweries was nine, while in the decade after 1870 the number of breweries increased from 51 to 91 with numerous locally made beers available, and imported beers fell to 10% of beer sales. Beer drinking became prevalent, but it is interesting to note that the beer consumption in the 1870s were still under half that of the United Kingdom.

There has always been a considerable opposition to the alcohol trade in New Zealand. In 1885, it was the Women's Christian Temperance Union (WCTU) organised by Kate Shepherd (now better known for her efforts in achieving voting rights for women) that spearheaded her suffragette activities and gave her access to an organised women's association. The temperance movement was one of the most divisive movements of the late 1800s and early 1900s, as it was argued that alcohol fuelled poverty, ill-health, crime, and immorality. National prohibition was nearly achieved in 1911, and the prohibition vote reached 55.8%, but below the 60% required. In 1919 the prohibition vote was 49.7%, tantalising below the 50% required at that time, with the vote being heavily influenced by soldiers returning from World War 1. So New Zealand never introduced prohibition, although controversy on the topic remained for many years after.

We see then that in colonial New Zealand alcohol was plentiful and drinking laws permissive. Because of the related abuse, the temperance movement helped introduce the 6 o'clock swill during World War I as a means to support war efforts. The six o'clock swill was an Australian and New Zealand slang term for the last-minute rush to buy drinks at a hotel bar before it closed. During a significant part of the 20th century, most Australian and New Zealand hotels shut their public bars at 6 pm. A culture of heavy drinking developed during the time between finishing work at 5 pm and the mandatory closing time only an hour later. Also laws were introduced to separate drinking from entertainment and to "civilise" culture. Drinking establishments could no longer provide food or entertainment, could not serve women, and could not employ women as servers. All of this led to a male-oriented, beer-focused, binge drinking culture.

A key writer on alcohol matters was John A. Lee, a Labour politician, who wrote a book centred mainly about Sir Ernest Davis (Mr Booze). He canvassed against alcohol, but became a friend of Sir Ernest and described how in many ways the alcohol industry infiltrated the political systems in NZ. Every effort was made by the leaders of the brewing industry to protect "the Trade (of alcohol)." Lee writes in 1975:

> New Zealand has retreated from temperance and prohibition and has gone over to what is called 'civilised drinking'. For half the community the ideal life has become the way of Coronation Street; the mass mind tends to inhabit the slum Pub.

He goes on to state:

> Already Sir Ernest Booze is scarcely remembered, and yet there was no more sinister figure in New Zealand's political life: a man who owed loyalty only to 'The Trades' investments. Sir Ernest was maybe the greatest shadowland manipulator of politics New Zealand is ever likely to see.

In an attempt to modify the excesses of alcohol consumption the Alcohol Liquor Advisory Council (ALAC) was formed in 1976 to promote moderation in drinking, and reduce the harm of alcohol. (It was later absorbed in 2012 into the Health Promotion Agency (HPA), a wing of the Department of Health.) In 1984 the Labour government came to power in a landslide victory and quickly began setting up a number of economic reforms, which have become known as neo-liberalism. These concepts, championed by Roger Douglas the Labour minister of finance at the time, focused on the idea that decreasing regulation in the economy would allow the free market to be more efficient and deliver the best solutions for society.

A review of the liquor laws was established by the new government, headed by Sir George Laking. The group ignored the established association between increased availability of alcohol and alcohol-related harm and argued for the liberalisation of the supply and sale of alcohol. The Sale of Liquor Act of 1989 thus came into being and liberalised the environment in which alcohol was sold and supplied in New Zealand. For example, it saw the presence of wine in supermarkets followed by a proliferation of alcohol outlets, extension of trading hours, and increasingly sophisticated marketing techniques that encourage a culture of heavy drinking. Food and entertainment were allowed back into drinking establishments along with women waitresses. Alcohol was made more affordable, more available, and advertised more widely than ever before.

An organisation was formed in the early 1990s called the Group Opposed to Advertising of Liquor (GOAL) led by Mr Cliff Turner of Hamilton who was awarded an MBE for his efforts. With the new problems arising, another group founded in Auckland in 1990 was the Group Against Liquor Advertising (GALA), which grew from the success of ASH (Action on Smoking and Health). In 1990 the Smokefree Environments Act was passed by the Labour Government. Deirdre Kent had been director of ASH for the past 8 years and perceived the need for a similar law to stop the advertising and sponsorship of alcohol. Like tobacco, alcohol was having serious ill effects on the health of New Zealanders.

In 1991 Deirdre called together a meeting in Auckland of relevant health groups and groups in the Temperance Movement. GALA was established with Deirdre as volunteer chairperson, and a constitution was written. A committee with representatives of women's groups, health promotion, churches, nurses, Samoan, Māori, and temperance organisations was established. One of the first actions of GALA was to massively support the Private Member's Bill of Joy McLaughlan requiring health and safety warnings to accompany broadcast liquor advertisements. In spite of many well-argued submissions to the select committee the bill was not passed.

During her time with ASH, Deirdre wrote many newsletters. In one of them she described Michael Thompson, Head of the Tobacco Institute, as "a friendly international drug pusher." He took exception and threatened to sue for libel for $250,000. After a painful twenty months, during which she had to retire from ASH and was working on foetal alcohol syndrome for GALA, ASH had to employ a QC, and soon this was settled out of court for an undisclosed sum. One of the unspoken but independently verified conditions of settlement was that Deirdre should also stop working for GALA.

In 1993 Deirdre called on Viola Palmer, a medical doctor and fellow activist in Tauranga, with the request that she take over the chair of GALA. Viola had lost a son 10 years previously in an alcohol related car crash. She led GALA for the next 19 years. The committee at this time consisted of Viola Palmer (chair) Graham Creahan, Phil Groom, Averill Groom, John Potter, Judy McAnulty, Paul Town-Treweek, Jeanette McIntosh, June Mariu, and Susanna Lavea. It was later joined at various stages by others including Harold Coop, Graeme Woodfield, and George Seber.

There was a further wave of liberalisation ushered in by the National-led coalition government in 1999 under Jenny Shipley involving liquor sales in grocery stores in addition to supermarkets, adding beer to wine for these sales, and lowering the overall purchase age of alcohol from 20 to 18 years. During this time GALA, led by Dr Viola Palmer, was very active in lobbying against alcohol advertising, and made many submissions to government. Later, it played a part in encouraging the development of the alcohol law reform study chaired by Sir Geoffrey Palmer in 2010, which is discussed later.

In 2014 GALA joined with Alcohol Action New Zealand (AANZ) led by Dr Doug Sellman, a professor of Otago University. This organisation proved to be very effective in Government lobbying at high levels, and organised annual conferences on the various aspects of alcohol harm, working closely with Alcohol Healthwatch (AHW) in Auckland, an Auckland Hospital Board organisation. In 2015, the Health and Safety at Work Act helped put a dampener on alcohol in the workplace, as an employer had to take all "reasonably practicable steps" to eliminate risks in the workplace. That includes employees becoming a hazard to themselves or colleagues due to alcohol intake (NZ Herald, January, 2018). The wording of the act made organisations nervous and many took a long, hard look at their alcohol policies. Many big names have made changes, for example Fonterra has a policy of no alcohol at work.

### Early research on alcohol

What research was being done on alcohol in those earlier years? Huckle, Pledger and Casswell (2012) looked at 11 comparable general population alcohol surveys conducted between 1990 and 2000 in Auckland, New Zealand, during the period when the liberalising alcohol policy changes occurred. They found considerable increases in alcohol consumption and alcohol-related problems particularly among young people and women. The youngest age group, those 14–19 years old, experienced the most marked increases in quantity. The proportion of them experiencing threshold problems was observed to be higher in each year compared with those 40–65 years old, and the 14- to 19-year-olds experienced a greater year-on-year increase. Drinking remained relatively stable between 2000 and 2004, but with increases in quantity for men 30–39 and 40–49 years, and increases in proportions of heavier drinkers among men aged 40–49 and 50–65 years (Huckle, You, and Caswell, 2011). From 1998 to 2008, per capita alcohol consumption in New Zealand increased by about 10% having previously been declining (New Zealand Law Commission, 2009).

## 5.2 THE LAW COMMISSION

Sellman, Connor, et al. (2018) discussed attempts at alcohol law reform in New Zealand between 2008 and 2017, and some of what follows is based on their paper. Two decades on from the 1989 liberalisation, in the face of mounting concerns about alcohol-related harms, the government of the day entrusted the New Zealand Law Commission, led by Sir Geoffrey Palmer, to undertake a rigorous and comprehensive review of the liquor laws in 2009/2010. The resulting review set out a progressive reform of the alcohol laws regulating marketing, price, accessibility, and age of purchase. It led to an extensive book (New Zealand Law Commission, 2010) which made 153 recommendations. While several of these were adopted in whole or in part in the new Sale and Supply of Alcohol Act 2012 (implemented during 2013), some of the most effective recommendations to reduce alcohol-related harms were ignored (see Kypri, Maclennan et al. (2011) for examples). Sellman, Connor, et al. (2018) commented that the

> non-reform bill was the outcome of a political process of obfuscation, delay and inaction led by then prime minister, John Key.

They concluded that "the love of money" is at the heart of the barriers to change. Sellman, Connor, et al. (2017) document

> how the government engaged in a drawn-out process with significant time delays, largely ignoring the main evidence-based recommendations of the Law Commission, withholding vital information from the public, dismissing concerns expressed by both the public and opposition parties, and using a combination of the conscience vote and an unusual voting procedure in Parliament to deliver a Bill that was favourable to the alcohol industry.

Sellman, Connor, et al. (2018) described the main features of the process as follows:

- Setting the bar of expectations low at the outset by agreeing that New Zealand was in the mood for change but not a "major overhaul."

- Using the well-known industry assertion that major reform would be unfair to "responsible drinkers."

- Declaring early on that the government had no intention of raising alcohol taxes, and thus dismissing the single most effective and easily enacted measure advocated for in the Law Commission report.

- Including the possibility of a raising of the purchase age in the Alcohol Reform Bill to deflect attention away from the lack of marketing and pricing reforms.

- Establishing a very liberal default for on- and off-licence alcohol sales (7am–4am), while putting the responsibility for establishing more restricted hours on to local government, thereby setting up drawn-out, expensive processes involving communities, local councils, and the alcohol industry.

- Breaking an undertaking to introduce new legislation within six months by delaying by over a year and a half.

- Timing public submissions on the new bill to coincide with the Christmas/New Year holiday period.

- Introducing more delays by timing the second reading of the bill for the month before the general election in November 2011 and therefore leaving no time for it to be debated.

- Withholding publication of the results of a Health Sponsorship Council survey showing that the majority of the public wanted strong reforms around alcohol.

- Introducing further delays before the bill was finally debated and passed in August 2012.

- Using the conscience vote and an unusual two-step voting strategy to see off the raising of the age of purchase of alcohol.

- Using parliamentary processes to sweep away 22 supplementary order papers on the bill.

- Falsely claiming the bill was a great success when the truth was that this so-called reform bill contained no reforms, the minister resorting to the well-known alcohol industry mantra of striking a balance between reducing harm and not penalising responsible drinkers.

Sellman, Connor, et al. (2017) mentioned that the alcohol industry has a series of stock-phrases, revealed from alcohol-industry internal documents (Bond, Daube, and Chikritzhs, 2010), designed to be repeated as much as possible in public in order to counter effective alcohol reform. Here are a sample of these phrases

- "the majority of people who drink do so responsibly".

- "unfair to penalise the majority to pay for the actions of a few".

- "excise taxes are regressive, forcing a disproportionate burden on those least able to afford it".

- "advertising affects brand performance not consumption or abuse. advertising is used to remind drinkers about the importance of drinking responsibly".

- "more research is needed".

The role of marketing of alcohol with regard to the Law Commission was discussed by Casswell (2014) who noted that the Commission's final report recommended a three-stage reform which, if carried through, would result in some effective restrictions on exposure to alcohol marketing. She suggested that there were two major influences that could have led to this recommendation: (1) the level of popular support for change (3000 submissions, with 86% of these recommending banning or restricting alcohol advertising of all alcohol in all media), and (2) recent research such as by Baber, Caetano, et al. (2010), who established both that exposure to alcohol advertising recruits young people to drink earlier and to drink larger quantities, and that voluntary codes such as that operated by the ASA (Adverting Standards Authority) are ineffective.

All that occurred was (Casswell, 2014)

> an extension to pre-existing regulation, focussed on the retail sector, which prohibits promotions promoting excessive drinking, having special appeal to minors, offering free alcohol or discounts of 25% or more or offering free goods or services with the purchase of alcohol. The promotion which is so powerful in building brand relationships and normalising drinking was left untouched.

Casswell noted that the the marketing of alcohol in its unrestricted state is to

> first, protect the profits of the transnational corporate producers by allowing them to appeal to new cohorts of young people with marketing which recruits them as consumers as early as possible and encourages drinking of larger amounts and second, to protect the financial interests of the advertising and media industries.

How to control internet marketing is a world-wide problem. For example Russia has instituted bans originating from sites inside Russia, and Finland has passed legislated restrictions on alcohol advertising. In the end legislation is needed as self-regulation by the industries is ineffective.

High quality research has revealed that at least 25% of drinkers in New Zealand are heavy drinkers, in that they score above the threshold for hazardous drinking on the World Health Organisation screening tool, the Alcohol Use Disorders Identification Test or AUDIT (Wells, Baxter, and Schaaf, 2006). This translates into a national group of at least 700,000 heavy drinkers. Two other reports have since contained several recommendations for reducing the harms from alcohol to children and young people, but they have either been ignored or are yet to be fully implemented.

### 5.2.1 Act of 2012

The Act of 2012 specifies that anyone who is aged 18 years or over and shows approved ID can enter licensed premises and buy alcohol. In some circumstances, people under 18 may be allowed in licensed premises, even though they are not allowed to buy alcohol. It is illegal to supply alcohol to someone under the age of 18 years unless the person supplying the alcohol is the parent or legal guardian and the alcohol is supplied in a responsible manner, or the person supplying alcohol has the express consent of the young person's parent or legal guardian and the alcohol is supplied in a responsible manner. (See also www.alcohol.org.nz/help-advice/advice-on-alcohol/for-parents-and-caregivers.) There is no age at which it is illegal to drink alcohol in New Zealand.

With regard to drinking and driving, the legal alcohol limit for drivers under 20 years of age is now a blood alcohol (ethanol) concentration (BAC) of zero, while for drivers 20 years and over, 250 mcg per litre of breath or 50mg of blood per 100 millilitres of blood (commonly expressed as a percentage such as 0.05%). The purchase age in New Zealand was lowered from 20 to 18 in 1999, and this has been associated with increased assaults resulting in hospitalisation among young males aged 15 to 19 (Kypri, Davie et al., 2014), and an increased likelihood of alcohol-involved crashes among drivers aged 18 to 19 years (Huckle and Parker, 2014). Begg, Brookland, and Connor (2017) found that in New Zealand

> high alcohol use was common among young newly licensed drivers and those who repeatedly reported high alcohol use were at a significantly higher risk of unsafe driving behaviors.

### 5.2.2 Ministerial Forum, 2014

A ministerial forum on alcohol advertising and sponsorship was organised in October 2014. It came up with the following recommendations among others:

(1) Ban alcohol sponsorship of all streamed and broadcast sports. As noted in a previous chapter, in New Zealand there is a strong cultural connection between alcohol and sport which needs to be addressed. The Forum is concerned that young people are not protected from exposure to alcohol sponsorship when viewing sport.

(2) Ban alcohol sponsorship of sports (long-term). The objective of this recommendation is to break the connection between alcohol consumption and sport.

(3) Ban alcohol sponsorship (naming rights) at all venues. The objective of this recommendation is to prevent a situation where alcohol producers and retailers redirect funds to sponsoring venues. This recommendation includes the naming of all venues.

(4) Ban alcohol sponsorship of cultural and music events where 10% or more of participants and audiences are younger than 18.

(5) Introduce a sponsorship replacement funding programme. This recommendation is designed to specifically reduce the impact of funding lost as a direct result of the ban on alcohol sponsorship of sport.

(6) Introduce a targeted programme to reduce reliance on alcohol sponsorship funding. The objective of this recommendation is to work closely with community sporting clubs and associations to develop the capacity and skills to generate alternate sponsorship funding.

(7) Ban alcohol advertising during streamed and broadcast sporting events.

(8) Ban alcohol advertising where 10% or more of the audience is younger than 18. The proposed restriction would mean alcohol advertising could not be placed in public areas including billboards and advertisements in transit hubs such as bus stops and train stations. In addition, it is likely to capture some radio audience, readers or print publications and websites with a high youth audience.

(9) Further restrict the hours for alcohol advertising on broadcast.

(10) Continue to offset remaining alcohol advertising by funding positive messaging across all media. The objective of this

recommendation is to secure the "moderation time" arrangements in light of the fact that some alcohol advertising, albeit restricted, will still be permitted.

(11) Introduce additional restrictions on external advertising on licensed venues and outlets. The objective of this recommendation is to ensure that all measures available to reduce youth exposure to alcohol are exercised and avoid gaps and loopholes in the system.

(12) Establish an independent authority to monitor and initiate complaints about alcohol advertising and sponsorship.

(13) Establish a mechanism to identify and act on serious or persistent breaches of advertising standards. A criticism of the current approach to self-regulation is that there is limited impact from breaching the Advertising Standards Authority (ASA) codes. The logic is that by the time the ASA has heard a matter the advertising campaign in question has usually aired for some time already and may even have come to an end. There is a strong perception that by this stage the damage from exposure to inappropriate alcohol advertising is already done.

(14) Establish a multi-stakeholder committee to periodically review and assess advertising standards complaints board decisions and pre-vetted advertising. This recommendation responds to the criticism that alcohol advertising self-regulation offers no effective restriction on advertising content. In particular the criticism suggests that advertisers actively find ways to circumvent existing restrictions intended to limit intentional or perceived associations between alcohol consumption and positive outcomes and lifestyles.

Here (1)–(6) endeavour to reduce youth exposure through sponsorship, while (7)–(11) endeavour to reduce youth exposure through advertising, and (12)–(14) endeavour to strengthen the current system of co-regulation. The above as a whole would tighten up the recommendations of the ASA Code, but were not taken up and enacted.

### 5.2.3 Alcohol Action NZ

At the beginning of 2009, a new alcohol law reform group was set up led by Dr Doug Sellman, a professor of Otago University and director of the National Addiction Centre, Christchurch School of Medicine and Health Sciences, since its inception in 1996. The organisation was called Alcohol Action NZ (AANZ), and began advocating for scientifically-based alcohol law reform. This organisation has proved to be effective in Government lobbying at high levels, and has organised annual conferences on the various aspects of alcohol harm. It has co-ordinated closely with Alcohol Healthwatch (AHW) in Auckland, a Hospital Board organisation. In 2014 GALA joined forces with AANZ which had formulated an easy-to-remember summary of the most effective measures for reducing population-based alcohol harm called the "5+ Solution", as follows:

(1) Raise alcohol prices.

(2) Raise the purchase age.

(3) Reduce alcohol accessibility.

(4) Reduce alcohol advertising and sponsorship.

(5) Increase drink-driving countermeasures.

These recommendations were incorporated in the New Zealand Medical Association's guidelines discussed in chapter 7.

## 5.3   LOCAL COUNCILS

As part of the 2012 Act, there was an emphasis to promote increased community input into local licensing decisions through the devolution of policy-making from a central body to local government. could adopt local alcohol policies (LAPs) to make local rules for alcohol licensing. Alcohol promotions are controlled so that they do not encourage excessive alcohol consumption or drinking by people under 18. Regulations may be made to ban some alcohol products. Supermarkets and grocery stores are required to limit the display and advertising of alcohol to a single non prominent area of their store. A visit to supermarkets indicates that this has not routinely happened. However, the main effect of the Act was to restrict very late-night trading (after 4am) in a relatively small number of on-licence venues in New Zealand's main cities. New research from Massey University (Randerson, Casswell, and Huckle, 2018) showed little evidence that changes introduced by the Act have affected New Zealand's alcohol environment between 2013 and 2015, apart from a small reduction in on-licence trading hours in New Zealand's main cities.

Casswell (2018c) reported that although the Sale and Supply of Alcohol Act was passed in 2012, by 2016 less than 30% of local authorities had successfully implemented LAPs (Jackson, 2016). She said that the "decision to allow an appeal against local authorities" (LAPs) in the Sale and Supply of Alcohol Act has resulted in unusual visibility of the influence process. The opportunity to engage legal representation to challenge proposed restrictions on trading hours has illustrated the very different financial resources available to the retailers of alcohol versus those supporting strategic restriction of availability. As a result, some of the councils have faced ongoing and expensive lengthy legal battles. This has happened with proposed local alcohol policy limits on trading hours and premise locations being delayed and weakened by extensive legal appeals from alcohol suppliers, who had greater resources than those of local authorities and health agencies.

### Dealing with LAPs

The process of objecting to an alcohol licence application is not an easy one, and can be very stressful. The number of alcohol licenses continues to increase. For example, sixty-seven new alcohol licences have been issued in Queenstown in just two years; up from 192 to 259 (Otago Daily Times, 28 July 2019). Also the number of people seeking treatment for addictions in Queenstown has doubled in two years (Otago Daily Times, 18 May, 2018).

We now give a few recent examples of what can happen as battles are going on all over the country. A Stuff news item (April 12, 2019) said:

> A liquor store will be able to open near a medical centre and five other grog shops in Levin, despite the fact it clashes with the area's proposed alcohol policy.

We also have the opening of a large liquor barn in Whanganui where there were already about 10 outlets and liquor stores within a 1km radius, which caused outrage (NZ Herald, 30 April, 2019). Dunedin mayor in the Otago Daily Times (12 October, 2018) said that there needed to be a "complete change" in approach at a national level when it came to LAPs, "because at the moment they are a farce." He said that the burden of proof was on councils to prove their policies would reduce alcohol-related harm, despite an earlier royal commission having already identified the factors exacerbating that harm. The Council policy was stripped of key changes earlier that year after being successfully appealed by a group including supermarket chains and liquor stores, leaving only uncontested aspects of the policy to be rolled out in Dunedin.

Commercial interests are effectively being put ahead of community wellbeing. By 2108, the alcohol industry had appealed 30 of 32 alcohol policies proposed by councils to reduce harmful drinking. Their appeals generally focussed on a lack of *local* evidence linking reduced availability to reduced harm. Unfortunately evidence comes from large scale studies rather than local ones.

A small study (104 participants)) involving Colmar Brunton, Social Research Agency (Ryan-Hughes, 2018), summarised comments made by community members who experienced anxiety/stress in objecting to new liquor outlets suggested that difficulties arose due to the following:

- The intimidating courtroom setting and lawyers.

- Not knowing the required actions and feeling unprepared.

- Not knowing the sequence of events for the hearing.

- Opposing parties having more resources to represent their views.

- Feeling disrespected by other parties involved.

- Inconvenient hearing times.

Legal costs can also be a problem. Gathering supporting evidence in time for a District Licensing Committee hearing or a LAP hearing was considered difficult by the majority of those who had to undertake these tasks. Suggested priority areas for improvement in participation from the highest to the lowest are:

(1) The fairness of the way in which the process is conducted.

(2) Equal weight given to the views of community members and others.

(3) Community members views being taken into consideration in decision making.

(4) The enjoyability of the process.

(5) Feeling at ease during the process.

(6) Easy to understand information on the process and what to do.

(7) Easy access to people who can explain the process and give advice.

(8) The amount of time it takes for community members to participate.

A number of useful recommendations for achieving some of the above were also given. A very useful document for advising how to object to a licence is given by the Health Promotion Agency (2015a). Justice Minister Andrew Little said he's concerned about the alcohol industry using its "deep pockets" to "overpower" local communities - and warns a review of the current law is on the cards (Newshub, 26 August, 2019). For further statistical information about LAPs see NZIER (2019).

## 5.4  LABELLING OF ALCOHOL CONTAINERS

Health warnings on alcohol beverage containers exist in many countries. For example, the International Alliance for Responsible Drinking gives a table (http://www.iard.org/resources/health-warning-labeling-requirements/) listing 39 countries plus three pending describing warnings that must be used. Because of Ireland going ahead with legislation at the time to have warnings, there was opposition from 11 European Union countries and the European Commission to alcohol warnings on the grounds that the legislation would create barriers to free trade. Manufacturers who imported alcohol into Ireland would be required to include health labels on their products. A Dublin MEP, Brian Hayes, said:

> The legislation is a landmark piece of public health legislation. It contains many measures including minimum pricing, advertising rules and restrictions on promotions. The most controversial element is the requirement to have health labels on all alcoholic drinks.This means all alcoholic drinks sold in Ireland must contain a label showing the grams of alcohol, calorie count, health warnings as well as an address to a public health website. No such laws exist in any other EU country.

(Spirits Business, 31 May, 2016). On 12 March 2018, the European associations representing the alcoholic beverages sectors presented their self-regulatory proposal to the Commission, and is being assessed. It contains a common commitment applying to the wine, cider, spirit and beer sectors. However, their emphasis is on ingredients rather than health warnings (https://alcoholireland.ie/eu-labelling-regulations/).

### *New Zealand*

Locally, one concerning fact is that current health warning labels on alcohol beverage containers in New Zealand are highly deficient and inconsistent among brands. This was the conclusion of a study by Tinawi, Gray et al. (2018) of examining the labelling of such containers. They selected a purposive (and low-cost) sample of 59 local and imported beers, wines, and ready-to-drink alcoholic beverage containers available in New Zealand in 2016–2017. They collected information about the type and location of health warnings on the containers as well as about alcohol content, and found 80% had a pregnancy-related warning (predominantly found on beer, a product more commonly marketed to men), 73% had industry-led initiatives (e.g. advising "responsible" consumption) and 19% had drink-driving/heavy machinery warnings. These labels were very small and inadequate, and occupied less than 1/400th of the available label space; some had no warnings. They contrasted strongly with the more graphic warnings on cigarette packets.

### Voluntary recommendations

What seems clear is that voluntary recommendations do not work, and some legislation is needed with regard to having compulsory standardised labelling outlining alcohol-related risks to avoid the inconsistencies found in the study. Nutrition information, although given by very few beer producers (e.g., sugar content, preservatives, carbohydrate content, and total kilojoules) but absent on wine, is also needed, as with nonalcoholic drinks. (For example, a bottle of wine or six small beers contain the same calories as a burger and fries.) The study found that around three quarters of beverages had industry-led messages such as "Cheers!" or "Enjoy responsibly", which seem somewhat ambiguous from a health perspective. An extensive list of references with regard to labelling is also given by the study.

A recent news item from Stuff Business (March 11, 219) referred to a 19-week-pregnant woman thought she was buying a healthy drink Kombucha (a fermented tea) for her baby only to taste alcohol when she took a sip. After reading the label on the back of the bottle, she found an alcohol warning in "very small print" saying there was a trace amount less than she felt from it, being quite sensitive to alcohol and being five months pregnant; probably a bit more sensitive. In Australia, Kombucha has come in for criticisms about labelling and alcohol content.

### Health warnings

The 2018 Global Drug Survey (Guardian 8 May, 2018)) looked at information from 130,000 people across 44 countries (including 3,200 New Zealanders) to see if health warning labels on alcohol would increase awareness of alcohol harm and whether the messages were believed and whether people's attitudes towards drinking would change. The survey found that most people will ignore some warnings on bottles and drinks about the damaging effects of alcohol on health. However, the type of message was important in making an impact. The CEO of the survey, Professor Adam Winstock, said:

> It is clear that the link between alcohol consumption and increased cancer risk is a message that is still not reaching UK drinkers and where it does, many chose to react to the message with scepticism. The alcohol industry which makes profits from selling its product will never embrace anything

that might lead to people drinking less. A self-regulated industry will always regulate to optimise profits not public health.

Some health messages could be:

**Cancer** Drinking less reduces your risk of 7 different sorts of cancer.

**Heart** Heart disease is a major cause of death among people with heavy alcohol use.

**Liver** People with heavy alcohol use can reduce their risk of liver disease by cutting down even by a small amount.

**Calories** A bottle of wine or 6 bottles of beer contain as many calories as a burger and fries.

**Violence** Alcohol use increases the risk of violence and abuse.

**Pregnancy** No level of alcohol is safe for a pregnant woman as it can affect the growing baby.

Dr Baddock, chair of New Zealand Medical Association (NZMA) argued that current voluntary labelling is sending mixed messages (Stuff news, June 25, 2018). For example, the green colour of the DrinkWise Australia pictogram, which appears on some products in New Zealand, causes confusion and the NZMA favours a red pictogram which she says is commonly used on packaged alcohol internationally and is mandatory in France. She said: "Virtually all people associate red with a warning."

A study supported by the Health Promotion Agency in New Zealand (Rout and Hannan, 2016) looked at how women recalled and understood pregnancy warning labels for alcohol. The best kind of label was a pictogram showing a silhouette of pregnant women in a circle with diagonal line across it indicating don't drink. The Drinkwise text of "It is safest not to drink while pregnant" was sometimes misconstrued that it is still okay to drink while pregnant. An alternative text "Don't drink pregnant" did better in getting the message across especially when the pictogram was also added. What was disappointing was that:

> Few consumers recall pregnancy warning labels without prompting, but with visual prompting more than four in ten consumers recall at least one of the three alcohol pregnancy warning labels tested.

Clearly the choice of label(s) is an important factor in getting a health message across. Dr. Baddock suggested we need to use stronger language such as "Alcohol could kill your baby" as with the message "Cigarettes kill you."

## Australia and New Zealand

Unfortunately New Zealand and Australia are joined together at the hip with regard to legislation on labelling. However, they recently (11 October 2018) put out a joint communique from the Australia and New Zealand Ministerial Forum on Food Regulation. It commented that:

> The Forum agreed that, based on the evidence, a mandatory labelling standard for pregnancy warning labels on packaged alcoholic beverages should be developed and should include a pictogram and relevant warning statement. The Forum requested Food Standards Australia New Zealand (FSANZ) develop this mandatory labelling standard as a priority and that the work be completed expeditiously.

See https://foodregulation.gov.au/internet/fr/publishing.nsf/Content/forum-communique-2018-October for further details and proposed further actions.

The Australian Daily Mail (August 4, 2019) said that bottles of alcohol will finally be carrying information on healthy drinking guidelines more than three years after the new rule was introduced. The alcohol industry's standards body told its members in 2017 they were not obliged to print the new limits because the guidance was voluntary. However the Portman Group has changed its advice. Firms were told they had until September 2019 to update packaging, but until now virtually all labels have carried the old guidance. The change in alcohol guidance marked the biggest shake-up for 30 years and was driven by new evidence linking alcohol and cancer. Katherine Severi, of the Institute of Alcohol Studies, said:

> These proposals fail to provide details on calories and ingredients, meaning that shoppers who buy alcohol get less information than when they buy milk or orange juice.

It is interesting to note that Ireland has recently enacted legislation for mandatory health warnings on alcohol packaging that, among other requirements, enforces the display of cancer warnings. This policy action is supported in the UK via recommendations from the UK House of Lords, Royal Society for Public Health and Public Health England. Given the similarities between the self-regulatory systems of alcohol labelling in New Zealand and the UK, it is likely the NZ results are generalisable to the UK environment, providing further support for UK action on alcohol labelling. For further information on labelling in various countries see http://www.iard.org/resources/beverage-alcohol-labeling-requirements

## 5.5   CONCLUSION

It would seem that the National-led government's weak response to the Law Commission's recommendations on alcohol law reform, which have been shown to be supported by a majority of the public, must have involved successful lobbying by the alcohol industry behind closed doors. Judging what happened with tobacco, nothing will change unless alcohol reform becomes important to the government as with the Labour Government when Helen Clark was minister of health and introduced smoke-free legislation. The Smoke-free Environments Act 1990 initiated bringing about observable improvements in the health of New Zealanders over the subsequent decades. Although different, this can be used as a model for alcohol as it provides a thorough coverage of all marketing and sponsorship, including internet marketing.

Alcohol needs to be treated like smoking and have a complete ban on all marketing and sponsorship. According to Fuseworks Media in New Zealand, (Voxy.co.nz, 29 May 2019), Alcohol Healthwatch (AHW) is alarmed that "further consideration" is needed to reduce the impact of alcohol use on mental health and addiction. Of the 40 recommendations in the Mental Health and Addiction Inquiry report, the Government has "agreed" or "agreed in principle" to the majority, leaving the recommendations that relate to taking strong action on alcohol needing "further consideration". Executive Director Dr Nicki Jackson for AHW said:

> The Inquiry's recommendation was simple and well-considered — we absolutely need to take a stricter regulatory approach to the sale and supply of alcohol.

Also

> Alcohol is already the second strongest risk factor for suicide and plays a major role in family violence and homicide. We can turn down the tap of addiction in our country by addressing alcohol use in adolescence. This means having strong policies in place to protect New Zealanders.

A recent poll showed that 80% of New Zealanders believe New Zealand needs to take action to reduce alcohol-related harm.

Unfortunately the current Labour government is stalling on dealing with alcohol problems. A very recent editorial in the New Zealand Medical Journal by four psychiatrists and a psychologist from the university of Otago (Sellman, Adamson, et al., 2019) have outlined their concerns about the Government failing to act on the key recommendation relating to alcohol in the recent inquiry into mental health (www.mentalhealth.inquiry.govt.nz/inquiry-report/). It was the fourth government-initiated report in the past decade that recommended stronger regulation of alcohol, and our politicians have managed to ignore the key strategies that are known to work. The experts said stricter regulation of the sale and supply of alcohol was one of the easiest and most effective ways a government could improve the nation's wellbeing and reduce misery. The editorial stated that alcohol "is the cause of widespread damage and suffering, and costs the country an estimated $7.85 billion per year." Also:

> Apart from various emotional and mental health sequelae of injury, violence and chronic disease including carcinogenicity, alcohol can directly cause clinical depression, is associated with a number of anxiety syndromes and is a significant factor in causing about a third of completed suicides.

The latest recommendation referring to the mental health report above says that the government should enact everything from the previous three inquiries! The government can ban guns quickly and spend time over legalising marijuana, and yet ignore a major health problem of the damage done both individually and socially by alcohol. Some would argue that there are vested interests.

The latest editorial mentioned above was followed up by a press release from the Royal Australian and NZ College of Psychiatrists (RANZCP) supporting the call for strengthening of alcohol regulations to reduce the negative impact of alcohol on New Zealanders' mental health and wellbeing (Scoop Health news, 8 July, 2019). "Alcohol harm remains the most pervasive addiction problem in New Zealand," and "We need a public health focus on reducing alcohol harm." said Dr Every-Palmer, Deputy Chair of the New Zealand National Committee-Tu Te Akaaka Roa. He suggested: (1) raising the cost of alcohol by including a minimum price per unit of alcohol and by curtailing the hours and limiting the number of outlets selling alcohol, and (2) calling for a ban on alcohol advertising including stopping alcohol sponsorship at all sporting events. Dr Sam McBride of the New Zealand Faculty of Addiction Psychiatry explained:

> The relationship between alcohol and poor mental health outcomes is stark and occurs through multiple pathways ... Alcohol is directly associated with development of depression and anxiety as well as being used as a means of managing distress associated with these conditions. Its use has been associated with suicide and self-harm.

Dr John Gregson, Deputy Chair of the New Zealand Faculty of Child and Adolescent Psychiatry said:

> The RANZCP urges the government to immediately raise the purchase age for alcohol back to 20 years.

When will the message get through?

# CHAPTER 6

# ALCOHOL ADDICTION

---

## 6.1 INTRODUCTION

Some people will not read this chapter because they believe they are not addicted or, at worst, are just simply a moderate or heavy drinker. It is true that some heavy drinkers can perform successfully, but that does not rule out the health effects which can be intertwined with other factors. If you ask a drinker how much alcohol they drink they are just as likely to say "not much." The problem is that most people underestimate the amount they drink (cf. section 1.1.2), and will sometimes say, "I can stop at any time." They will often like to drink with others for a variety of reasons, one of which may not be mentioned is that it legitimises their own drinking. It helpful therefore for the reader's own sake or for the sake of friends and family to be aware of the material in this chapter.

*Alcohol: A dangerous love affair.*
By George A. F. Seber and D. Graeme Woodfield Copyright © 2019

## 6.2 NATURE OF ADDICTION

A number of definitions are given for an addiction. It is basically an overpowering, repetitive, excessive need for something. There are two main types of addiction, substance and behavioural addictions. For example, a substance addiction might be an addiction to caffeine, smoking, alcohol, or cannabis, while a behavioural addiction might be doing something like shopping or gambling. In the end they are all basically substance addictions as substances (neurotransmitters) are produced in the brain such as adrenaline and dopamine, which can be addictive. Also some substance addictions have a behavioural or repetitive action effect such as lighting up a cigarette.

Addictions can also have a crossover effect. To give up smoking a person should not continue to drink strong coffee. It is therefore not uncommon for a person to have multiple addictions or even conquer one addiction, but then move on to another. The Guardian (5 July, 2019) published an article by Emily Reynolds, the author of "A Beginner's Guide to Losing Your Mind." She recounted her experience with her own mental health and alcohol problems, and the under-resourced mental health system in England. She emphasised that just treating the alcohol problem is not enough as comorbidity (i.e., existence of other problems) is common and the whole person needs to be helped; not just the alcoholic part.

A good place to start discussing addiction is to consider Sellman (2010), a professor of psychiatry and an expert on addiction who lists the following ten most important things known about addiction. We also mention how they pertain to alcohol.

(1) *Addiction is fundamentally about compulsive behaviour.* What happens is that a compulsive circuit in the brain gets set up causing compulsive behaviour where the addicted person continues to carry out their addiction even when they know it is harmful. We see this with alcohol, where the desire to drink becomes so overwhelming that it begins to seriously affect a person's life, especially with regard to health, work, finances, and relationships.

(2) *Compulsive drug seeking is initiated outside of consciousness.* It seems that the addiction is triggered subconsciously before it is registered by the conscious brain. We can react to things before the thinking part of the brain takes over. For example a person can be walking overseas and suddenly react because of the amygdala in the brain sending a message that there is a snake in their path. After a slight delay, the neocortex cuts in

and says it is only a stick. The same thing can happen with the nucleus accumbens, which can put drug seeking behaviour into motion without conscious initiation. This delay is exaggerated for people with an addiction.

(3) *Addiction is about 50% heritable and complexity abounds.* Some years ago alcoholism was demonstrated to be a strongly familial disorder. Now a variety of studies have subsequently shown that alcohol dependence is a genetically influenced disorder for both men and women, with heritability estimates ranging from 40 to 60%. We find an interaction of environment and genes; a combination of nature and nurture. It does not mean that genes make a person drink, but they raise the probability that a person will do so.

(4) *Most people with addictions who present for help have other psychiatric problems as well.* Selman (2010) said:

> It is somewhat unusual to encounter a person presenting to out-patient addiction services with addiction problems alone.

This means that other psychiatric problems (so-called comorbidity) can be present, the three most common disorders being social phobia, major depression, and post-traumatic stress disorder. Also addiction can be linked with diseases such as Type 2 diabetes, hypertension, and asthma (McLellan, Lew, et al., 2000). Alcohol can become a form of medication.

(5) *Addiction is a chronic relapsing disorder in the majority of people who present for help.* With alcohol, the way forward is abstinence, not moderation. Unfortunately relapses are common with people who have an alcohol addiction.

(6) *Different psychotherapies appear to produce similar treatment outcomes.* The most important part of counselling is the relationship between the counsellor and the client.

(7) *'Come back when you're motivated' is no longer an acceptable therapeutic response.* Treatment should be where the client is and not where the therapist thinks they should be.

(8) *The more individualised and broad-based the treatment a person with addiction receives, the better the outcome.* People are unique and need individually tailored therapy (cf. Seber, 2013, Chapters 12–14 for a discussion of various addictions and associated counselling).

(9) *Epiphanies are hard to manufacture.* Sudden and dramatic recoveries do occasionally happen, but generally they are hard to come by. Sellman (2010) comments:

> Recovery from addiction involves a re-orientation from self-deception to the pursuit of higher ideals. New meaning and hope in life is required, a spiritual experience, which for some is best described as 'finding God'.

(10) *Change takes time.* Recovery from addiction is not so much a matter of changing one's mind but changing one's brain, and a life-style change takes time; in fact considerable time. Patience is needed to practice new behaviours for a long period of time.

Sellman (2010) describes the following four phases of treatment: (i) picking up the pieces of a failed life-style (Treatment); (ii) assembling a new life-style (Rehabilitation); (iii) practising the new life-style (Aftercare); and living the new life-style (Self-management).

To label alcohol as an addiction for someone, at least three of the following occur (the International Classification of Diseases, IC-10):

(1) A strong desire or sense of compulsion to drink.

(2) An impaired capacity to control drinking.

(3) Withdrawal symptoms if drinking is stopped.

(4) Evidence of tolerance, i.e., the amount of alcohol consumed tends to increase.

(5) Preoccupation with alcohol and a decreased interest in other activities.

(6) A persistent use of (excessive) alcohol in spite of clear evidence of its harmfulness.

Because alcohol is addictive, early initiation into alcohol use is a risk factor for alcohol-related harm in young people, and for heavy drinking and alcohol dependence in adulthood (Zeigler, Wang et al., 2005). Data from the Dunedin Multidisciplinary Health and Development Study in NZ showed that adolescents with no history of conduct problems but exposed to alcohol and other drugs before the age of 15 years were two to three times more likely than non-early exposed adolescents at age 32 to be substance dependent, to have herpes infection, to have had an early pregnancy, and to have failed to obtain educational qualifications (Odgers, Caspi, et al., 2008).

Only a small proportion of people with drinking problems seek help or are ever diagnosed, suggesting that the actual unmet need for treatment services is very large indeed. In New Zealand, around 32,000 people (1% of the population aged 16–64 years) want help to reduce their alcohol use every year but do not receive it (Ministry of Health, 2009). Also, those from the most deprived neighbourhoods were over four times as likely to report lack of help than those living in the least deprived areas.

Those seeking to identify older drinkers, who are becoming our problem drinkers and consuming at higher frequency (but not higher quantity), should consider screening males who are at the younger stage of older adulthood (i.e., approximately between the ages of 60–70), with a moderate to high level of education, and who likely have a high economic living standard (Towers, Sheridan et al., 2018). There is good evidence to show that brief interventions in a primary care setting, consisting of one or more sessions of advice and feedback from a health professional, can significantly reduce drinking and alcohol-related problems (O'Donnell, Anderson, et al., 2014).

## 6.3   WHY IS ALCOHOL ADDICTIVE?

What happens is that ethanol produces chemical reactions in the brain that lead to addiction. It becomes needed to feel normal, just like tobacco addiction. Messages telling our body to function (e.g., heart beat, breathe, blink etc.) get delivered from one brain cell (neuron or neurone) to another via a connection ("wire") called an axon. At its end it reaches a gap called a synapse and then crosses the gap from the transporter site to the receptor site via a chemical called a neurotransmitter to reach the next cell. There are various neurotransmitters that can be put into two categories, inhibitory (e.g., melatonin for sleep) and excitatory (e.g., adrenaline for action), where the former helps to calm the brain down, and is associated with balance and ease, while the latter stimulates the brain necessary for mental and physical action.

The main inhibitory neurotransmitter in the human body, known as GABA, is gamma-aminobutyric acid. This is increased by alcohol and substantially inhibits the brain, which is why drunken people have trouble walking, talking, and remembering things later. The increased signalling of GABA sedates the brain, and this happens every time someone consumes alcohol, and happens more intensely as more alcohol is consumed. Long term abuse stirs up the brain to counter this by producing more glutamate, an excitatory transmitter. The more alcohol consumed, the more GABA is transmitted, and the more glutamate is then transmitted in order to keep the balance. It is this chemical chain reaction that causes a tolerance to alcohol. This means it takes more and more drinks to produce the same effect. The strength of the tolerance grows over time.

Another neurotransmitter alcohol affects is dopamine, which is released when we do anything we consider pleasurable such as having a hug. Because some of the initial effects of alcohol are pleasurable, the brain considers alcohol use to be rewarding, and reinforces this by releasing dopamine. However, over time, alcohol abuse wears down the brains dopamine transporter and receptor sites, and subsequently inhibits the individual's ability to feel pleasure. With the decrease in dopamine and the consequent inability to feel pleasure without dopamine is what actually causes increased drinking, and the build up of tolerance.

Then there are endorphins. These are morphine-like molecules produced by the central nervous system and are released by the body to counteract physical pain, or in response to activities such as working out (e.g., running) and laughing. They can also create a feeling of euphoria, which can be felt after physical activity. Alcohol abuse also releases endorphins. Different parts of the brain release endorphins according to different responses, and alcohol releases endorphins in two different parts: the nucleus accumbens, which produces pleasure, and the orbitofrontal cortex, which controls decision-making. With so many neurotransmitters being released, along with endorphins, it is not surprising that alcohol is so addictive.

The brain does not feel normal without alcohol, and the brain becomes used to it in order to function properly. Being drunk feels normal! The same happens with tobacco for a different reason. It mimics the neurotransmitter acetylcholine as well as creating dopamine and prevents the mopping up of excess dopamine. Clearly drinking and smoking are not a good mix as they can feed off each other.

Why is it that some people become addicted and others do not? It is because so many factors are involved such as how much a person drinks, how often they drink, their age and health status, and their family history.

## 6.4 LOW-RISK DRINKING

If alcohol is a bit of a problem, there is a need to reduce how frequently one drinks and reduce how many drinks one has. The following are tips for low-risk drinking, including those based on Health Promotion Agency (HPA) recommendations in New Zealand.

- Know what a standard drink is and have just one an hour when drinking several. Standard drinks of beer, wine, spirits have the same amount of pure alcohol. Space out alcoholic drinks.

- Avoid such things as salted peanuts or potato chips while drinking as they can increase thirst.

- Keep track of how much, daily and weekly, is drunk.

- Set personal limits and stick to them.

- Start with non-alcoholic drinks and alternate with alcoholic drinks. Having a small glass of water between every alcoholic drink can help replenish what is lost because of dehydration caused by the alcohol.

- Accept a drink only when it is decided that it is time for another.

- When needing to tell friends about not being able to drink or needing to drink less, rehearse a few standard responses. This may be helpful if people are bugging one to drink more.

- Practice saying "no". It may be difficult at first, but it is surprising s how quickly it can become comfortable to say "no"; others will get used to it.

- Do not engage in drinking games.

- Do not drink in rounds if heading out on Saturday night. Drinking in rounds is also one of the behaviours that makes a person drink more than they would want to.

- Drink slowly (sip your drinks).

- It can be hard to avoid drinking too much on social occasions. A good strategy is not finish off an alcoholic drink, and do not allow hosts to pressure acceptance of a fresh one.

- Beware of alcoholic punches and stick with standard drink sizes.

- Try drinks with a lower alcohol content as the alcohol is less quickly absorbed.

- Eat before or while drinking (especially at home) as food dilutes the alcohol and dramatically slows its absorption into the bloodstream by preventing it from passing quickly into the small intestine.

- See if a friend/partner/family member can help keep up accountability for reducing either frequency or quantity.

- Stay active. This helps one be more aware of any physical or mental effects of alcohol that may be happening.

- It is not true that switching between beer, wine, and spirits will lead to intoxication more quickly than sticking to one type of alcohol beverage if one keeps to standard drinks. Do not switch. The advice "beer before wine and feel you'll fine, wine before beer and you'll feel queer" has been followed by drinkers eager to avoid a hangover. Research, however, suggests that the order of drinking does little to stave off nausea and a throbbing head.

- Never drink and drive (be a designated driver), or do anything like operate machinery where there is risk or skill involved.

- Follow any medical advice received about drinking when taking medications.

- After drinking alcohol, drinking coffee, exercising, showering and similar behaviours have no effect on alcohol metabolism. Only time can do that. There is no evidence that any of the hangover remedies on the market are of any value. Alcohol leaves the body of virtually everyone at a constant rate of about .015 of blood alcohol concentration (BAC) every hour. This means that a person with a BAC of 0.015 would be completely sober in an hour while a person with a BAC of ten times that (0.15) would require 10 hours to become completely sober. This is true regardless of sex, age, weight, and similar factors (Avis, 1999: 40.)

### General strategies

There are also some general strategies that can be used.

- Set a budget on how much you will spend on alcohol in any period.

- Find ways to change your routine. For example, pack a beach bag with a picnic, joggers or exercise clothes in the morning and drive straight to your special place from work rather than via home. Physical exercise can help relieve tension, depression, and relax your mind.

- Try not to keep alcohol in the house. Only head to the bottle shop if you specifically need drinks for an occasion.

- Have alcohol-free days. When you have one, plan it. When your mind is tempted to drink, remember your intention and your plan and why it is important to you. Start putting the kettle on when you get home, instead of going straight to the fridge on those alcohol-free days.

- Go somewhere where you don't have to drink such as the movies, or picnic at the beach or park.

- When out for dinner, wait until dinner is served before drinking. If having wine, drink only one glass as it is usually about 1.5 standard drinks.

- If going to a friend's house, take less alcohol with you and take some non-alcoholic drinks that you enjoy drinking.

- Using phone apps if possible can be helpful, as apps can help people set goals, intentions, reasons not to drink, and track success so far. They can become a good reminder of your intentions to reduce your drinking when out, and it is very socially acceptable to reach for your phone.

- Be a responsible host.

A good idea is to join the many others to have an alcohol-free month (e.g., July in New Zealand or Australia) to see what happens to how you feel, how you sleep, what happens to your weight, your skin, and your energy levels. You may be pleasantly surprised. However, heavy drinkers need to be careful about stopping suddenly as it can be detrimental if the body is strongly used to having alcohol in the system. Also, be aware that you may be more affected by alcohol because of reduced tolerance of both brain and liver, so that binge or heavy drinking should initially be avoided. A well known NZ psychiatrist said that

> In a month it is likely that your [alcohol] tolerance will reduce; the amount is uncertain.

(NZ Herald, 3 March 2019).

Research from the University of Sussex involving 800 people who took part in what is referred to as Dry January in 2018, also reported drinking less later, regaining control over their drinking, having more energy, having better skin, and losing weight. These changes in alcohol consumption were also seen in the participants who did not manage to stay alcohol-free for the whole month, although they were a bit smaller (The New Times, Ruwanda, January 20, 2019). Mention should be made of Alcoholics Anonymous, mentioned briefly in chapter 5 and now discussed.

### Alcoholics Anonymous

Alcoholics Anonymous is famous for their 12-step programme, as follows:

(1) We admitted we were powerless over alcohol–that our lives have become unmanageable.

(2) We came to believe that a Power greater than ourselves could restore us to sanity.

(3) We made a decision to turn our will and our lives over to the care of God as we understood Him.

(4) We will make a searching and fearless moral inventory of ourselves.

(5) We admitted to God, to ourselves and to another human being the exact nature of our wrongs.

(6) We were entirely ready to have God remove all these defects of character.

(7) We humbly asked Him to remove our shortcomings.

(8) We made a list of persons we have harmed, and became willing to make amends to them all.

(9) We made direct amends to such people wherever possible, except when to do so would injure them or others.

(10) We continued to take a personal inventory and when we were wrong promptly admit it.

(11) We sought through prayer and meditation to improve our conscious contact with God as we understood Him, praying only for knowledge of His will for us and the power to carry that out.

(12) Having had a spiritual awakening as the result of these steps, we tried to carry this message to alcoholics and to practice these principles in all our affairs.

Step 1 requires honesty, step 2 requires faith, step 3 requires surrender, step 4 means soul searching, step 5 can be hard and requires integrity, step 6 requires acceptance, step 7 focusses on humility, step 8 means willingness, and step 9 is the difficult forgiveness. The first nine steps help a person to see the truth about one's behaviour and how the rest of the world responds to one's actions. Step 10 demonstrates to a person that they have the ability to control their actions and focusses on maintenance, step 11 is about contact, and step 12 is about service. Although the 12 Steps are heavy on spirituality, many nonreligious people have found the program immensely helpful.

Al-Anon, a helpful friend and family support group that is an offshoot of Alcoholics Anonymous also has a 12-step program readily available on the internet. It is designed for those who live with alcoholism in their home or interact with alcoholics. There are many 12-step programs for various addictions and compulsive behaviours, such as Narcotics Anonymous, Cocaine Anonymous, Overeaters Anonymous, and Debtors Anonymous, all using the same 12 Step methods.

## 6.5   MEDICATIONS FOR ALCOHOL USE DISORDER

If a person sees a doctor about a possible alcohol problem, the doctor may ask several questions related to drinking habits, perform a physical exam, carry out some laboratory tests, complete a questionnaire (some are given in the appendix), and perhaps use some international criteria such as the DSM-5 (cf. Kranzler and Soyka (2018) for a list of the criteria). Alcohol use disorder (AUD) commonly occurs along with other mental health disorders such as depression and anxiety, and usually counselling is the first approach. If there is a serious problem, a medication may be prescribed.

Such medications (pharmacotherapy), used for moderate to severe AUD, work in different ways. The oldest, disulfiram (Antabuse), inhibits an enzyme from breaking down alcohol to a toxic byproduct of alcohol (acetaldehyde dehydrogenase), and its administration needs to be supervised to ensure adherence. As a result, people who drink experience symptoms like nausea, headaches and weakness, which may discourage some people from drinking. It means that many of the effects of a "hangover" are felt immediately after alcohol is consumed.

Naltrexone (oral and long-acting injectable formulations), which blocks some of the naturally occurring opioids in the brains pleasure centre is available as a short-acting pill or a long-acting injection, and is useful to reduce the risk of binge drinking. By dulling the pleasure of drinking, this drug may help some people avoid binges.

A third drug, acamprosate, appears to help abstinent patients maintain their avoidance of alcohol by attacking pathways in the brain that may make people more prone to alcoholism. Unlike disulfiram and naltrexone, acamprosate does not cause nausea after taking a drink. (Further information is available on the internet.)

The extensive review by Kranzler and Soyka (2018) indicated that the four methods of medication are all useful, are approved by the US Food and Drug Administration to treat AUD, and are generally equally effective. They gave a useful table comparing them in different ways, as well as giving their side effects. Four other contenders, Nalmefene, Baclofen, Gabapentin, and Topiramate were mentioned briefly.

The authors said medications were under-prescribed, and noted that patients with an AUD often have co-occurring psychiatric disorders (eg, depressed mood). However, a reduction in heavy alcohol use or abstinence from alcohol would often diminish or resolve the psychiatric symptoms. The optimal duration of treatment has not been determined, but the current recommendation by the authors is at least 6 months. Currently ketamine, which acts as a rapid-acting anti-depressant drug is being investigated as to its efficacy in reducing problematic alcohol and drug use.

To get prescriptions to more patients who might benefit from these drugs, primary care providers will need to make a concerted effort to screen patients. Then patients with a diagnosis of alcohol use disorder can be given counselling and prescribed medications. For many people, gaining greater insight into their spiritual side is a key element in recovery.

Saitz (2018) noted that in spite of the large number of those with AUD, affecting 1 in 7 in the United States, there is a lack of information about morbidity and mortality. He states that only about 20,000 patients with AUD have been studied in various trials, with only 10% of people with recognised AUD receiving any treatment, and few receiving any pharmacotherapy. He recommends:

> When screening findings are positive, brief counselling is appropriate for risky alcohol use, and treatment is the next step for AUD. Medications should be offered to all patients, and simple medication management counselling can be performed by the prescribing physician. Achieving treatment goals can be further helped by more intensive counselling to motivate change, provide tools and methods, and help with challenging social situations. Patients can also avail themselves of sober social networks and layperson groups.

Some people with AUD, especially those hospitalised, can have major problems with withdrawal when "drying out." Wood, Albarquon, et al. (2018) discussed the problem of trying to predict who will develop severe alcohol withdrawal syndrome, and identified a number of risk factors for the syndrome. Predicting its occurrence is important because the mortality rate is high when untreated. More research is needed on this topic.

## 6.6   SIGNS OF ALCOHOL POISONING

Alcohol poisoning is more common and life-threatening than people realise. Drinking too much can lead to death or even permanent brain damage. A fatal dose of alcohol can lead a person to stop breathing or choke on their vomit while unconscious. A person who looks asleep may very well be unconscious. If they are passed out, medical help should be sort immediately. To avoid alcohol poisoning a person should know how much they are drinking, and realise that "sleeping it off" is not a safe option. Critical signs of poisoning are: mental confusion, slow or irregular breathing, blue skin colour or low body heat, vomiting, seizures, or a person won't wake up.

## 6.7   GIVING UP ALTOGETHER

One of the authors (GAFS) watched a British TV programme called "Trust me, I'm a doctor" in November 2018. A small group of people were involved in a study where they did not drink alcohol for a month. The overwhelming response was that they felt so much better! Not a detailed scientific study, but an interesting result nevertheless. Perhaps some drinkers should experiment if they are able to do so. The Guardian, Monday 27 August 2018, had an article by Catherine Gray entitled "I'm surprised how happy I am after giving up alcohol". She said:

> It wasn't only the health risk that made me go teetotal. But now that I am, my family and friends like me a lot more ... Drinking is not socially essential. I am living proof, as are millions of others, that you can be 100% teetotal and have an infinitely more interesting social life.

We find the same ideas expressed in the book by Ruby Warrington (2018) with a subtitle of "The Blissful Sleep, Greater Focus, Limitless Presence, and Deep Connection Awaiting Us All on the Other Side of Alcohol." She found that removing alcohol from her life completely transformed her life. Warrington, who had a history of drinking alcohol asked (her italics)

> why don't more people see quitting drinking as a positive health-affirming *choice*? Why do we assume a person must have had a 'problem' with alcohol when he or she quits? And why do so few people talk about the clarity, the self-assurance, the *presence* that becomes your very own lighthouse when you remove the booze?

Grace (2018a) suggested:

> We continue drinking to get rid of the empty, uneasy feeling that alcohol created [after it left our system]. When we enjoy the 'pleasure' of a drink, we restore the wholeness and peace of mind we knew our entire lives before we drink a drop.

Annie Grace was a successful high flyer, being the youngest Vice President in a multinational company. In a global C-level marketing role she was responsible for 28 countries and was drinking almost two bottles of wine a night. She no longer drinks and has never been happier. Her book (Grace, 2018a) breaks down how alcohol changes us both physically and mentally and describes how to reprogram our unconscious allowing us to break free from alcohol. She has also written a second book (Grace, 2018b) which gives a 30-day programme for dealing with an alcohol problem.

British journalist Rosamund Dean decided to cut down, but found drinking in moderation harder than giving up altogether (Stuff news, February 19, 2018). She said:

> It's hard because abstinence is just one decision, so you've decided that you don't drink, ever. ... Whereas, with moderation, every single day is a series of decisions, because you have to decide 'Am I going to drink today? What am I going to drink? How much am I going to drink? What am I going to say to the person who is going to try and make me drink?'

A National Public Radio health news item in the US (June 23, 2019) in a article entitled "Breaking The Booze Habit, Even Briefly, Has Its Benefits" said there was a movement that has spread across the US, with people challenging each other to see what life is like without alcohol and sharing in that experience. First there was "Dry January," when people could brag on social media about how they were taking a break from booze, and now there is "Dry July" and even "Sober September."

A study by de Visser, Robinson, and Bond (2016) studied 249 men and 608 women, who participated in the "Dry January" alcohol abstinence challenge and found reductions in alcohol consumption and increases in drink refusal self-efficacy. Ten of the New Scientist's staff members took part in a month of alcohol abstinence, while four continued to drink as normal. The abstainers saw their liver fat drop from an average of 15%, and up to 20% for some; on average, the abstainers saw their blood glucose levels drop by 16% and their blood cholesterol dropped by almost 5%; and reported higher sleep quality and better concentration, but there was one universal downside; they reported having less social contact (NZ News Hub, 2 January, 2018).

There is also a growth in the number of alcohol-free bars beginning in London and New York where entertainment and socialising can be enjoyed without alcohol. The Guardian (8 May 2019) referred to the opening in Dublin, Ireland, of apparently the first pub with alcohol free drinks. The Guardian said that Irish drinking habits are changing in that the overall consumption of alcohol has fallen by 25% from 2005 to 2016, with a further reduction of 1.4% in 2017. Another Guardian article (14 June 2019) said that according to the German Association of Brewers (DBB), now as many as one in 15 beers of the estimated annual 6.2 million hectolitres consumed in Germany contain no alcohol. The makers of one such brand found sales up 40%. Two reasons given for the change are an increase in health awareness, and

> as an improvement in the quality of a beverage with a reputation for being flat and tasteless, typically drunk only out of necessity.

Three articles in the New Zealand website Spinoff told the story of Mike Metcalfe and how he handled life after almost 20 years with a drinking problem. As a "functional" alcoholic he found a number of things (October 2, 2018). Firstly, you begin to smell, not just with the liquor drunk, but underneath there was a persistent chemical odour of alcohol coming, for example, from pores of the skin, clothing, bedding etc. Secondly, people will notice that you have been drinking no matter how hard you try to hide it. It is not just the smell, but also your physical demeanour and behaviour, like not shaving. Thirdly, you are going to lie a lot, especially to avoid anyone questioning your drinking habits. This could refer to hiding bottles around the house, making excuses about money, and calling in sick to work. Fourthly, you are going to be caught out. He said: "Sooner or later the lies on top of lies are going to collapse like a house of cards." Finally, eventually you are going to screw everything up, which may include your health, relationships, accidents, and even involvement with the police.

In a second article (January 24, 2019), Mike noticed the following changes after giving up alcohol. Firstly, you have more energy. Secondly, your beer belly begins to disappear. Thirdly, you look better, healthier; and other people notice. Fourthly, drunks can be extremely annoying! Fifthly, drinkers really do not understand someone who is sober. People can be shocked when you tell them you do not drink!

In a third article, Mike writes about some psychological effects from giving up alcohol (May 18, 2019). As with all substance addictions there is often a behavioural addiction. Mike found that he needed something else to keep his hands occupied. He said:

> The number of times, particularly in the early days, I reached down to grab the beer that wasn't there are too numerous to count. I'd be watching a movie and without thinking, I'd grasp at thin air where my beer would've been.

He then found he needed something else to binge on. Again this is not surprising as addicts may find that when they give up one addiction they can get hooked on another. Mike found it was zero % beers, then smokes, followed by candy. Finally he settled on music, which he loved. He says he does have rapid mood swings and can "go from happy-go-lucky to brooding anger within minutes."

Alcohol gave him a modulating effect, but he began sinking into depression and got mad at himself for letting it happen. However, he found he was helped by cognitive behavioural therapy, which helps to change one's beliefs and behaviours. Forgiving himself was also therapeutic, and he found that there were people there to help him.

Finally we note that a heavy drinker should be careful about giving up alcohol immediately because of the body's dependancy on regularly having high concentrations of alcohol in the blood. The intensity of withdrawals can range from mild to severe, and can be dangerous for some people. People with an alcohol dependency problem should always seek support from their doctor before going through detox.

## 6.8   CONCLUSION

Alcohol is highly addictive and can destroy a person's life. The nature of the addiction is described, and how it affects the brain. Some tips for low risk drinking are given as well as some strategies for controlling alcohol consumption including having alcohol-free months and obtaining help from Alcoholics Anonymous. If alcohol is a serious problem and becomes a disorder then there are some medications that can be helpful. Alcohol poisoning is something that people need to aware of.

Although not usually the favourite option, giving up alcohol altogether is endorsed by several people who have found that it has transformed their lives.

# CHAPTER 7

# WHERE TO NOW?

## 7.1 NEW ZEALAND MEDICAL ASSOCIATION

In looking into the future, a good place to start is with the New
Zealand Medical Association recommendations (2015) for reducing alcohol-related harm (www.nzma.org.nz/advocacy/advocacy-
issues/reducing-alcohol-related-harm) that collectively seem to be
generally accepted worldwide for reducing harm from to alcohol.
Although the Association's recommendations are directed primarily at doctors, policy makers and politicians, it does indicate how
serious the Association is about the whole problem. The statistics
also mentioned are alarming. At the time, the incoming NZMA
Chair, Dr Stephen Child said that while alcohol is responsibly consumed and enjoyed by many of us, well over half a million New
Zealanders consume alcohol in a hazardous way. He said:

> Alcohol is not an ordinary commodity. It is a toxin, an intoxicant, and
> an addictive psychotropic drug. Such a significant risk to the health of
> our people must be of concern to doctors—we see the effects every day
> in our hospitals and consulting rooms. Our commitment to the health of
> our patients means we must individually and collectively do as much as

*Alcohol: A dangerous love affair.*
By George A. F. Seber and D. Graeme Woodfield Copyright © 2019

we can to reduce this harm that often occurs to people other than the individual drinker.

## Ten recommendations

The following are from ten recommendations given by the report.

(1) Doctors and other healthcare professionals should take every opportunity to provide screening and/or brief interventions for patients with suspected harmful alcohol consumption.

(2) The government should introduce a specific health target that incorporates the provision of better help to address harmful drinking, like the target on advice for smoking cessation.

(3) Expand treatment services for alcohol dependence (including people convicted of criminal offences).

(4) The government should raise the excise taxation on alcohol and introduce minimum unit pricing. Also a greater proportion of revenue gained from alcohol taxation should be utilised towards alcohol harm-reduction.

(5) All forms of alcohol marketing, including sponsorship of sporting and cultural events, should be phased out. In the interim, restrictions on the content and quantity of alcohol advertising need to be supported by statutory regulation rather than industry self-regulation.

(6) Women who are pregnant or are considering pregnancy should be advised against drinking any alcohol. This should be part of an action plan developed to combat the harm caused by Foetal Alcohol Spectrum Disorder in New Zealand.

(7) Local authorities should support calls by health professionals for (a) restrictions in the density of alcohol outlets and (b) reductions to maximum trading hours when developing their Local Alcohol Policies (LAPs).

(8) When negotiating international trade agreements, the government should ensure that it retains the ability to implement best-practice public health policies for reducing alcohol-related harms.

(9) Enforce drink-drive countermeasures in a rigorous and highly visible manner.

(10) The minimum purchase age for alcohol should be raised to 20 years for on-licensed as well as off-licensed premises. This

should be viewed by parliamentarians as a health and social policy issue rather than a conscience issue.

The World Health Organization (WHO) released an action package called SAFER with the aim of supporting a global target of reducing harmful use of alcohol by 10% by 2025 by helping governments to reduce the harmful use of alcohol and related health, social, and economic consequences. It had the following five recommendations:

(a) Strengthen restrictions on alcohol availability.

(b) Advance and enforce drink driving counter measures.

(c) Facilitate access to screening, brief interventions and treatment.

(d) Enforce bans or comprehensive restrictions on alcohol advertising, sponsorship, and promotion.

(e) Raise prices on alcohol through excise taxes and pricing policies

The most cost-effective actions (or "best buys") include increasing taxes on alcoholic beverages, enacting and enforcing bans or comprehensive restrictions on exposure to alcohol advertising across multiple types of media, and enacting and enforcing restrictions on the physical availability of retailed alcohol. According to WHO Assistant Director-General Dr Svetlana Axelrod, the package was introduced as,

> We have seen too little progress since the endorsement of the 'Global strategy to reduce the harmful use of alcohol' by the World Health Assembly eight years ago. But SAFER brings new impetus for action.

Chisholm, Moro et al. (2018) said that their study involving 16 countries spanning low-, middle-, and high-income settings indicated that pricing policies and restrictions to alcohol availability and marketing continued to represent a highly cost-effective use of resources. They also added the policies of enforcement of drink-driving laws and blood alcohol concentration limits via sobriety checkpoints, and brief psychosocial treatments as cost effective policies. Anderson, Bitarello do Amaral-Sabadini, et al. (2011) mentioned some of the above recommendations but also included the importance of where alcohol was consumed. They said:

> Even though more people drink at home, consumers frequently go out to drink, and the design of where that drinking takes place matters. Having fixed alcohol prices to avoid price promotions, making low-alcohol beers available, having fixed salaries for managers, with commissions on food and soft drinks rather than on alcohol, having light and airy bars with

comfortable seating and tables, and providing leisure facilities all help reduce drinking.

It appears that in formulating policy some subgroups in the population should be especially targeted, such as with Polynesian people in New Zealand. In this respect some mention perhaps needs to be made of a theory of collective drinking behaviour due to Skog (1985). The theory asserts that changes in per capita alcohol consumption are accompanied by equivalent changes across all levels of the drinking distribution, including the heaviest drinkers. This means that if there is a reduction of per capita consumption, this leads to a reduction among all levels of drinking. The population *as a whole* tends to move up and down the scale of consumption. At a personal level this means that an individuals drinking habits are strongly influenced by the drinking habits of his friends, or more generally by the drinking habits in his personal social network. Consequently public health strategies such as limiting the availability of alcohol aimed at reducing alcohol-related harms will often have a reduction in per capita consumption as their primary goal.

Skog's model has not been supported in some recent literature where it has been found that consumption can vary considerably among subgroups of a population. For example Hallgren, London, et al. (2018) gave several examples of this such as in the World Health Organization European Region between 1990 and 2014, where per capita consumption decreased, but alcohol-attributable mortality increased, mainly driven by countries with the heaviest drinking level. They mentioned that prevention policies oriented both at the aggregate level and towards high-risk sub-groups may be needed. Probst, Parry, et al. (2018) found that in South Africa: "Alcohol use contributed to vast socioeconomic differences in mortality."

We now consider each of the above policy items from the New Zealand medical Association separately along with some additional topics.

### 7.1.1 Screening for Alcohol Problems

Referring to (1) above, we have seen previously from Towers, Sheridan et al. (2018) that a high proportion of New Zealanders aged 50 or more drink hazardously, and many of those who are most at-risk see their GPs at least three times a year. Clearly there is a need to screen all older patients for alcohol use, regardless of their presenting problem. Some of these would not normally be screened, but really should be. They might drink frequently, but not a lot at one time, and may have health conditions such as heart disease or depression. The report also includes a useful flow chart that will help with diagnostics.

The Alcohol Use Disorders Identification Test or AUDIT (Babor, Higgins-Biddle, et al., 2001) and its short versions, such as the 3-item AUDIT-C (Bush, Kivlahan, et al., 1998) are standardised alcohol screens assessing hazardous drinking at the primary healthcare level and in research in New Zealand (cf. Appendix A.2). However, the authors point out that:

> these screens focus only on levels of alcohol consumption, and are insensitive to the factors that might place older adults at significantly increased risk of harm even when drinking small amounts of alcohol (e.g., reduced metabolism, health conditions, and alcohol-interactive medication use). In this respect, there is concern that using a screen not measuring older adult-specific risk factors may result in inaccurate assessments of hazardous drinking rates in this population.

Another older screen, the Comorbidity Alcohol Risk Evaluation Tool or CARET (Moore, Beck et al., 2002; Moore, Giuli, et al., 2006) is an adult-specific alcohol screen that assesses alcohol-related risks both based on consumption levels and the presence of factors increasing potential harm. It also includes health conditions, medications, frailty (e.g., low mood, memory problems, and falls), and alcohol risk behaviours (such as drink-driving). Towers, Sheridan, et al. ( 2018) compared the screens AUDIT-C and CARET and found that there was a 90% agreement between these screens in classifying non-hazardous drinkers and 77% in classifying hazardous drinkers. Also 10% of older drinkers were classified as non-hazardous by the AUDIT-C, but as hazardous by the CARET because of health-related risk factors. It is clear that both screens are helpful for the older person.

### 7.1.2 Legislation not Self-regulation

In relation to (2) above, it was mentioned several times in this book that self-regulation and voluntary codes for alcohol do not work. Casswell (2011) stated that the alcohol and allied industries promoted ineffective voluntary codes on marketing to keep governments from imposing stricter regulations. We first consider the situation in countries other than New Zealand.

### *South Africa*

Parry, Burnhams, and London (2012) said that:

> While abstention from drinking is high, South Africa is among the countries having the highest consumption of absolute alcohol per drinker per year, the second highest category of harmful patterns of drinking, and the highest category for past year heavy episodic drinking.

About 130 people die daily as a result of alcohol-related causes, 46% from injuries, 35% from tuberculosis (TB) and HIV/AIDS, and 15% from non-communicable diseases such as cancer and liver and cardiovascular diseases. They noted that a comprehensive review of policies and programmes indicates that making alcohol less available and more expensive and placing a ban on alcohol advertising are the most cost-effective ways to reduce the harm caused by alcohol. Also, the resulting economic costs are enormous, with alcohol estimated to have cost provincial health departments and the national Department of Health in 2009 R6.1 billion and R0.5 billion, respectively. Currently, about R2 billion is spent annually on alcohol marketing in South Africa, with sports sponsorships accounting for some 30% (where R is the Rand).

In South Africa, alcohol advertisements are subject to the code of the Advertising Standards Authority of South Africa (ASA), a body set up and paid for by the marketing communication industry to ensure that its system of self-regulation works in the public interest. The Industry Association for Responsible Alcohol Use (ARA), which is funded by the major alcohol producers in South Africa, is a member of the ASA. Parry, Burnhams, and London (2012) said it is not surprising that alcohol advertisements are permitted

> that link their (alcoholic) products to things that have nothing to do with the intrinsic properties of the products or their manufacture, but rather to notions such as financial and social success (even happiness), sex, patriotism, and mocking people who buy beer in 340 ml containers rather than 750ml bottles, or who choose to drink milk rather than beer while watching sporting events.

Morojele, Lombard et al. (2018), in studying the effect of alcohol marketing on adolescent alcohol consumption, concluded that:

> Exposure to alcohol marketing and not being strongly averse to advertisements of alcohol brands and products were associated with alcohol use among adolescents.

### Australia

Pierce, Stafford, et al. (2019) looked at the rules in Australia regarding the placement of alcohol advertisements (Placement Rules) that were added to the industry-managed Alcohol Beverages Advertising Code Scheme in November 2017. They concluded that the objectives and key terms of the Placement Rules are inadequately defined and narrow in scope, resulting in the dismissal of almost all relevant complaints. There was lack of transparency and independence in the Scheme's administration, and limited monitoring and enforcement options. The authors said that the Rules were unlikely to reduce young people's exposure to alcohol marketing and hence fail to meet public health objectives. They concluded that their review adds to the body of literature that demonstrates that industry-managed systems fail to effectively regulate alcohol marketing.

### Europe

A comprehensive project investigating alcohol marketing in five European countries was reported by De Bruijn, van den Wildenberg, and van den Broek (2012). It concluded that self-regulation for alcohol advertising and promotion does not protect young people against exposure to alcohol commercials.

### Poland

At the beginning of 2018 the Polish president signed new laws which allow local government to limit alcohol sales such as putting a cap on the number of concessions for alcohol sales that are issued. Concessions will also be required for the sale of beer and other beverages with less than 4.5% alcohol content. Current laws say that drinking is illegal on streets and in squares and parks. The new law, under which the sale of alcohol between 10 pm and 6 am can be capped, aims to prevent a large number of liquor stores operating in a single area. The move particularly affects major city centres and tourist resorts (Radio Poland, 31 January, 2018).

### Lithuania

Lithuania, home to the world's heaviest drinkers, has passed a detox bill banning alcohol advertisements and limiting booze at public events like music festivals (Deutsche Welle, 1 June, 2017). Also the legal drinking age was raised from 18 to 20, and the sale of alcohol to under-20-year-olds will be prohibited at public events. Additionally, alcohol sales will be restricted to 10:00 am to 8:00 pm Monday through Saturday and 10:00 am to 3:00 pm on Sundays, rather than 8:00 am to 10:00 pm every day.

#### 7.1.3 Better Treatment Services

Concerning (2) and (3), it is clear that only a small proportion of people with drinking problems seek help or are ever diagnosed, suggesting that the actual unmet need for treatment services is very large indeed. Further details about addiction are given in chapter 6, and some standard screening questionnaires are referred to in the Appendix.

### 7.1.4 Pricing

In considering (4) above, we note that Meir, Purshouse, and Brennan (2010), in a policy appraisal for the UK government, pointed out that the range of alcohol pricing policies has expanded to include targeted taxation, inflation-linked taxation, taxation based on alcohol-by-volume (ABV), minimum pricing policies (general or targeted), bans of below-cost selling, and restricting price-based promotions.

Pricing is a complex process, involving purchasing preferences in terms of the types and volumes of alcoholic beverages, prices paid, and the balance between bars, clubs and restaurants as opposed to supermarkets and off-licenses. Age, sex and level of drinking will also fundamentally affect such things as beverage preferences, drinking location, prices paid, price sensitivity and tendency to substitute for other beverage types. They concluded that:

> Policy appraisals must account for population heterogeneity and complexity if resulting interventions are to be well considered, proportionate, effective and cost-effective.

The debate is usually whether price-based policies concern who would be most affected—harmful or low-income drinkers. For example, an Australian study (Callinan, Room, et al., 2015) involving 1681 Australians aged 16 and over who had consumed alcohol and purchased it in off-licence premises found that the answer was not simple, but involved a number of factors that emphasised the need to allow for population heterogeneity. One finding was that respondents from low-income groups were more likely to be abstainers than those in middle- or high-income households, in line with previous research. Below we consider policies relating to excise tax, minimum pricing, and taxation generally. In New Zealand, Wall and Casswell (2013) concluded that:

> The affordability of alcohol is more important than real price in determining consumption of alcohol. This suggests that affordability needs to be considered by policymakers when determining and pricing policies to reduce alcohol-related harm.

### 7.1.5 Excise Tax

Further to (4), alcohol has become more affordable in New Zealand due to incomes increasing more than alcohol prices (Health Promotion Agency, 2018). For example, Dr. Jackson from Alcohol Healthwatch (NZ Newswire, Section Health, 27 February, 2018) said that

> the real price of wine is 30 per cent lower today than it was in 1988. This is reflected in supermarket prices where bottles of wine can now be purchased for $5.99.

The current widespread availability of cheap alcohol products contributes to the excessive and harmful consumption of alcohol. Cheap alcohol products are favoured by heavy as well as young drinkers. Alcohol in New Zealand became more affordable over the 10 years between 1999 and 2009, with heavily discounted alcohol cheaper than averagely priced bottled water (Gunasekara and Wilson, 2010).

Raising alcohol prices is internationally recognised as one of the most effective and cost-effective ways to reduce alcohol related harms. Raising prices preferentially reduces consumption in high-risk groups such as heavy drinkers—about 1% for each percentage rise in price —and the young. It also reduces the likelihood of young or moderate drinkers becoming heavy drinkers. The evidence for this is extensive, for example Anderson, Chisholm, and Fuhr (2009), Wagenaar, Salois, and Komro (2009), and Wagenaar, Tobler, and Komro, (2010).

The alcohol industry lobbies to get rid of excise tax, and the struggle with this issue is well described by Casswell and Maxwell (2005a). For example, combined industry groups argued in a submission to a national tax review in 2001 that the excise tax had "no sound economic and social rational" and recommended that it should be progressively phased out. Typically, they favoured "policies that target misuse" (Beer Wine and Spirits Council et al., 2001). However, as mentioned elsewhere, the industry profits greatly from misuse.

Following the Law Commission's Report, The New Zealand Medical Association 2105 report recommended that the government adopt the recommendations of an increase in alcohol excise tax by 50% to achieve a 10% average increase in the price. This would likely have net economic benefits to New Zealand of around $72 million each year via reductions in alcohol-related harms. Twenty percent of New Zealanders drink 75% of the country's alcohol, yet are not paying to clean up the mess. Because excise tax is levied on the amount of pure alcohol in a product, those who drink the most alcohol pay the most tax, both proportionately and absolutely. Furthermore, excise tax forms a substantially larger proportion of the price of cheap alcohol products. So any increase in excise tax will make relatively little difference to prices paid by consumers in pubs and bars, but will significantly affect the prices of cheap alcohol favoured by heavy drinkers and the young. "Responsible" drinkers will not be penalised.

It is also suggested that a greater proportion of revenue from the excise tax on alcohol be used for prevention, treatment and rehabilitation services, and to replace alcohol sponsorship of sporting and cultural events. Earmarking a greater proportion of excise tax for mitigating alcohol-related harms should help make the increase in price more acceptable. This has been demonstrated for tobacco products in the New Zealand setting. The Ministry of Justice (2014) concluded that an excise increase has a greater impact on harmful drinkers, while a minimum price is estimated to have a greater impact on low risk drinkers compared to harmful drinkers. Any increase should be carried out to pre-empt the signing of any free trade deals.

### 7.1.6 Minimum Pricing

Again focussing on (4), minimum pricing and minimum unit pricing (MUP) have been debated in many countries for some time, the argument being put forward that it will not make a difference and that it unfairly punishes those who can drink responsibly, particularly if they are on low incomes. At the same time it does little to help those with serious drink problems. The Scottish Parliament voted for a price minimum in 2012 but legal challenges by the alcohol industry delayed the policy's implementation until May 2018; Wales is coming on board in 2019. Similar delays occurred with England until May 2014.

Countries with some form of minimum pricing include the majority of Canadian provinces, certain states of the USA, Russia, Moldova, Ukraine, and Uzbekistan. (There may be others since this was written.) Apart from Ireland, European countries (e.g., France, Spain, Italy, Portugal and Bulgaria) have opposed MUP on the grounds that it is contrary to EU law, is unfair and ineffective, and could be hurtful for the wine and spirits industry. Bans on selling alcohol below cost price have also been debated.

An article in the Guardian (19 June 2019) stated that alcohol sales in Scotland have fallen to their lowest level in 25 years (a 3% fall) after the introduction of price controls, with the reduction in the unit minimum price in May 2018. Supermarkets and off-licences are banned from selling cheap or discounted spirits, wine, beers and cider, although online sales from suppliers outside Scotland are not affected. There are on average 22 alcohol-specific deaths every week in Scotland, and 683 hospital admissions. Increases in the minimum price of alcohol have produced benefits in other parts of the world, for example, a shift in consumption patterns toward beverages with lower alcohol content.

Stockwell, Auld, et al. (2012) found in Canada that increases in minimum prices of alcoholic beverages can substantially reduce alcohol consumption. Lonsdale, Hardcastle, and Hagger (2012) investigated public opinion concerning UK government proposals to introduce new price controls to curb alcohol consumption. They found participants expressed some qualified support for the policy, but stated that it would only work as part of a wider campaign including other educational elements. The main objections were: (1) scepticism of minimum pricing as an effective means to reduce harmful alcohol consumption; (2) a dislike of the policy for a number of reasons (e.g., it was perceived to "punish" the moderate drinker); and (3) concern that the policy might create or exacerbate existing social problems. There was a general perception that the policy was aimed at "problem" and underage drinkers.

Using a mathematical model, Holmes, Meng, et al. (2014) predicted that in England minimum pricing could lead to a reduction in alcohol consumption, with the greatest effect being for the heavier drinkers. As already noted, Scotland had been successfully fighting legal challenges from the industry for the right to use minimum pricing since 2012 and it has now been implemented as with Wales and Ireland (Connor, 2017).

In Australia, where the alcohol taxation is complex, Chalmers, Carragher, et al. (2013) commented that taxes on alcohol can be raised to increase prices. However, this strategy can be undermined if the industry absorbs the tax increase and cross-subsidises the price of one alcoholic beverage with other products. Such loss-leading strategies are not possible with minimum pricing. The authors argued that a minimum (or floor) price for alcohol should be used as a complement to alcohol taxation. They discussed three possible impediments to implementing such a policy: (1) public opinion and misunderstandings or misgivings about the operation of a minimum price; (2) the strength of alcohol industry objections and measures to undercut the minimum price through discounts and promotions; and (3) legal obstacles including competition and trade law.

A survey study by Falkner, Christie, et al. (2015) in New Zealand involving 115 clients undergoing medical detoxification concluded that:

> Although the majority of our group would be financially impacted by an increase in the minimum price per standard drink, any potential impacts would be most significant in those buying the cheapest alcohol (who also drink the most), suggesting that minimum pricing may be an important harm minimisation strategy in this group.

It can be expected that a minimum price per standard drink would limit the possibility of switching to an alternate cheaper product and probably leading to an overall reduction in alcohol consumption in this group.

### 7.1.7 Taxation

We have already referred to excise tax. Wagenaar, Maldonado-Mollna, and Wagenaar (2009) mentioned more than 100 studies on the subject that concluded, with few exceptions, that increasing prices (or tax rates as a surrogate for prices) reduced various indices of sales or consumption of alcohol. Using an interrupted time series approach they found that reductions in alcohol-related mortality occurred after two tax increases almost 20 years apart. They concluded that taxing alcoholic beverages is an effective public health strategy for reducing the burden of alcohol-related disease. The World Health Organisation (WHO) recommends increasing alcohol taxes as a "best-buy" approach to reducing alcohol consumption and improving population health. Alcohol may be taxed based on sales value, product volume or alcohol content, and EU countries have very different alcohol taxation policies (Angus, Holmes, and Meier, 2019). The authors state that:

> There is only limited evidence that alcohol duties are designed to minimize public health harms by ensuring that drinks containing more alcohol are taxed at higher rates. Instead, tax rates appear to reflect national alcohol production and consumption patterns.

Gale, Muscatello, et al. (2015) examined the effects of tax changes on ready-to-drink (RTD) beverages or alcopops with regard to emergency department (ED) admissions for acute alcohol problems in 39 Australian EDs over 15 years. After a Goods and Services Tax introduced in 2000 led to a decline in the price of RTD beverages relative to other alcohol products there was statistically significant increase in ED presentations among 18-24 year old females. In 2008 an RTD tax increase increased RTD prices and led to

> declining presentations in young to middle-aged persons of both sexes, including under-age drinkers.

Albers, Siegel, et al. (2015) found that different types of flavoured alcoholic beverages (as is the case with RTDs and cocktails, for example), were associated with episodic heavy drinking and injuries requiring medical attention among underage drinkers. However, simply increasing the cost of RTDs without increasing the cost of other alcoholic beverages may simply lead to a shift to other forms of alcohol as shown in Australia (Doran and Digiusto, 2011). However Hall and Chikritzhs (2011), in noting this, found that the consumption of spirits did increase, but not by enough to offset the reduction in alcopops drinking. The result was a 2% reduction in alcohol consumption per head, the first in Australia for 4 years. The data from the Australian Bureau of Statistics showed that taxation increases can reduce the consumption of specific alcoholic beverages.

Hall and Chikritzhs (2011) referred to other studies about the effects of price increases for cask wine and beer with 3% or more alcohol content, showing that increases reduced the use of wine and beer, and their related harms. As an aside, Canada have taken a more hard line approach with RTDs. In a news item (May 23, 2019) by the Canadian press it was stated that on April 23, new federal restrictions on sugary alcoholic beverages took effect that day, following at least two deaths in 18 months. The alcohol content in what Health Canada describes as "single-serve flavoured purified alcoholic beverages" can no longer exceed 25.6 ml for each container of one litre or less. This amounts to about one and a half standard drinks, whereas previously a single serving could previously contain up to four standard alcohol drinks. Given the "seriousness of the situation," Health Minister Ginette Petitpas Taylor said in a statement that the rules are effective immediately and there will be no transition period. A government can act quickly!

Getting back to taxation, a review of 54 studies by Patra, Giesbrecht, et al. (2012) concluded that:

> In order to reduce alcohol-related trauma, chronic disease, and other consequences of high-risk drinking, an increase in pricing/taxation is a central component of an overall alcohol strategy.

They give a large number of examples from different countries showing how increasing alcohol prices and taxes leads to a reduction in various alcohol-related harms.

Nelson and McNall (2016) also provided a review of a large number of studies. They commented that previous reviews tended to concentrate on the effects of policy changes in demand elasticities for whole populations (combining light and heavy drinkers), where an "elasticity" is the percentage change in quantity demanded in response to a one percent change in price. The authors preferred to focus on "natural" experiments where the emphasis is on alcohol-related harms, such as mortality and crime statistics. They concluded that more attention needs to be given to effects on subgroups such as heavy drinkers and critical subpopulations such as, for example, women, youth, and unemployed with regard to price changes. Although they agree that increasing alcohol prices reduces alcohol consumption in the total population, reductions in total consumption do not necessarily imply reductions in harmful consumption or comprehensive reductions in specific alcohol-related harms. They believe that policy changes need to be targeted better towards certain subgroups.

Wall, Casswell, et al. (2018) found there is considerable variation in alcohol tax systems and prices across a number of countries, and there is scope for increasing taxation with some middle and high-income countries. For example, a study in Australia involving 2020 English-speakers (age 16+) suggested that

> alcohol price policies, such as increasing alcohol taxes or introducing a minimum unit price, can reduce alcohol demand. Price appears to be particularly effective for reducing consumption and as well as alcohol-related harm among harmful drinkers and lower income drinkers.

(Jiang, Livingston, et al., 2016). Kuo, Heeb, et al. (2006) found that the consumption of spirits increased after the price of spirits decreased in Switzerland. The increase in spirits consumption was consistent across subgroups, with the exception of the group aged 60 or older. They concluded that:

> price should be considered an effective policy to reduce alcohol misuse and alcohol-related problems, especially among the younger population.

In New Caledonia, as part of measures to curb excessive drinking, especially among the young, the tax on alcoholic beverages was raised by 20 percent at the start of 2018.

The value of taxation was emphasised by Marten, Kadandale et al. (2018) who gave examples from countries where taxes on sugar, tobacco, and alcohol (STAX) have been effective. They commented that:

> Evidence from Chile, South Africa, Ukraine, and other countries shows that the impact of tobacco tax increases are progressive as health benefits exceed increases in tax liability, and these benefits accrue disproportionately in lower-income households.

They pointed out that, despite their potential, taxes on sugar, tobacco, and alcohol are underused by policy makers. Emerging evidence suggests the same progressive impact with tobacco is probably true for taxes on sugar and alcohol (Sassi, Belloni et al., 2018; Summers, 2018). Professor Sally Casswell, the New Zealand member of the STAX team said (18 June, 2018),

> New Zealand has done relatively well in tobacco taxation but less so in alcohol and sugar. The current Tax Working Group in New Zealand could pay close attention to STAX.

Raising the excise tax on alcohol and increasing alcohol licence fees would help to pay for alcohol-related harm in New Zealand (Auckland 1 News Now, January 23, 2018). Why should tax payers foot the bill?

### 7.1.8 Advertising and Marketing

With regard to (5) above, there is a need for controls on advertising and marketing for at least two reasons. First, as mentioned in section 3.5.1, there is problem drinking among players and spectators of sport, especially in team and contact sports. Second, as noted by Casswell (2014), alcohol marketing is broader than just advertising, as it involves sponsorship where there is branding of teams and events (e.g., use of logos), branding merchandise (e.g., hats and t-shirts), price promotions (e.g., supermarkets), competitions on social media (e.g., post a drinking picture) or using social networking sites such as Facebook, Twitter and YouTube by both users and marketeers, and so on (e.g., Winpenny, Marteau, and Nolte, 2013). It is not a question of simply attempting to affect the content of advertising, but rather preventing all exposure to alcohol marketing. Also, as with research on tobacco and food, it is advertising that encourages young people into the market, not particular channels of advertising or types of message.

Casswell (2014) pointed out that:

> The response on sites such as Facebook has dramatically increased since 2012 and underage users can access alcohol material, while this remains largely under the parental radar.

Jernigan and Rushman (2014) commented that:

> Looking at brand and user activity on Facebook for 15 alcohol brands most popular among US youth, we have found that activity had grown dramatically in the past three years, and underage users may be accounting for some of this activity.

With regard to television marketing, policies to reduce exposure to alcohol marketing on television include complete bans and restrictions on time and content. Countries such as Denmark, Finland, Norway, Sri Lanka, Turkey and France have implemented complete bans on televised alcohol marketing. However, the European Union Court overturned bans in Denmark and Finland due to their incompatibility with European Union regulations. France, under pressure from alcohol industry lobbying, introduced a 2016 amendment to the Loi Évin that allowed alcohol marketing on television for the first time since 1991. However, France has strict statutory regulations on the content of alcohol marketing messages, prohibiting marketing that associates alcohol with pleasure, glamour, success, sport, sex or opinion leaders.

In the Ukraine, Belarus and the Netherlands time restrictions are mandated by law, with alcohol marketing not permitted between the hours of 6.00am to 11.00pm, 7.00am to 10.00pm, and 6.00am to 9.00pm, respectively. However, in the Netherlands, the alcohol industry's response to the introduction of legislated time restrictions on televised alcohol marketing between 6.00am to 9.00pm was to increase the number of advertisements broadcast after 9.00pm from 7,500 to 23,000. In New Zealand, the self-regulatory ASA (Advertising Standards Authority) codes prohibit any alcohol marketing on television between the hours of 6.00am and 8.30pm. Unfortunately children frequently watch television outside these times and are therefore likely to be exposed to alcohol marketing on television (apparently about once every 7 minutes). Collectively, the evidence suggests that restrictions on the time and content of televised alcohol marketing are ineffective, even when mandated by law.

The focus on branding and intense advertising with young people was spelt out clearly by Casswell (2004) who noted that the advertising to sales ratio for the alcohol industry in New Zealand was then approximately 9% compared with 3% for the average advertising to sales ratio generally. She gave some examples of the sorts of promotions that were carried out such as one Australian radio campaign whose main message was that (Jones and Donovan, 2001)

> the product delivered mood effects: both removal of negative emotions, such as stress reduction, and inducing positive states such as feeling carefree and gaining increased enjoyment. Consumption of the product was perceived to offer self confidence, sexual, relationship and social success.

Advertising affects not only the young, as Bosque-Prous, Espel, et al. (2014) found that:

> advertising restrictions in European countries is associated inversely with prevalence of hazardous drinking in people aged 50–64 years.

### EU regulations

Most attempts at regulation have focused on traditional electronic, print, and outdoor media rather than the full marketing mix (Casswell, 2009). The EU (www.wipo.int/edocs/lexdocs/laws/en/eu/eu128en.pdf) has had a policy on the advertising of alcohol described by article 15 of the Council Directive 89/552/ EEC on the coordination of certain provisions laid down by law, or briefly "Television without Frontiers Directive". This is: Television advertising for alcoholic beverages shall comply with the following criteria:

(a) it may not be aimed specifically at minors or, in particular, depict minors consuming these beverages;

(b) it shall not link the consumption of alcohol to enhanced physical performance or to driving;

(c) it shall not create the impression that the consumption of alcohol contributes towards social or sexual success;

(d) it shall not claim that alcohol has therapeutic qualities or that it is a stimulant, a sedative or a means of resolving personal conflicts;

(e) it shall not encourage immoderate consumption of alcohol or present abstinence or moderation in a negative light;

(f) it shall not place emphasis on high alcoholic content as being a positive quality of the beverage.

The World Health Organization (WHO) adopted a Framework for Alcohol Policy in 2005. Included in this statement were their five ethical principles, including:

> all children and adolescents have the right to grow up in an environment protected from the negative consequences of alcohol consumption and, to the extent possible, from the promotion of alcoholic beverages.

On the other hand, Difford's Guide for discerning drinkers made the comment that (https://www.diffordsguide.com/encyclopedia/499/bws/alcohol-advertising-and-dark-markets):

> The major problem with a ban on alcohol advertisements is that, while they push brands, they also help to educate and inform. By the time most of the population are ready to purchase alcohol they have a basic understanding of aged spirits and un-aged, gin compared to vodka and perhaps even the knowledge that bourbon and Scotch are whiskies, they are quite different.

Not a helpful comment for a young person who will generally already know about alcohol if they are drinking.

### Industry submissions

The alcohol industry makes submissions against marketing regulations. Martino, Miller, et al. (2017) examined submissions invited by the Australian National Preventive Health Agency when alcohol marketing regulations were reviewed in 2012. They concluded that the submissions were a direct lobbying tactic, making claims to government that were contrary to the evidence-base. They identified five main themes in submissions from nine major groups about the increased regulation: (1) it is unnecessary; (2) it is not backed up by sufficient evidence; (3) it will lead to unintended negative consequences; and (4) it faces legal barriers to implementation; underpinned by the view (5) that the industry consists of socially responsible companies working toward reducing harmful drinking. The article is worth reading for examples of submission comments, for example:

> The small percentage of alcohol advertisements complained about each year ... reinforces the industry view that there is no widely held community concern about alcohol advertising ...

and

> when consumed in moderation, [alcohol] can be part of a healthy, balanced lifestyle.

Martino, Miller, et al. (2017) made the comment that:

> The alcohol industry repeats the mantras that 'most people drink responsibly' and that alcohol consumption can be 'part of a healthy lifestyle', claiming then that the majority of the population should therefore not be 'punished for the sins of the few' through policies that reduce the promotion of alcohol.

As noted above in section 7.1.2, South Africa's severe public health burden from hazardous alcohol use requires some action. Parry, Burnhams, and London (2012) commented that the proposed government ban on alcohol advertising had been stalled for many years as there has been strong opposition from the alcohol industry, sporting bodies, and the advertising sector. The arguments put forward include some of the usual ones, namely: possible communication sector job losses (though the authors say "these are likely to have been exaggerated"), advertising only affects brand selection with youth (and not consumption), and sporting organisations and events will lose financial sponsorship support (as seen previously, other supporters usually step in). However, at the very least it appears that tighter restrictions on alcohol advertising will eventually come.

Apart from Islamic countries, several others restrict alcohol advertising. France, for example, restricts the content of radio and print advertisements to specific elements such as product name, ingredients, alcohol strength, method of production and conditions of sale; and requires that advertisements include moderation messages. Norway and Sweden prohibit advertising to the public of alcoholic beverages over 2.5% alcohol by volume in Norway, and 3.5% in Sweden.

### New Zealand

In New Zealand, Lin, Casswell, et al. (2012) examined the relationship between measures of awareness to marketing and drinking among a sample of young people in New Zealand. The sample consisted of 1302 males and 1236 females predominantly aged between 13 and 14 years and drawn from a number of schools in a metropolitan city. The results showed that awareness of each alcohol marketing channel increased the odds of being a drinker by 8%. Engagement with web-based marketing increased the odds of being a drinker by 98% while engagement with traditional marketing increased the odds by 51%. Brand allegiance increased the odds of being a drinker by 356% and increased the likelihood of non-drinkers reporting future drinking intentions (by 73%). It was also associated with more frequent alcohol consumption (1.65 times more drinking occasions per year) and 86% more alcohol consumed on a typical occasion.

From October 1, 2018, all Auckland Transport infrastructure, facilities and public transport services were made free from alcohol advertising. Such a step was good news given the strong evidence of the harms from alcohol advertising particularly to young people, women, and those with alcohol dependencies.

In summary, the New Zealand results suggested that while exposure to all forms of marketing are associated with drinking by young people, measures of more active engagement such as owning merchandise and downloading screen-savers are stronger predictors of drinking. It was found that having established a brand allegiance at this early age was related to not only drinking and future intentions to drink, but also drinking patterns including consuming larger quantities. The internet does make a difference!

In Australia, Queensland recently joined the Australia Capital Territory, Victoria, and Western Australia in moving to protect children from alcohol industry advertising. The removal of alcohol advertising from Government owned property will commence with the Queensland's rail network and be extended to busways, bus shelters, roadsides, and outside major hospitals. New York City banned alcohol advertising on city property in April 2019, citing health risks posed by excessive drinking. The ban, which takes effect immediately, applies to bus shelters, news stands, Wi-Fi kiosks and recycling kiosks. Other US cities that have moved to ban alcohol advertising on city property include Philadelphia, San Francisco, and Los Angeles.

### 7.1.9   Off-Trade Discounting

A study in the UK by a team at Sheffield University (University of Sheffield, 2008) used mathematical models to examine the effect of price changes. It referred to restrictions on the extent of discounted price-based promotion in the off-trade (supermarkets, off-licenses etc.). The idea is to put a ban on promotions for reductions, especially for higher-priced alcohol, of more than a certain percentage (e.g., 20%) below the regular price as this would achieve a reduction in consumption.

### 7.1.10   Pregnancy

With regard to (6), the Ministry of Health (2010) recommended a three-step process that can be used as an intervention guide for health professionals when working with women who are planning a pregnancy, or who are pregnant. This short resource is as follows:

(a) **Ask** about alcohol use, and record and assess the level of alcohol consumption.

(b) **Advise** about not drinking alcohol if a woman is planning to be, or is, pregnant and explain why.

(c) **Assist** women to stop drinking alcohol while pregnant, and arrange referrals to addiction treatment services for those who are unable to stop.

The above is particularly important for women with a history of risky drinking and who have an unplanned pregnancy, for women who already have a child with FASD, and women who have FASD themselves. Help can also be obtained from the National Addictions Treatment Directory which is available at www.addictionshelp. org.nz and from contacting the Alcohol Drug Helpline (0800 787 797). Resources are discussed further in Appendix section A.4.

### 7.1.11 Density of Outlets

*New Zealand*

New Zealand has 218 breweries, more per capita than the UK, Australia and the US (NZ Herald, 18 February, 2019). Concerning recommendation (7a), in New Zealand the number of outlets licensed to sell alcohol more than doubled from 6,296 in 1990 to 14,424 in February 2010 (New Zealand Law Commission, 2010: 59). A more recent report sponsored by the Health Promotion Agency (M.E. Consulting, 2018), in which there was a tidying up of the data, found almost 11,400 premises in New Zealand selling or supplying alcohol through a combination of an estimated 12,390 licences (The Treasury, 2017). This worked out about one licence per 390 persons, nationally. Of these, 6,911 or 56% were on-licences (about one licence per 640 persons), while 3,442 (28%) were off-licences (one per 1,300 persons), and the remaining 2,037 (16%) were club licences (one per 2,200 persons). Also there were some 58 different licence type and category combinations including, for example, restaurants (29%), taverns (15%), sports clubs (13%), bottle stores (8%), hotels (8%) and grocery stores (4%). Together, these six outlet types accounted for over three quarters of all licences in 2014.

It was found that supermarkets accounted for an estimated 31% of national alcohol sales by total beverage volume, bottle stores an estimated 33%, taverns 6% and restaurants 4%. Combined, these four types of premises accounted for 74% of total volume of alcohol sold in 2014. Total sales of alcoholic beverages for 2014 was estimated as $5,747 million covering a reported 450 million litres. Also, referring to the Sale and Supply of Alcohol Act (SSAA) of 2012

> ... while some changes are able to be observed pre and post the enactment of the SSAA, the research shows - within the limitations of the data - no substantial shifts in demand patterns in licensed premises based solely on a 2014 comparison with 2013 data.

Legal battles are going on all round New Zealand where people are trying to stop the renewal of liquor licences or stop new ones often because there are already more than enough in the particular area, or because there are community problems, or the location of a proposed new licence is inappropriate. It is interesting to note that for New Zealanders, 85% live within 2-minutes drive of an alcohol outlet (in 2012/13), 66% live within 2-minutes of an on-licence (bars, clubs, restaurants and cafs), and 67% live within 2-minutes of an off-licence alcohol outlet. (Not exactly a shortage of outlets).

The relationship between outlet density and alcohol-related harm is complex and context specific. It was considered in considerable detail by Cameron, Cochrane, and Livingston (2016) in a substantial report commissioned by the Health Promotion Agency in New Zealand. The report had three overall objectives: (1) To investigate the impacts of alcohol outlet density on police activity at the local (Census Area Unit) level across New Zealand, especially with regard to violence events; (2) To evaluate how these impacts have changed between the period before passing of the Sale and Supply of Alcohol Act 2012 (SSAA) on 18 December 2012, and after; and (3) To evaluate the direct and mediating effects of local alcohol policies (LAPs) on the relationships between alcohol outlet density and police activity. They used nation-wide longitudinal panel data for the period 2007-2014 to evaluate the relationships between alcohol outlets (by type) and both police events (by type) and motor vehicle accidents. For some areas, a higher density of outlets is associated with increased consumption, particularly among young people.

With regard to the objectives, off-licence outlets appeared to have a number of positive relationships with alcohol-related social harms, while the relationships for on-licence outlets are more mixed. Although the period of time from the SSAA was relatively short, the research added to the weight of evidence that links alcohol outlets and social harms. Because of lack of data from the period after the first LAPs became operative (in 2014), the third objective was not evaluated.

New Zealand research has demonstrated that higher outlet density is more common in lower socio-economic (poorer and more disadvantaged) neighbourhoods than in higher socio-economic neighbourhoods. Unsurprisingly, higher outlet density is associated with lower alcohol prices and longer opening hours. Where there are several outlets in one area, particularly off-licence outlets, alcohol discounting is one commonly used means for outlets to compete with each other. Lower prices can stimulate demand and facilitate heavier consumption. Regulating the physical availability of alcohol is therefore a major tool available to reduce alcohol-related harms. Restrictions on maximum trading hours and curbing outlet density are key ways to reduce alcohol-related harms (Connor, Kypri et al., 2011); see also Day, Breetzke et al. (2012) and Miller, Palmer et al. (2011).

While public health interests have called for reductions to both trading hours and outlet density in LAPs, these provisions have frequently been appealed by segments within the industry. It seems that local authorities need to be further empowered to ensure that the harm reduction objectives of the Sale and Supply of Alcohol Act 2012 take precedence over other interests. This may require alterations to the terms of engagement between councils and industry during the LAP process. (See www.legislation.govt.nz /act/public/ 2012/0120/latest/DLM3339340.html).

A number of local battles have been going on to try and stop further applications for liquor shops and bars. For example, Turehou Maori Wardens Kiatara Trust have been putting a up a fight to prevent more such places opening in South Auckland (e.g., Mangere, Otahuhu, Otara, Manurewa, Papakura, and Pukekohe), as the area has a high Maori population and a high deprivation level as well. David Ratu, a warden, said,

> Alcohol is a major curse on our people. We believe that Maori were more prone to alcohol harm than anybody else. The legislation needs to be changed to reflect that.

Recently (www.stuff.co.nz/auckland/local-news/manukau-courier/ 105573811/liquor-licence-for-south-auckland-tavern-declined-again) it was said that two licences have been declined. After years of battling with a liquor store operating right outside the front gate, a Mangere school has decided to move its entrance on to another road.

## Overseas evidence

There is substantial overseas evidence that increasing the density of outlets is associated with higher levels of harmful drinking as evidenced by more alcohol-related crime or anti-social behaviours, or a variety of secondary harms that can undermine community wellbeing (Babor, Caetano, et al., 2010: 131). An extensive study in England showed a possible relationship between alcohol outlet density and alcohol related hospital admissions (Maheswaran, Green et al., 2018). A study in the US by Toomey, Erikson, et al. (2012) showed a positive association between the density of alcohol establishments and each of five non-violent crime categories. In Scotland, Richardson, Hill, et al. (2015) found that:

> Alcohol-related hospitalisations and deaths were significantly higher in neighbourhoods with higher outlet densities, and off-sales outlets were more important than on-sales outlets.

Also in the US, a downloadable publication entitled Strategizer 55-Regulating Alcohol Outlet Density: An ActionGuide (2011), found that higher concentrations of alcohol outlets are associated with increased alcohol consumption and related harms. It also recommended increasing alcohol taxes, dram shop (alcohol outlet) liability, maintaining minimum legal drinking age laws, maintaining limits on hours of sale and days of sale, and enhanced enforcement of laws prohibiting sales to minors.

### 7.1.12  Trading Hours

With regard to recommendation (7b), a number of reviews have highlighted the effectiveness of policies that restrict trading hours on reducing alcohol-related harms with recent evidence from Australia, Norway, and the Netherlands demonstrating a reduction of between 16% to 37%. One reason for this might be that heavy drinkers were more likely to buy cheaper alcohol and purchase at later times, as shown by the international study by Casswell, Huckle, et al. (2014). Later times of purchase predicted larger quantities consumed (on and off premise) and more frequent drinking (on premise only), as noted by Casswell, Huckle, et al. (2016). Policies regulating alcohol availability, including reductions in trading hours, have been promoted as key strategies for reducing alcohol-related harms and have been reported to be second only to pricing policy in terms of their effectiveness.

In Australia, Wilkinson, Livingston, and Room (2016) identified 21 studies, including seven from Australia, and there were 14 studies published since previous reviews. A series of robust, well-designed Australian studies demonstrated that reducing the hours during which on-premise alcohol outlets can sell alcohol late at night can substantially reduce rates of violence.

The Australian studies were supported by a growing body of international research. For example, Wicki and Gmel (2011) concluded that modest restrictions on opening hours and the density of off-premise outlets were found to be of relevance for public health in the canton of Geneva. In particular,

> in the experimental site the policy change was found to have a significant effect on admission rates among adolescents and young adults. Depending on the age group, hospitalisation rates for alcoholic intoxication fell by an estimated 25-40% as the result of restricted alcohol availability.

Menéndez, Kypri, and Weatherburn (2016) found that restrictions in two inner-city entertainment areas in Sydney, Australia, reduced the incidence of assault in the areas and increased the incidence of assault in nearby areas where the restrictions did not apply. A similar result showing the effectiveness of small changes in bar closing hours on violence in Norway was obtained by Rossow and Nörstrom (2012). Their findings suggested that a one-hour extension of bar closing hours led to an increase of violence by approximately 16%.

### 7.1.13 International Trade Agreements

With regard to (8) above, Casswell and Thamarangsi (2009) stated that one of the problems with the development of a global market place, free trade agreements, and the World Trade Organization (WTO) is that it has led to the expansion of alcohol corporations in emerging markets, thus contributing to increased availability and affordability of alcohol. The effects of trade agreements are felt nationally and locally because alcohol policy has to meet conditions of the treaties by allowing equal access to foreign imports; this includes alcohol. For example, in Thailand a newspaper reported that a group of foreign operators had threatened taking the Thai Government to the WTO if a proposed ban on alcohol advertising was to come into force. In Australia the tobacco countries have challenged the new laws about packaging. Casswell and Thamarangsi (2009) gave two further examples, but with a more positive outcome.

The first is France's alcohol policy law Loi Évin of 1991 restricting alcohol advertising (Rigaud and Craplet, 2004), which was challenged by the European Commission and the UK. However, the European Court decided that the law was justified on the grounds that it protected health and was an effective strategy. Originally the French were asked to change their previous law of 1980, which happened in 1985, but was not satisfactory. During a ten-year interim period producers and advertisers flagrantly used this legal loophole to full advantage. This situation led the French Parliament to pass the Loi Évin. That history, unlike most European countries, explains why the advertising of alcohol in France does not depend on self-regulation or voluntary codes of practice depending on the good will of the producers. Instead it is controlled by law, and illegal advertisements can be brought before the courts with significant penalties for infringement.

The second example relates to a challenge to Sweden's regulations on alcohol. Sweden was able to retain most of its restrictions by rewriting the legislation to state clearly that the policy was necessary to achieve public health goals. Some trade agreements have excluded alcohol (and tobacco) from their scope of concern, at least temporarily, which is the best response from a public health perspective.

### Trade treaties

Continuing on with (8) above, particular attention is needed when dealing with trade treaties and developing a policy for alcohol control. Casswell and Thamarangsi (2009) noted that:

> Representatives of the global alcohol industry, especially the distilled spirits sector, were strong supporters of trade treaties that expanded their access to rapidly emerging markets. The World Spirits Alliance lobbied for the General Agreement on Trade in Services (GATS), seeking liberalisation or elimination of barriers to tariffs and non-tariffs, including all restrictions on distribution and advertising.

The alcohol industry will campaign against effective strategies and for ineffective strategies like education (Foxcroft, 2005; Casswell, 2005; Room, 2005) and voluntary codes. For example, Anderson, Chisholm, and Fuhr (2009) said that

> school-based education does not reduce alcohol-related harm, although public information and education-type programmes have a role in providing information and in increasing attention and acceptance of alcohol on political and public agendas.

The authors gave some examples from Brazil, the UK, and some African countries where the industry has intervened to change proposed alcohol policy.

A major influence on the scene is the International Council on Alcohol Policy (ICAP) established in 1995, that operates from Washington DC and is funded by the ten largest alcohol corporations. Such organisations want to be included in health policy development when there should be no such collaboration because of different aims, except possibly for consultation (e.g., WHO Executive Board, 2008). It is a bit like a committee of hens having a fox on their committee! What is needed is a negotiated international health law covering alcohol control as it would make nations more likely to respect other nations' laws and policies in this area. Casswell and Thamarangsi (2009) suggested that a good time to do this is when free-trade ideology is being challenged by economic circumstances. Connor (2017) emphasised that "alcohol policy is time-sensitive." She noted that:

> Provisions in the previous version of the Trans-Pacific Partnership Agreement would have made it impossible for the government of any partner country to introduce regulation of the alcohol marketplace without being subject to litigation from alcohol corporations.

Care is therefore needed when countries like New Zealand are negotiating free trade agreements as a healthy alcohol policy needs to be incorporated. We conclude with a quote from the World Health Organization (2018: chapter 2):

> Given the increasing encroachment of international trade and investment on the ability of national and subnational governments to control their alcohol markets, and the increasingly consolidated global alcohol producers, a strong public health case for considering the negotiation of a Framework Convention on Alcohol Control, or alternatively for including alcohol within other international control systems ..., has been repeatedly presented and discussed by public health entities, experts and advocates .

The above WHO reference has very considerable international data.

### 7.1.14  Drink-Drive Countermeasures

As raised by (9), a variety of punitive measures for drink driving have been suggested, namely:

- Court appearance, especially for hard-core repeat offenders. They could also be electronically monitored.

- Licence suspension or revocation.

- Distinctive licence plate marking for an alcohol offence.

- License plate confiscation or impounding.

- Mandatory ignition interlock devices, which prevent a person from starting a vehicle.

- Vehicles impoundment or vehicle immobilisation.

- Increased penalties for drunk driving.

- Restricting nighttime driving by young people.

- Mandatory alcohol education.

- Enforcement of seat belt laws.

- Expanded use of designated drivers.

Other measures that improve road safety include improved roads, with raised lane markers that are easier to see and make a startling sound when a tire wanders over them, as with corrugations along the edges of roads emitting a sound when driven over. There are also improvements in vehicles. In the US it has been found that jail or prison sentences for alcohol offences for high over the limit drivers and large fines are not effective. The one voluntary action which we consider is the use of designated drivers, for which there has been considerable debate.

The alcohol industry has supported the idea of designated drivers (DDs) who are supposed to stay alcohol free to drive drinkers home safely home. It sounds a good idea but does it work? Barry, Chaney, and Stellefson (2013) sampled 1071 adult restaurant and bar district patrons ages 18 years or older and found that of 165 DDs, approximately 40% did not abstain from drinking and nearly 20% were alcohol impaired. Some believe that rather than having total abstention from alcohol it is alright if the DD is below the legal limit. However, what is not realised is that whatever the legal limit for drivers (BAC of 0.05% for most countries), studies indicate that alcohol begins to affect driving skills at 0.02%. The authors echoed those of previous investigations that document DDs failure to abstain from drinking or consuming alcohol at a level that minimises psychomotor impairment. Their results support Grube's (2007: 23) contention that laypersons

do not have a good idea of what constitutes a safe designated driver.

Although designated driver programs appear to be quite widespread around the world, only a limited number have been subject to rigorous evaluation. However, they seem to have done little to prevent drunk driving.

With regard to attached devices for motor vehicles, France required from 1 July 2012 that all motorised vehicles on French roads, except 2 or 3 wheeled vehicles with an engine capacity of less than 50cc, must be equipped with a government-approved portable breath testing device. Drivers are meant to use the devices to check that they are not exceeding the French legal limit for driving of 0.05. They are instructed to breathalyse one hour after consuming the last alcoholic drink. Announcing the move, the French Interior Ministry stated that in 2010, alcohol was responsible for 31%of fatal accidents, and if drivers had complied with the legal limit for driving, 1,150 lives could have been saved since 2006 (The Globe, 2012, issue 3, page 13).

In The Age newspaper (May 20, 2019) there was an article entitled "Low-range drink-drivers to lose licences immediately" that said that drink-drivers in New South Wales (NSW), Australia, will lose their licences on the spot from May 20 and cop a fine of almost $600 under tough new laws that take a zero-tolerance approach to drink- and drug-driving. Drivers can appeal against the suspension through the courts but all drivers will initially lose their licences. Previously, they could keep their licences if they challenged the matter in court. A low-range reading is considered anything between .05 and .079. Previously, only those with a blood alcohol concentration of .08 or higher had an immediate licence suspension. Alcohol-related crashes killed at least 68 people on NSW roads last year, accounting for nearly one in five road deaths, including 55 lives lost on country roads.

### 7.1.15 Minimum Purchase Age

Evidence supporting (10) comes from several sources. For example, a study by Gruenewald, Treno, et al. (2015) showed that lowering the minimum purchase age (MPA) for alcohol from 20 to 18 in 1999 in New Zealand led to increases in the proportion of 18–19-year-old drinkers, increases in frequencies with which this age group drank in different contexts, especially commercial contexts such as pubs and night clubs (rising an average 15 occasions per year), and problem risks associated with drinking in these contexts. With 16–17-year-old drinkers, there was more frequent drinking, greater drinking quantities, and more use in non-commercial social contexts such as in one's own home, others' homes, and other drinking contexts. They concluded:

> From the perspective of protecting youth, the natural experiment posed by the MPA-reduction appears to have failed, presenting more drinking and more problems among 16–19-year-olds.

Wall, Casswell, and Yeh (2017) noted that over half of those between the ages of 15 and 17 consumed alcohol in the last year.

Almost all European and North American countries have minimum purchasing ages (MPA) for alcohol, typically ranging from 16 to 21 years. Bendtsen, Damsgaard, et al. (2014) in a survey covering 37 countries, made the general observation that low MPA is associated with a higher proportion of young people who buy and drink alcohol and the proportion who experience problems from their alcohol use such as injuries and drunk driving.

### 7.1.16 Legal Drinking Age

This differs from the minimum purchase age. A majority of countries have a minimum drinking age of 18 years, though it is 21 in the US, except people can legally drink below that age under many different circumstances. An interesting discussion giving the pros and cons of lowering the age to 18 is given by drinkingage.procon.org

/#arguments. There is no age set in China and parts of Africa, for example, while alcohol is generally banned in Muslim countries. Most such laws apply only to drinking alcoholic beverages in public locations. The only country with a minimum legal age for consuming alcohol at home is the United Kingdom, which prohibits drinking below the age of six. In fifty countries the minimum age is lower than 18, and in 12 countries it is higher than 18. For a list see www.alcoholproblemsandsolutions.org/LegalDrinkingAge.html.

There are regular problems New Zealand with liquor outlets selling alcohol to under age youth. We give just one recent example from the Northern Advocate (2 April, 2019) which said that the police reported that three of 31 Northland stores sold alcohol to minors.

### 7.1.17  Labelling

In section 5.4 we stressed the need for appropriate information on alcoholic containers such as health warnings and nutritional information, and labels needed to be of appropriate size. It is not enough just to have the number of standard drinks, as a study by Jones and Gregory (2009) found that Australian university students used the standard drink labels to predominantly help them choose the strongest drinks for the lowest cost! The authors concluded that:

> This study provides initial evidence to support the view that standard drink labelling, in isolation of other modifications to product packaging and marketing, is likely to serve to further increase heavy drinking among young people.

### 7.2  FUTURE TRENDS

Where is the world heading as far as alcohol is concerned in the future? Predictions need to be treated with caution as the globalisation of the world can bring about change surprisingly quickly. One set of predictions has been made by Manthey, Shield, et al. (2019) who present estimates on the main indicators of alcohol exposure for 189 countries from 1990–2017, with forecasts up to 2030. The forecasting models they used were based on economic and religious indicators, and not on alcohol policies. Also, there is considerable variation among different regions, and a rise in a country's economy tends to lead to an increase in alcohol use.

Some country predictions were given. For instance, consumption in New Zealand has come down apparently because millennials have an increased focus on health, but it is predicted to go back up again. One of the problems in considering overall consumption per capita is that it sometimes hides a heavy drinking culture. Australian consumption has come down, and is going to remain about where it is for the next decade or so. In the United Kingdom it is actually going to fall a bit further. In both the last two cases, the drop is driven by sharp declines in drinking among young people. Alcohol use has dropped in Europe, most notably in Eastern Europe. At the same time it has increased considerably in several middle-income countries such as China, India, and Vietnam. In the US, a high-income country, current increases in mortality rates and decreases in life expectancies are primarily due to alcohol-related causes of death.

Globally, adult per capita alcohol use is estimated to have risen from 5.9 litres in 1990 to 6.5 litres in 2017, and is forecast to rise to 7.6 litres by 2030. The prevalence of current drinking increased from 45% in 1990 to 47% (44–50) in 2017, and is forecast to be 50% (46–53) by 2030 (annualised 0.2% increase). In 2017, 20% (1724) of adults were heavy episodic drinkers compared with 1990 when it was estimated at 18.5% (15.3–21.6), and this prevalence is expected to increase to 23% (19–27) in 2030. The gap between male and female drinkers is forecasted to decrease by 2030, in part related to an increase of female participation in remunerated work.

The three most important factors affecting the level of alcohol use are economic wealth, religion, and the implementation of alcohol policies. In low-income countries, most people simply do not have sufficient income to buy alcohol, so that levels of lifetime abstention are high. Political will can bring about about a change to reduce harm from alcohol, though it is often absent. However, change can happen, and Russia is a good example where interventions such as taxation, availability restrictions, a ban on marketing, and minimum pricing were implemented resulting in marked changes in both alcohol use and the alcohol–attributable burden of disease (Neufeld, Rhem, 2018).

What is disturbing is that alcohol companies are entering the cannabis market. Forbes news (December 19, 2018) has an article entitled "Cannabis Attracts Big Tobacco, Alcohol, and Pharma. Which Big Industries Will Join Next?" It stated that:

> By the end of 2019, there is a realistic chance that two of the largest cannabis companies in the world will be owned by two of the largest alcohol and tobacco companies in the world. The era of big business entering cannabis officially began in 2018.

We refer to the Global Drug Survey (GDS) for 2019 recently released and quoted by Stuff news (May 16, 2019). It said that 42.5% of New Zealand respondents said they would like to drink less next year. Globally, half of all those in India, Finland, and Ireland also wanted to drink less. A graph showing all countries is available at www.stuff.co.nz/life-style/food-wine/drinks/112723464/kiwis-want -to-drink-less-new-global-drug-survey-finds. The survey found that overall, 37% of all recent drinkers wanted to drink less next year. However, only one in 10 people wanted help to do so. Globally, slightly more than one in three people reported having never regretted getting drunk.

## *Law Commission*

Finally, we refer to a speech (13 August, 2019) by Sir Geoffrey Palmer who reflected on the Law Commission report he coauthored in 2010 entitled "Alcohol In Our Lives: Curbing the Harm", which is still regarded as a blueprint for alcohol law change in New Zealand. He said:

> My first observation is that there appears little or no interest in further reforms of New Zealand alcohol law in political circles. I do regard this as a pity.

He noted that:

> evidence gathered by the Commission was extraordinarily persuasive in presenting the case why law change was needed. The Law Commission recommended an Alcohol Harm Reduction Act. That is not what we got. The Government said they had accepted 133 of 154 recommendations. This, however, was misleading when one considers that the ones not accepted would have made the biggest difference.

The Law Commission recommended:

- increasing the price of alcohol through excise tax by 50% to reduce consumption. This was rejected.

- a minimum price policy for alcohol should be investigated, but none has eventuated.

- the regulation of promotions that encourage increase consumption or purchase of alcohol. This was not done as recommended.

- moving over time to regulate alcohol advertising and sponsorship. This was not done.

- increasing the purchase age to 20. This was not done.

- cutting back on the hours that licensed premises are open. This was done, but not to the extent recommended.

- that there should be more local input into licensing decisions. This was largely followed, although alcohol policies are optional, not mandatory as had been recommended.

- a streamlined enforcement system through a new alcohol regulatory authority and this recommendation was not followed either.

He finally commented that:

> Time passes on, the 2010 report is not a sufficient base now for future action. We need a new look at the evidence as things are now. All statutes should be regularly reviewed and it is time this was done for liquor.

For the speech see:
(https://mailchi.mp/314a3653cfc3/rt-ho-sir-geoffrey-palmer-speech-to-alcohol-action-conference-august-2019?e=%5bUNIQID).

Drawing from the experience of tobacco, real change in New Zealand will probably require alcohol reform to become a special interest for the government in the same way as tobacco reform became important to the fourth Labour government. Helen Clark was then minister of health and introduced smoke-free legislation. The resulting Smoke-Free Environments Act 1990 initiated observable improvements in the health of New Zealanders over the subsequent decades. A true alcohol reform bill, which includes reforms of marketing, pricing, and accessibility, in contrast to the fake Alcohol Reform Bill introduced by the previous government in 2010, would significantly improve the health and well-being of New Zealanders in the years to come, as well as raise the quality of social life in this country.

## 7.3   CONCLUSION

Casswell and Thamarangsi (2009) pointed out that in spite of alcohol's economic cost and harm, the focus on alcohol control is inadequate internationally and in most countries. There has been an expansion of industrial production and marketing of alcohol driving alcohol use to rise, both in emerging markets (especially populous markets such as Brazil, Russia, India, and China), and in young people in mature alcohol markets. There is therefore a need to put adequate policies in place, which in 2009 most countries did not have, and generally do not have now. Factors impeding progress include a failure of political will, unhelpful participation of the alcohol industry in the policy process, and increasing difficulty in free-trade environments to respond adequately at a national level.

The authors maintained that an effective national and international response will need not only governments, but also nongovernmental organisations to support and hold government agencies to account. There is also a need for local government support and community-level responses. The introduction of SAFER by WHO described above is a step forward. WHO directs and co-ordinates international health within the United Nations system. Working with its 194 Member States, WHO's mission is to promote health, keep the world safe, and serve the vulnerable.

### Alcohol and tobacco

Casswell (2013) asked the key question,

> Why do we not see the corporate interests of the alcohol industry as clearly as we see those of the tobacco industry?

Some of the reasons she gives are that the alcohol industry has

- sponsored intergovernmental events, along with funding of educational initiatives, research, publications, and sponsoring sporting and cultural events.

- framed arguments to undermine perceptions of the extent of alcohol-related harms to health by promoting ideas of a balance of benefits and harms.

- emphasised the heaviest drinkers in order to promote the erroneous idea that "moderate" drinkers experience no harm and that a goal of alcohol policy should be to ensure they are unaffected by interventions.

- ensured they have representatives on policy and government bodies (e.g., the United Nations). This is in contrast to tobacco companies who do not have representatives. The alcohol industry should be kept out of the policy arena.

- ensured that alcohol retained its positive image in the public mind by putting money into alcohol education and other projects in order to neutralise the pressures for more restrictions.

In contrast to tobacco, Casswell (2013) noted that the societal goal for alcohol in many countries will be different from that of tobacco, namely a reduction in harm rather than an eradication of use. However, the

> drivers of alcohol-related harm are the same, over-supply and marketing practices, as are used in tobacco promotion, and the policy tools available to reduce harm are also the same.

Some of the threats to the tobacco industry are similar to those perceived by the alcohol industry, which we now consider.

### Threats to the industry

The alcohol industry has known for some time that the key threats to their industry are tighter restrictions on advertising, marketing and sales; strong enforced labelling, including health warnings; blood alcohol content lowering; and measures to increase taxes and legal drinking age (Bond, Daube, and Chikritzhs, 2009). The industry will focus on individual controls (blaming the person who misuses alcohol) rather than population aspects (overall harm), as the latter tend to lead to population restrictions. Similar problems arise with other unhealthy commodities such as ultra-processed food and drink, as well as alcohol and tobacco.

### Self regulation

Moodie, Stuckler, et al. (2013) assessed the effectiveness of self-regulation, public and private partnerships, and public regulation models of interaction with these industries and concluded that these unhealthy commodity industries should have no role in the formation of national or international non-communicable diseases (NCDs) policies. They emphasised that these transnational corporations are major drivers of global epidemics of NCDs, and self regulation does not work. In 2012 at a Global Alcohol Policy Conference, the Director General of WHO, Dr. Anarfi Asamo-Bash, in welcoming delegates declared (The Globe, 2012, issue 2, page 4):

> We must not underestimate the alcohol industry. They will hit back, attack our evidence, attack our science and attack our policies. Resistance will come from well-financed lobby groups.

The alcohol industry is under pressure and needs to develop new sources of growth and profits. According to the South African paper, The Citizen (1 February, 2018):

> Markets in the developed world are under threat as a result of saturation. This is coupled with the fact that only a limited numbers of new drinkers are entering the market each year due to low population growth rates

This is particularly the case in Africa and Asia.

### Non-communicable diseases

When it comes to NCDs, Tangcharoensathien, Chandrasiri, et al. (2019) extended the discussion to include unhealthy food and tobacco industries, where all three industries have used aggressive marketing in emerging countries with fast economic development. In referring to interference by these industries in government policies aimed at containing consumption of unhealthy products, they list four groups of tactics: (a) interfering with the legislative process; (b) using front groups to act on their behalf; (c) questioning the evidence of tobacco harm and the effectiveness of harm-reduction interventions; and (d) appearing responsible in the eyes of the public, journalists and policy-makers. The question is how to robustly regulate multinational corporations with their undue influence on law and policy-making.

In commenting on this study, Reeve and Gostin (2019) raised two further issues. First there is the need to design voluntary industry initiatives to make them more effective, transparent, and accountable, and give a table of recommendations. They comment that

> governments should (credibly) threaten legislation if voluntary or collaborative initiatives fail to meet public health objectives.

Second, should public officials ever engage with industry and, if they do, how do they manage conflicts of interest and undue industry influence? The WHO Framework Convention on Tobacco Control strictly forbids engagement with the tobacco industry. In relation to the alcohol industry, the authors say that

> a stronger case can be made that engagement is never appropriate, given the status of alcohol as 'no ordinary commodity', that alcohol cannot be said to be crucial to human health and existence in the same way as (some) foods, and the lack of any evidence that collaboration with the alcohol industry leads to public health benefits.

### Alcohol Beverages Council (NZ)

Recently the alcohol industry set up an organisation in New Zealand called the Alcohol Beverages Council to provides an active voice in the media debate on alcohol policy in New Zealand. Casswell (2018c) in discussing the Council's messages said they are the usual ones:

> a focus on the drinker, not the product; protection of the rights of the moderate drinker; arguments for education; and erroneous statements about evidence-based policies. At the global level these messages, in the context of corporate social responsibility and lobbying activities, have been successful in subverting effective policy.

This has happened in New Zealand where 46% of the industry's sales and profits have been from very heavy alcohol consumption. The chief executive of the Council said in a TV interview that

> the vast majority of (drinkers) do so really responsibly and the alcohol industry is keen on promoting sensible drinking and education ….

Responsible drinkers are to be protected from regulation. As shown elsewhere in this book, Casswell commented that:

> Education, promoted as the only strategy by the industry, is not a cost effective, or even effective, solution.

As we have said over an over again, effective policies to reduce alcohol-related harm are the restriction of availability, banning or comprehensively restricting marketing, and decreasing affordability by increasing excise tax and price. The question now is:"Why isn't the world getting on board?"

## *Where is the international response?*

The remains one important problem raised by Casswell (2011, 2012a). Why is there is a marked absence of an international response to alcohol marketing, even though national restrictions have been upheld by some regional courts. For example, the Loi Évin involving both alcohol and tobacco in France in 1991, one of the most restrictive of alcohol marketing policies, has withstood court challenges by the alcohol industry. The law restricted exposure to the less powerful print media and also controlled content, restricting the advertising to facts, and thus excluded all life-style elements so popular with young people. Casswell and Thamarangsi (2009) commented that:

> Despite clear evidence of the major contribution alcohol makes to the global burden of disease and to substantial economic costs, focus on alcohol control is generally inadequate internationally and in most countries.

Also:

> Most countries do not have adequate policies in place. Factors impeding progress include a failure of political will, unhelpful participation of the alcohol industry in the policy process, and increasing difficulty in free-trade environments to respond adequately at a national level.

Those comments still apply today.

The global alcohol market is now dominated by a handful of large corporations that have so much influence that their accountability to national governments is limited. Their activities need to be regulated by global governance. Free trade agreements have contributed to a wide expansion of alcohol products and brands, both in the established markets of Europe, North America and Australasia but also into emerging markets. An example of this has been the Trans-pacific Partnership Agreement that has been under negotiation with New Zealand as part of group of nations. The globalisation and expansion has brought substantial profits that have been fed back into extensive marketing. The marketing is deliberate and sophisticated, and irrespective of the well-documented resulting harm. Casswell (2011) said:

> Alcohol is now one of the most heavily marketed commodities globally, and the industry is alarmingly skilled at exploitation of the full range of marketing possibilities which new communications technology allows, including the use of the new social media.

Au Yeung and Lam (2019) commented that:

> In the 2012 UN Political Declaration, when describing the main contributors to the four most prominent non-communicable diseases, the term harmful use is only used to describe alcohol use. Such a term implies that alcohol use can be safe and beneficial. This assumption could be partly driven by the findings of conventional epidemiology studies indicating moderate drinkers have a lower risk of cardiovascular disease than non-drinkers.

We have shown in sections 2.4 and 2.6 that this is generally not the case because of the confounding of other factors such as life style and genetics for example. The authors advocated for a Framework Convention for Alcohol Control (FCAC), already referred to in The Lancet editorial (2007), and urged WHO to start the process as soon as possible, especially as total alcohol consumption is increasing in all countries.

Whether the question of any international response can be answered in the near future remains to be seen, given the struggles currently going on over alcohol issues in many countries. It is a bit like asking for world peace. However, given the changes in legislation on smoking, we have some hope in New Zealand where there is some support for alcohol policy changes. This support is seen in other countries.

### Policy support

Parry, Londani, et al. (2018) investigated what support there was for alcohol policies among drinkers in Mongolia, New Zealand, Peru, South Africa, St. Kitts and Nevis, Thailand, and Vietnam using data from an extensive international alcohol control study. Their aim was to determine the magnitude of public support for 12 alcohol policies and whether it differed by country, demographic factors, and drinking risk (volume consumed). They found that drinking risk was substantial, and was particularly high in South Africa.

Across countries, policy support was generally higher for policies addressing drink driving and increasing the alcohol purchase age. There was less support for policies increasing the price of alcohol, especially when funds were not earmarked. Policy support differed by country, and was generally higher in the five middle-income countries than in New Zealand. Support from drinkers for a range of alcohol policies was extensive across all countries and could be used as a catalyst for further policy action. Casswell (2018b), in an editorial, noted that a non-communicable disease target of 10% relative reduction in alcohol consumption has been established by the World Health Organization (2013), and that alcohol is also recognised by the United Nations as a threat to sustainable development and contributes economic costs of approximately 1–2% of gross domestic product in several countries where these have been assessed.

Chaiyasong, Huckle, et al. (2018) used the same international study as Parry, Londani, et al. (2018) involving the countries Australia, England, Scotland, New Zealand, St Kitts and Nevis (high-income), Thailand, South Africa, Mongolia, and Vietnam (middle-income). They found that percentages of high-frequency, heavier-typical quantity and higher-risk drinking were greater among men than in women in all countries. Older age was associated with drinking more frequently, but smaller typical quantities especially in high-income countries. Middle-income countries overall showed less frequent but heavier typical quantities; however, the lower frequencies meant the percentages of higher risk drinkers were lower overall compared with high-income countries (with the exception of South Africa). Gray-Phillip, Huckle, et al. (2018) found from the study that in nine out of ten countries the vast majority of alcohol consumed was take-away. What is concerning is that alcohol was readily available and relatively easy for underage drinkers to access, particularly in the middle-income countries.

Also using the same study, Casswell, Huckle, et al. (2018) investigated behaviours related to four alcohol policy variables (policy-relevant behaviours) and demographic variables in relation to typical quantities of alcohol consumed on-premise in six International Alcohol Control study countries. They found that the three best policies in reducing consumption and harm are restrictions on availability (which relates to trading hours), increasing price, and restrictions on marketing, particularly with high-income countries, where it appears that better educated drinkers drink more frequently but in smaller quantities. In middle-income countries, it is the better educated who may find alcohol more affordable.

## 7.4  SUMMARY

We see then that a great deal needs to be done in most countries including New Zealand to reduce the harm from alcohol. It seems that government regulation is needed as self-regulation does not work. Although education has not been successful, it is clear that appropriate education is not reaching the right people, and many do not know about the the risks of drinking alcohol. People are not going to readily give up alcohol, but it is hoped that this book will provide sufficient information so that informed decisions can be made and the risks understood.

# SOME GENERAL RESULTS

## A.1 MAST AND VARIATIONS

How can you tell whether you have a drinking problem? One way is to take the revised Michigan Alcohol Sensitivity Test (MAST) with 22 yes-no questions. This can also can be downloaded from the internet. Several shorter versions are given below.

The full test can be downloaded from www.outcometracker.org/library/MAST.pdf. It is also given below.

Please answer YES or NO to the following questions:

(1) Do you feel you are a normal drinker? ("normal" means drinking as much or less than most other people).

(2) Have you ever awakened the morning after some drinking the night before and found that you could not remember a part of the evening?

(3) Does any near relative or close friend ever worry or complain about your drinking?

(4) Can you stop drinking without a struggle after one or two drinks?

(5) Do you ever feel guilty about your drinking?

(6) Have you ever attended a meeting of Alcoholics Anonymous (AA)?

(7) Have you ever got into physical fights when drinking?

(8) Has drinking ever created problems between you and a near relative or close friend?

(9) Has any family member or close friend gone to anyone for help about your drinking?

(10) Have you ever lost friends because of your drinking?

(11) Have you ever gotten into trouble at work or school because of drinking?

(12) Have you ever lost a job because of drinking?

(13) Have you ever neglected your obligations, your family, or your work for two or more days in a row because you were drinking?

(14) Do you drink before noon fairly often?

(15) Have you ever been told you have liver trouble such as cirrhosis?

(16) After heavy drinking have you ever had delirium tremens (D.T.s), severe shaking, visual or auditory (hearing) hallucinations?

(17) Have you ever gone to anyone for help about your drinking?

(18) Have you ever been hospitalized because of drinking?

(19) Has your drinking ever resulted in your being hospitalized in a psychiatric ward?

(20) Have you ever gone to any doctor, social worker, clergyman or mental health clinic for help with any emotional problem in which drinking was part of the problem?

(21) Have you been arrested more than once for driving under the influence of alcohol?

(22) Have you ever been arrested, even for a few hours, because of other behavior while drinking?

Score one point if you answered "no" to the following questions: 1 or 4. Score one point if you answered "yes" to the following questions: 2, 3, 5 through 22. A total score of six or more indicates hazardous drinking or alcohol dependence, and further evaluation by a healthcare professional is recommended.

If 24 questions seem like too many, the reader can download the short version with just seven key queries (SMAST) referring to the last 12 months:

(1) Do you feel that you are a normal drinker? ("normal" = drink as much or less than most other people)

(2) Do friends or relatives think you are a normal drinker?

(3) Are you able to stop drinking when you want to?

(4) Can you stop drinking without a struggle after one or two drinks?

(5) After heavy drinking, have you ever had delirium tremens or severe shaking, or heard voices or seen things that are really not there?

(6) Have you ever been arrested for drunk driving, driving while intoxicated, or driving under the influence of alcoholic beverages? (If yes, how many times?)

(7) Have you ever been arrested or taken into custody, even for a few hours, because of other drunk behaviour? (If yes, how many times?)

For the first four, a yes answer is good. For questions (5), (6), and (7), a yes answer is really bad.

If 24 or seven questions are still too many, try the CAGE questionnaire based on an acronym with four simple yes-no questions:

(1) Have you ever felt that you should **C**ut down on your drinking?

(2) Have people **A**nnoyed you by criticising your drinking?

(3) Have you ever felt bad or **G**uilty about your drinking?

(4) Have you ever had a drink first thing in the morning to steady your nerves or get rid of a hangover (i.e, an **E**ye-opener)?

Two or three yes answers, means you have a problem. A yes answer to number (4), means you have a big problem. There is also the helpful FAST Alcohol Screening Test with four questions namely:

(1) How often do you have eight or more drinks on one occasion?

(2) How often during the last year have you been unable to remember what happened the night before because you had been drinking?

(3) How often during the last year have you failed to do what was normally expected of you because of your drinking?

(4) Has a relative or friend, a doctor or other health worker been concerned about your drinking or suggested you cut down?

For the method of scoring see
(www.verywellmind.com/the-fast-alcohol-screening-test-69495).

## A.2 AUDIT-C Test

The Alcohol Use Disorders Identification Test is a publication of the World Health Organization, and the AUDIT-C test is a subset at
https://www.integration.samhsa.gov/images/res/tool_auditc.pdf.
It asks the following three questions.

**Q1: How often did you have a drink containing alcohol in the past year?**

| Answer | Points |
| --- | --- |
| Never | 0 |
| Monthly or less | 1 |
| Two to four times a month | 2 |
| Two to three times a week | 3 |
| Four or more times a week | 4 |

**Q2: How many drinks did you have on a typical day when you were drinking in the past year?**

| Answer | Points |
| --- | --- |
| None I do not drink | 0 |
| 1 or 2 | 0 |
| 3 or 4 | 1 |
| 5 or 6 | 2 |
| 7 to 9 | 3 |
| 10 or more | 4 |

**Q3: How often did you have six or more drinks on one occasion in the past year?**

| Answer | Points |
|---|---|
| Never | 0 |
| Less than monthly | 1 |
| Monthly | 2 |
| Weekly | 3 |
| Daily or almost daily | 4 |

The AUDIT-C is scored on a scale of 0-12 (scores of 0 reflect no alcohol use). In men, a score of 4 or more is considered positive; in women, a score of 3 or more is considered positive. Generally, the higher the AUDIT-C score, the more likely it is that the person's drinking is affecting his/her health and safety.

The bigger test (AUDIT) is also available on line at https://www.drugabuse.gov/sites/default/files/files/AUDIT.pdf.

## A.3  EXPERIMENTAL DESIGN

Data are usually obtained from one of three sources; records (e.g., hospital or police records), self-reporting questionnaires (e.g., postal surveys), and telephone surveys. Records need to be examined carefully as sometimes information is incomplete, for example some deaths from alcohol may not recorded as such. Care is needed in designing questionnaires as the way questions are worded can affect the outcome. When a large number of people are involved (which is what we hope for), it is not possible to have the questionnaire administered by professional people but must rely on self reporting. Self-reporting questionnaires can introduce a bias as, for example, heavy drinkers are inclined to underestimate the amount they drink. Telephone surveys are a convenient method of obtaining information, but they often depend on the memory of the person called, and there is also the problem of nonresponse so that followup calls may be needed.

To obtain questionnaire information or telephone information one is usually required to take a sample of people from some well-defined population or group. Random methods are required to do this to get a representative sample, and in statistical jargon this is referred to as having a suitable experimental design. A suitable design might be described as follows. Suppose we wish to compare two "treatments" $A$ and $B$. A random sample of an even number of people is divided randomly into two equal-sized groups with one group being given treatment $A$ and the second group treatment $B$. This is called a randomised design and we want to find the difference in outcomes for the two treatments. This idea sounds simple in practice but often it is not feasible. For instance, the original sample may be a sample of abstainers from alcohol. The first group called group $A$ are required to drink one standard drink per day and the second group, group $B$, have to drink 4 standard drinks a day. We then see over a long followup time who gets cancer.

What is wrong with such a design? Firstly, as we have seen in this book, abstainers may not be a suitable sample to start with. Secondly, we cannot ethically require people to do something that may be detrimental to their health. Thirdly cancer can take a long time to develop. You may think of other problems.

A more practical approach might be to take the initial sample from a general population and then compare the health outcomes of those drinking just one standard drink per day with those drinking more than four standard drinks per day; this would get round the ethical issue. However, this design could be hard to carry out as people may drink variable amounts on a daily basis, for example drink sensibly but have the occasional binge. If we are interested in seeing if alcohol causes cancer we can turn the previous design on its head and begin with a sample of cancer cases. We then find out the alcohol consumption, if any, for each case.

The reader may see some problems with this approach. For example, what kind of cancer or what kind of lifestyle does each person have, as often there is an underlying factor that needs to be accounted for (e.g., smoker or nonsmoker?). If we allow for such factors, the statistical analysis becomes more complicated, but doable. Clearly researchers have to be careful how an experimental design is chosen and also be aware of any shortcomings (which are usually mentioned in good research articles). The above two studies are called observational studies as we are simply observing and have no control over who gets what.

## A.4   USEFUL CONTACTS IN NEW ZEALAND

Further information concerning pregnancy is given by Ministry of Health (2010), who list the following resources:

- Alcohol and Pregnancy: When you drink so does your baby—a health education pamphlet, available from www.healthed.govt.nz

- Food and Nutrition Guidelines for Pregnant and Breastfeeding Women—a guideline for health professionals, available from www.moh.govt.nz

- Your Pregnancy—an information booklet for women about pregnancy, available from www.healthed.govt.nz

- Eating for Healthy Pregnant Women—a health education pamphlet, available from www.healthed.govt.nz

If you are concerned about your own drinking or that of someone close to you, contact the free Alcohol Drug Helpline on Ph 0800-787-797 24 hours a day - 7 days a week, free text 8681 or visit their website alcoholdrughelp.org.nz or alcohol.org.nz for the Health Promotion Agency (Freephone, 0508 258 258). There are some apps that may be helpful, e.g., daybreak (https://medicalxpress.com/news/2019-09-daybreak-app-halves-alcohol-months.html).

## A.5   THE BIBLE AND WINE

This is a big subject and quite controversial so we will just give an overview for those interested. There is some ambiguity about wine in the Old Testament (OT) as seen in the following two verses (Psalm 104: 14–15):

> He (Yahweh or God) causes the grass to grow for the cattle and plants for man to cultivate so that he may bring forth food from the earth, wine which makes man's heart glad ...

and (Proverbs 20:1)

> Wine is a mocker, strong drink is a brawler; whoever is led astray by it is not wise.

There is another warning in Proverbs 21:17 "He who loves wine and oil will not be rich". Wine was meant to be a blessing but instead has been misused. Everything is good for the purpose for which it was created, but anything can be perverted.

The following general observations can be made.

(1) Drunkenness is strongly condemned in the Bible (e.g., 1 Samuel 1:14; Isaiah 5:11, 22; 28: 1–3,7–8; 29:9; 56:12; Luke 21:34: Ephesians 5:18) and some unseemly incidents involving drunkenness are recorded in the Old Testament (OT) associated with Noah (Genesis 9: 20–23), and Lot (Genesis 19:30–38). Noah got drunk with wine and lay naked in his tent, breaking the current code of conduct and causing problems with his sons. Lot's daughters got Lot blind drunk on two occasions, and both committed incest with him. Proverbs 23: 29–32 talks

about wine looking good but it then bites like a serpent and stings like an adder, affecting the eyes and the mind. Verse 20 admonishes not to be among winebibbers or gluttonous meat eaters as they will end up in poverty.

The Old Testament prophets frequently used drunkenness as a metaphor for God's judgment and curse on sinful human societies (Jeremiah 13:13–14; Ezekiel 23:38–33). Numerous passages use wine or drunkenness in an analogy about Gods wrath, etc. (cf. Revelation 14:8,10; 16:19; 17:2; 18:3). Drunkenness has other ramifications today; a drunk on a camel is not as lethal as a drunk in a motor car!

(2) The wine of the first century, though containing a degree of fermentation, did not have nearly the potency that modern wines possess. All the wine in Bible times was light wine, i.e., not fortified with extra alcohol. Natural wine strength is limited by two factors: (a) the percentage of alcohol will be half of the percentage of the sugar in the juice; and (b) if the alcoholic content is much above 10 or 11 percent, the yeast cells are killed and fermentation ceases. This means that ancient wines were probably 7-10 per cent.

To avoid the sin of drunkenness and for other reasons, mingling of wine with water was practiced. A favourite proportion according to one authority was three parts of water to one part of wine, though there were a number of other attested ratios. This means it was still possible to get drunk. The dilution was specified by the Rabbis in New Testament times for the wine used at Passover. However, wine as such is not condemned in the Bible.

(3) There are some situations where alcohol is not recommended. For example, in Proverbs 31:4 it says that it is not for kings to drink wine or for rulers to desire strong drink otherwise they will forget the decrees and pervert the rights of all the afflicted. It was also prohibited by prophets on occasions. Leviticus 10:8 and Ezekial 44:21 suggest that wine or strong drink and holiness do not mix. Levitical priests in service at the temple (Leviticus 10:8, 9), the Nazirites (Numbers 6:3), and the Rechabites (Jeremiah 35:13) abstained from wine. Daniel and his companions set a worthy example by refusing to drink the king's wine (see Daniel 1:5–16). When fasting later in life, Daniel abstained from wine (see Daniel 10:3).

In the New Testament John the Baptist also abstained. With regard to leadership in the early church, Paul stated that elders, bishops, deacons (1 Timothy 3:3,8), and older women

(Titus 1:7) should not be given to drinking much wine. Paul said that whether you eat or drink or whatever you do, do it all for the glory of God (1 Corinthians 10:31). We also have 1 Corinthians 11. In this chapter, Paul addresses some issues concerning the taking of communion. It is obvious in verse 21 that the wine was alcoholic because those partaking (albeit incorrectly) were getting drunk!

Wine was an important part of life because of the quality of the drinking water, which is no longer the case today in most countries. While it is true that the Bible does not condemn moderate drinking alcohol as a sin, it certainly does not celebrate it as something we should all be doing.

(4) The Hebrew word "yáyin" is used for wine 141 times in the Old Testament and can mean either (fermented) wine or unfermented grape juice, and it is not always clear which it refers to (Teachout, 1980). The words "strong drink" is also used for stronger alcoholic drinks. In the New Testament, the corresponding Greek word for wine is "oinos" and can also refer to fermented or unfermented grape juice.

In the OT there are some verses where wine appears to refer to grape juice, e.g., Isaiah 16:10, Jeremiah 40:10b, Lamentations 2:12, and Isaiah 65:8 (see also Genesis 40:11 where the saky, or cupbearer, took the bunch of grapes, pressed the juice into the cup, and instantly delivered it into the hands of his master). Grape juice was a common drink in a land of many vineyards. The evidence from ancient writers does indicate that nonalcoholic "wine" was commonly served mainly to women, children, and slaves. The Mishna, a collection of oral Jewish tradition, states that the Jews were in the habit of drinking boiled wine, which was nonalcoholic because it was boiled, if not also from the manner of preservation. The vine was an exceptionally important plant not only with reference to the economy, but also to the theology of the Jews. It interesting that Jesus said I am the true vine (John 15:1–8).

(5) Wine can be used as a sedative, antiseptic, and for pain relief. For example, Proverbs 31:6 says that strong drink should be given to someone who is perishing and wine to those in bitter distress so that they can forget their misery and poverty. The good Samaritan poured oil and wine on the wounds of a man who was mugged (Luke 10:25–37). Paul advised Timothy to drink not just water but also a little wine for his stomach and his frequent ailments (1 Timothy 5:23). Timothy lived in Ephesus, a decaying city with sewage problems that poisoned

some of the underground water supplies. Since the days of Hippocrates it was recognised that contaminated water could produce illnesses. Note that the text says "little", so obviously alcoholic. It seems that Timothy had refrained even from the medicinal use of wine, a perfectly legitimate remedy, for the sake of his influence, even if misguided here (cf. (3) above with regard to leadership).

(6) Jesus turned water into wine (John 2:1–11). What sort of wine was it? If it was grape juice then, because it was a large quantity (six water jars or 120 to 180 gallons), it would ferment quickly. However, although not stated in the Bible, the ancients did have ways of preserving grape juice. The ruler of the feast commented on the high quality of the wine and his senses were nor dulled from previous drinking. Commentaries suggest that the wine was alcoholic, but we cannot be definitive since it was created from water. It appears that Jesus drank wine (Luke 7:33–35) as he was accused of being a drunkard and a glutton (Matthew 11: 18–19), though this could simply be very insulting language in their culture.

(7) There are some positive things said about wine, e.g., (Psalm 104:15)

> wine to gladden the heart of man, oil to make his face shine and bread to strengthen man's heart,

as well as metaphors. For example, wine is viewed as the blessing of God (Genesis 27:28; Deuteronomy 7:13), while benefits or promises of wisdom are favourably compared to wine (Proverbs 9:2–5). Also the blessings of romantic love in marriage are compared with wine (Song of Solomon 1:4b). Do some of these refer to grape juice?

Many passages anticipate a great eschatological feast at the end of time when the nations will gather to enjoy a feast of rich food, a feast of well-aged wine prepared for God's people by the Lord himself (Isaiah 25:6-9; Amos 9:13-15).

Finally, Paul said (1 Corinthians 6:12):

> All things are lawful for me, but not all things are profitable. All things are lawful for me, but I will not be mastered by anything.

So maybe instead of asking if whether or not drinking is a sin, we should be asking if drinking is profitable.

# REFERENCES

Adams J., Coleman, J., and White, M. (2014). Alcohol marketing in televised international football: Frequency analysis. *BMC Public Health*, **14** (1), 473–480.

Advertising Standards Authority. (2016). Code for Advertising and Promotion of Alcohol. Available from: http://www.asa.co.nz/codes/codes/code-for-advertising-and-promotion-of-alcohol/.

Albers, A. B., Siegel, M., Ramirez, R. L., Ross, C., Dejong, W., and Jernigan, D. H. (2015). Flavored alcoholic beverage use, risky drinking behaviors, and adverse out- comes among underage drinkers: results from the ABRAND study. *American Journal of Public Health*, **105**, 810–815.

Alcohol Healthwatch. (2018). *Time for Evidence-Based Action on Alcohol is Now.* AHW submission forum, Christchurch. (http://www.ahw.org.nz/News-Events/Latest-News-Update.)

Alhabash, S., Mcalister, A. R., Quilliam, E. T., Richards, J. I., and Lou, C. (2015). Alcohol's getting a bit more social: when alcohol marketing messages on facebook increase young adults' intentions to imbibe. *Mass Communication and Society*, **18** (3), 350–375.

Allen, N. E., Beral, V., and 5 others. (2009). Moderate alcohol intake and cancer incidence in women. *Journal of the National Cancer Institute*, **101** (5), 296–305.

American College of Cardiology. (2019). Moderate alcohol consumption linked with high blood pressure: Study among the first to suggest moderate drinking harms, rather than protects, heart health. ScienceDaily, 7 March 2019. (See www.sciencedaily.com/releases/2019/03/190307081024.htm).

Anderson, P., Bitarello do Amaral-Sabadini, M., Baumberg, B., Jarl, J., and Stuckler, D. (2011). Communicating alcohol narratives: Creating a healthier relationship with alcohol. *Journal of Health Communication*, **16** (sup2), 27–36.

Anderson, P., Chisholm, D., and Fuhr, D. C. (2009). Effectiveness and cost-effectiveness of policies and programmes to reduce the harm caused by alcohol. *Lancet*, **373** (9862), 2171–2258.

Anderson, P., de Bruijn, K. A., Gordon, R., and Hastings, G. (2009). Impact of alcohol advertising and media exposure on adolescent alcohol use: a systematic review of longitudinal studies. *Alcohol and Alcoholism*, **44** (3), 229–243.

Anderson, P., Harrison, O., Cooper, C., and Jané-Llopis, E. (2011) Incentives for Health. *Journal of Health Communication*, **16** (sup2), 107–133.

Angus, C., Holmes, J., and Meier, P. S. (2019). Comparing alcohol taxation throughout the European Union. *Addiction*, **114** (8), 1489–1494.

Arcos-Burgos, M., Vélez, J. I., and 30 others. (2019). ADGRL3 (LPHN3) variants predict substance use disorder. *Translational Psychiatry*, **9** (1), 42 pp.

Asante, L. S., Chun, S., Yun, M., and Newell, M. (2014). Social supply of alcohol to Korean high school students: a cross-sectional International Alcohol Control Study. *BMJ Open*, **4**, e003462.

Athar, M., Back, J. H, and 5 others. (2007). Resveratrol: a review of preclinical studies for human cancer prevention. *Toxicology and Applied Pharmacology*, **224** (3), 274–283.

Au Yeung, S. L. and Lam, T. H. (2019). Unite for a framework convention for alcohol control. *Lancet*, **393** (10183), 1778–1779.

Augustin, J., Augustin, E., Cutrufelli, R. L., Hagen, S. R., and Teitzel, C. (1992). Alcohol retention in food preparation. *Journal of the American Dietetic Association*, **92** (4), 486+.

Avis, H. (1999). *Drugs and Life*. Boston, Massachusetts: McGraw-Hill.

Babor, T., Caetano, R., and 13 others. (2010). *Alcohol: No Ordinary Commodity: Research and Public Policy*, 2nd edit. New York: Oxford University Press.

Babor, T. and Robaina, K. (2013). Public health, academic medicine, and the alcohol industry's corporate social responsibility activities. *American Journal of Public Health*, **103**, 206–214.

Babor, T. F., Robaina, K., and 6 others. (2018). Is the alcohol industry doing well by 'doing good'? Findings from a content analysis of the alcohol industry's actions to reduce harmful drinking. *British Medical Journal, Open*, **8**, e024325, 1–8.

Bagnardi, V., Rota, M., and 13 others. (2015). Alcohol consumption and site-specific cancer risk: a comprehensive doseresponse meta-analysis. *British Journal of Cancer*, **112**, 580-593.

Ballard, C. and Lang, I. (2018). Alcohol and dementia: a complex relationship with potential for dementia prevention. *Lancet, Public Health*, **3** (3), e103-e104.

Barry, A. E., Chaney, B. H., and Stellefson, M. L. (2013). Breath alcohol concentrations of designated drivers. *Journal of Studies on Alcohol and Drugs*, **74** (4), 509–513.

Bates, S., Holmes, J., and 7 others. (2018). Awareness of alcohol as a risk factor for cancer is associated with public support for alcohol policies. *BMC, Public Health*, **18** (1), 688+.

Beaglehole R., Bonita R., and 42 others. (2011). Priority actions for the non-communicable disease crisis. *Lancet*, **377** (9775), 1438–1447.

Beer Wine and Spirits Council of New Zealand, Distilled Spirits Association of New Zealand and Wine Institute of New Zealand Incorporated. (2001). Submission to the tax review 2001 (www.beerwsc.co.nz/page.asp?pageid=49).

Begg, D., Brookland, R., and Connor, J. (2017). Associations of repeated high alcohol use with unsafe driving behaviours, traffic offences, and traffic crashes among young drivers: Findings from the New Zealand Drivers Study. *Traffic Injury Prevention*, **18** (2), 111–117.

Bellis, M. A., Phillips-Howard, P. A., Hughes, K., Hughes, S., Cook, P. A., and Morleo, M. (2009). Teenage drinking, alcohol availability and pricing: a cross-sectional study of risk and protective factors for alcohol-related harms in school children. *BMC, Public Health*, **9**, 230–242.

Bendtsen, P., Damsgaard, M. T., and 10 others. (2014). Adolescent alcohol use: a reflection of national drinking patterns and policy? *Addiction*, **109** (11), 1857–1868.

Bergmann, M. M., Rehm, J., and 36 others. (2013). The association of pattern of lifetime alcohol use and cause of death in the European Prospective Investigation into Cancer and Nutrition (EPIC) study. *International Journal of Epidemiology*, **42**, 1772–1790.

Blakemore, S.-J. (2019). *The Adolescent Brain*. Article by the Edge foundation.

Bond, L., Daube, M., and Chikritzhs, T. (2009). Access to confidential alcohol industry documents: from "big tobacco" to "big booze". *Australasian Medical Journal*, **1**, 1–26.

Bond, L., Daube, M., Chikritzhs, T. (2010). Selling addictions: Similarities in approaches between big tobacco and big booze. *Australasian Medical Journal*, **3** ( 6), 325–332.

Boniface, S., Kneale, J., and Shelton, N. (2014). Drinking pattern is more strongly associated with under-reporting of alcohol consumption than socio-demographic factors: evidence from a mixed-methods study. *BMC, Public Health*, **14**, 1297–1306.

Boniface, S., Scholes, S., Shelton, N., and Connor, J. (2017). Assessment of non-response bias in estimates of alcohol consumption: applying the continuum of resistance model in a general population survey in England. *PLoS ONE*, **12** (1), e0170892.

Borschmann, R., Becker, D., and 13 others. (2019). Alcohol and parenthood: An integrative analysis of the effects of transition to parenthood in three Australasian cohorts. *Drug and Alcohol Dependence*, **197**, 326–334.

Bosque-Prous, M., Espelt, A., Guitart, A. M., Bartroli, M., Villalb, J. R., and Brugal, M. T. (2014). Association between stricter alcohol advertising regulations and lower hazardous drinking across European countries. *Addiction*, **109** (10), 1634–1643.

Bowden, J. (2019). Damage done. *NZ Listener, June 15–21*, 14–18

Braillon, A. (2017). Pinnochio awards: Public health responsibility deal among the nominees! *Health Policy*, **121**, 92–93.

Braillon, A. (2018). Alcohol: cardiovascular disease and cancer. *Journal of the American College of Cardiology*, **71** (5), 582–583.

Bratberg, G. H., Wilsnack, S. C., and 5 others. (2016). Gender differences and gender convergence in alcohol use over the past three decades (1984–2008), The HUNT Study, Norway. *BMC, Public Health*, **16** (1), 723–735.

Burton, R. (1906). The causes of melancholy. In The Anatomy of Melancholy Vol 1, Part 1, Section 2, London: William Tegg (and various publishers). Originally published in 1621.

Burton, R. and Sheron, N. (2018). No level of alcohol consumption improves health. *Lancet*, **392** (10152), 987–988.

Bush, K., Kivlahan, D. R., McDonell, M. B., Fihn, S. D., and Bradley, K. A. (1998). The audit alcohol consumption questions (audit-c): An effective brief screening test for problem drinking. *Archives of Internal Medicine*, **158**, 1789–1795.

Caetano, R. (2017). Does a little drinking make your heart grow stronger? *Journal of Studies on Alcohol and Drugs*, **78** (3), 341–343.

Callinan, S. (2014). How big is a self-poured glass of wine for Australian drinkers? *Drug and Alcohol Review*, **34** (2), 207–210.

Callinan, S., Laslett, A.-M., and 16 others. (2016). Alcohol's harm to others: An international collaborative project. *International Journal of Alcohol and Drug Research*, **5** (2), 25–32.

Callinan, S., Livingston, M., Room, R., and Dietze, P. M. (2018). How much alcohol is consumed outside of the lifetime risk guidelines in Australia? *Drug and Alcohol Review*, **37**, 42–47.

Callinan, S., Room, R., Livingston, M., and Jiang, H. (2015). Who purchases low cost alcohol in Australia? *Alcohol and Alcoholism*, **50**, 647–653.

Cameron, M. P., Cochrane, W., and Livingston, M. (2016). The relationship between alcohol outlets and harms: A spatial panel analysis for New Zealand, 2007-2014. Wellington: Health Promotion Agency. (A few corrections in versions 2 and 3, 2017.)

Cao, Y., Willett, W. C., Rimm, E. B., Stampfer, M. J., and Giovannucci, E. L. (2015). Light to moderate intake of alcohol, drinking patterns, and risk of cancer: results from two prospective US cohort studies. *British Medical Journal*, **351**, h4238.

Carah, N. and Shaul, M. (2016). Brands and Instagram: Point, tap, swipe, glance. *Mobile Media and Communication*, **4** (1), 69–84.

Casswell, S. (2004). Alcohol brands in young people's everyday lives: New developments in marketing. *Alcohol and Alcoholism*, **39** (6), 471–476.

Casswell, S. (2005). ICAP's latest report on alcohol education: a flawed process. *Addiction*, **100**, 1069–1070.

Casswell, S. (2009). The alcohol industry and alcohol policy: the challenge ahead. *Addiction*, **104** (1), 3–5.

Casswell, S. (2011). Alcohol harm - the urgent need for a global response. *Addiction*, **106**, 1205–1207.

Casswell, S. (2012a). Current status of alcohol marketing policy—an urgent challenge for global governance. *Addiction*, **107** (3), 478-485.

Casswell, S. (2012b). Why have guidelines at all? A critical perspective. *Drug and Alcohol Review*, **31**, 151–152.

Casswell, S. (2013). Vested interests in addiction research and policy. Why do we not see the corporate interests of the alcohol industry as clearly as we see those of the tobacco industry? *Addiction*, **108** (4), 680–685.

Casswell, S. (2014). Profits or people? The informative case of alcohol marketing. *New Zealand Medical Journal*, **127** (1406), 87–92.

Casswell, S. (2018a). Alcohol harm—who pays? *New Zealand Medical Journal*, **131** (1470), 102–103.

Casswell, S. (2018b). International Alcohol Control Study: Analyses from the first wave. *Drug and Alcohol Review*, **37** (Suppl. 2), S4–S9.

Casswell, S. (2018c). Conflict of interest and alcohol discourse —a new face but familiar messages [Viewpoint]. *New Zealand Medical Journal*, **131** (1483), 59–62.

Casswell, S., Callinan, S., plus 8 others (2016). How the alcohol industry relies on harmful use of alcohol and works to protect its profits. *Drug and Alcohol Review*, **35** (6), 661–664.

Casswell, S., Harding, J. F., You, R., and Huckle, T. (2011). Alcohol's harm to others: self-reports from a representative sample of New Zealanders. *New Zealand Medical Journal*, **124** (1336), 75–84.

Casswell, S., Huckle, T., and Pledger, M. (2002). Survey data need not underestimate alcohol consumption. *Alcoholism: Clinical and Experimental Research*, **26** (10), 561–567.

Casswell, S., Huckle, T., Wall, M., and Parker, K. (2016). Policy-relevant behaviours predict heavier drinking in both on and off premises and mediate the relationship between heavier alcohol consumption and age, gender, and socioeconomic status—analysis from the international alcohol control study. *Alcoholism Clinical and Experimental Research*, **40** (2), 385–392.

Casswell, S., Huckle, T., Wall, M., and Yeh, L. C. (2014). International alcohol control study: pricing data and hours of purchase predict heavier drinking. *Alcoholism: Clinical and Experimental Research*, **38** (5), 1425–1431.

Casswell, S., Huckle, T., and 8 others. (2018). Policy-relevant behaviours predict heavier drinking and mediate the relationship with age, gender and education status: Analysis from the International Alcohol Control study: Policy-relevant behaviours and alcohol. *Drug and Alcohol Review*, **37**, 586–595.

Casswell, S. and Maxwell, A. (2005a). What works to reduce alcohol-related harm and why aren't the policies more popular? *Social Policy Journal of New Zealand*, **25**, 118–141.

Casswell, S., and Maxwell, A. (2005b). Regulation of alcohol marketing: a global view. *Journal of Public Health Policy*, **26** (3), 343–358.

Casswell, S., Meier, P., and 8 others. (2014). The international alcohol control (IAC) study—Evaluating the impact of alcohol policies. *Alcoholism: Clinical and Experimental Research*, **36** (8), 1462–1467.

Casswell, S., Morojele, N., and 10 others. (2018). The Alcohol Environment Protocol - a new tool for alcohol policy. *Drug and Alcohol Review*, **37** (S2), S18-S26.

Casswell, S. and Thamarangsi, T. (2009). Reducing harm from alcohol: call to action. *Lancet*, **373** (9682), 2247–2257.

Casswell, S., You, R. Q., and Huckle, T. (2011). Alcohol's harm to others: reduced wellbeing and health status for those with heavy drinkers in their lives. *Addiction*, **106** (6), 1087–1095.

Caughey J. E. and Ney, P. G. (1987). *Sense and Alcohol*. Invercargill, New Zealand: Craig Printing, Co.

Chaiyasong, S., Huckle, T., and 10 others. (2018). Drinking patterns vary by gender, age and country-level income: Cross-country analysis of the International Alcohol Control Study. *Drug and Alcohol Review*, **37** (Suppl. 2), S53–S62.

Chalmers, J., Carragher, N., Davoren, S., and O' Brien, P. (2013). Real or perceived impediments to minimum pricing of alcohol in Australia: Public opinion, the industry and the law. *International Journal of Drug Policy*, **24** (6), 517–523.

Chambers, T. J. (2018). The extent and nature of children's real-time exposure to alcohol marketing using wearable cameras and GPS devices. PhD Thesis University of Otago, Retrieved from http://hdl.handle.net/10523/8265.

Chambers, T., Signal, L., Carter, M.-A., McConville, S., Wong, R., and Zhu, W. (2017). Alcohol sponsorship of a summer of sport: a frequency analysis of alcohol marketing during major sports events on New Zealand television. *New Zealand Medical Journal*, **130** (1448), 27–33.

Chao, C., Haque, R., Caan, B. J., Poon, K.-Y. T., Tseng, H.-F., and Quinn, V. P. (2010). Red wine consumption not associated with reduced risk of colorectal cancer. *Nutrition and Cancer*, **62** (6), 849–855.

Chelimo, C. and Casswell, S. (2013). Effect of alcohol consumption on cancer risk: A review of meta-analyses (2007-2013). SHORE and Whariki Research Centre, School of Public Health, Massey University, New Zealand.

Cherpitel, C. J., Witbrodt, J., Korcha, R. A., Ye, Y., Kool, B., and Monteiro, M. (2018). Multi-level analysis of alcohol-related injury, societal drinking pattern and alcohol control policy: emergency department data from 28 countries. *Addiction*, *113* (11), 2031–2040.

Chikritzhs, T., Fillmore, K., and Stockwell, T. (2009). A healthy dose of scepticism: Four good reasons to think again about protective effects of alcohol on coronary heart disease. *Drug and Alcohol Review*, **28** (4), 441—444.

Chisholm D., Moro, D., and 5 others. (2018). Are the "best buys" for alcohol control still valid? An update on the comparative cost-effectiveness of alcohol control strategies at the global level. *Journal of Studies on Alcohol and Drugs*, **79** (4), 514–522.

Christensen, A. I., Nordestgaard, B. G., and Tolstrupa, J. S. (2018). Alcohol intake and risk of ischemic and haemorrhagic stroke: results from a mendelian randomisation study. *Journal of Stroke*, **20** (2), 218–227.

Colder, C. R., Shyhalla, K., and Frndak, S. E. (2018). Early alcohol use with parental permission: Psychosocial characteristics and drinking in late adolescence. *Addictive Behaviors*, **76**, 82–87.

Connor, J. (2017). Improved health and welfare will flow from reductions in drinking. *New Zealand Medical Journal*, **130** (1409), 8–10.

Connor, J. and Casswell, S. (2009). The burden of road trauma due to other people's drinking. *Accident Analysis and Prevention*, **41**(5), 1099–1103.

Connor, J. and Casswell, S. (2012). Alcohol-related harm to others in New Zealand: evidence of the burden and gaps in knowledge. *New Zealand Medical Journal*, **125** (1467), 11–27.

Connor, J. L., Kydd, R., Maclennan, B., Shield, K., and Rehm, J. (2017). Alcohol-attributable cancer deaths under 80 years of age in New Zealand. *Drug and Alcohol Review*, **36** (3), 415 423.

Connor, J. L., Kydd, R., Shield, K., and Rehm, J. (2015). The burden of disease and injury attributable to alcohol in New Zealanders under 80 years of age: marked disparities by ethnicity and sex. *New Zealand Medical Journal*, **128** (1409), 15–28.

Connor, J. L., Kypri, K., Bell, M. L., and Cousins, K. (2011). Alcohol outlet density, levels of drinking and alcohol-related harm in New Zealand: a national study. *Journal Epidemiology and Community Health*, **65** (10), 841–846.

Connor, J. L., You, R. Q., and Casswell, S. (2009). Alcohol-related harm to others: a survey of physical and sexual assault in New Zealand. *New Zealand Medical Journal*, **122** (1303), 10–20.

Cotter, T., Perez, D., Dunlop, S., Kite, J., and Gaskin, C. (2013). Knowledge and beliefs about alcohol consumption, longer-term health risks, and the link with cancer in a sample of Australian adults. *NSW Public Health Bulletin*, **24**, 81–86.

Crampton, E. and Burgess, M. (2009). *The Price of Everything, The Value of Nothing: A (Truly) External Review of BERLs Study of Harmful Alcohol and Drug Use*. Working Paper No. 10/2009, Department of Economics and Finance, College of Business and Economics. University of Canterbury.

Crawford A. (1987). Bias in a survey of drinking habits. *Alcohol and Alcoholism*, **22** (2), 167–179.

Dawson, D. A. (2000). Alcohol consumption, alcohol dependence and all-cause mortality. *Alcoholism-Clinical and Experimental Research*, **24**, 72–81.

Dawson D. A., Goldstein, R. B., Pickering, R. P., and Grant, B. F. (2014). Nonresponse bias in survey estimates of alcohol consumption and its association with harm. *Journal of Studies on Alcohol and Drugs*, **75** (4), 695–703.

Day, P., Breetzke, G., Kingham, S., and Campbell, M. (2012). Close proximity to alcohol outlets is associated with increased serious violent crime in New Zealand. *Australian and New Zealand Journal of Public Health*, **36** (1), 48–54.

DeBruijn, A. (2014). Commentary on O'Brien *et al.* Refuting arguments against a ban on alcohol sport sponsorship. *Addiction*, **109**, 1655–1656.

de Looze, M., Raaijmakers, Q., and 12 others. (2015). Decreases in adolescent weekly alcohol use in Europe and North America: evidence from 28 countries from 2002 to 2010. *European Journal of Public Health*, **25** (suppl. 2), 69–72.

De Pirro, S., Lush, P., Parkinson, J., Duka, D., Critchley, H., and Badiani, A. (2019). Effect of alcohol on the sense of agency in healthy humans. *Addiction Biology*, to appear.

De Santis, S., Bach, P., and 10 others. (2019). Microstructural white matter alterations in men with alcohol use disorder and rats with excessive alcohol consumption during early abstinence. *JMA Psychiatry*, **76** (7), 749–758.

De Visser, R., Robinson, E., and Bond, R. (2016). Voluntary temporary abstinence from alcohol during "Dry January" and subsequent alcohol use. *Health Psychology*, **35** (3), 281–289.

Degenhardt, L., Charlson, F., and many others (2018). The global burden of disease attributable to alcohol and drug use in 195 countries and territories, 1990-2016: a systematic analysis for the Global Burden of Disease Study 2016. *Lancet Psychiatry*, **5** (12), 987–1012.

Dickerman, B. A., Markt, S. C., Koskenvuo, M., Pukkala, E., Mucci, L. A., and Kaprio, J. (2016). Alcohol intake, drinking patterns, and prostate cancer risk and mortality: a 30-year prospective cohort study of Finnish twins. *Cancer Causes Control*, **27** (9), 1049–1058.

Dieze, P., Room, R., Jolley, D., Matthews, S., and Chikritzhs, T. (2011). The adverse consequences of drinking in a sample of Australian adults. *Journal of Substance Use*, **16** (2), 116–126.

Donald, K. A., Eastman, E., and 6 others. (2015). Neuroimaging effects of prenatal alcohol exposure on the developing human brain: a magnetic resonance imaging review. *Acta Neuropsychiatrica*, **27** (5), 251–269.

Doran, C. M., and Digiusto, E. (2011). Using taxes to curb drinking: a report card on the Australian government's alcopops tax. *Drug Alcohol Review*, **30** (6), 677–680.

Druesne-Pecollo, N., Tehard, B., and 5 others. (2009). Alcohol and genetic polymorphisms: effect on risk of alcohol-related cancer. *Lancet Oncology*, **10** (2), 173–180.

Easy, K. E., Dyer, M. L., Timpson, N. J., and Munafò, M. R. (2019). Prenatal alcohol exposure and offspring mental health: A systematic review. *Drug and Alcohol Dependence*, **197**, 344–353.

Eckhardt, L., Woodruff, S. I., and Elder, J. P. (1994). A longitudinal analysis of adolescent smoking and its correlates. *Journal of School Health*, **64**, 67–72.

Edenberg, H. J. (2012). Genes contributing to the development of alcoholism: an overview. *Alcohol Research: Current Reviews*, **34** (3), 336–338.

Ervasti, J., Kivimäki, M., and 12 others. (2018). Sickness absence diagnoses among abstainers, low-risk drinkers and at-risk drinkers: consideration of the U-shaped association between alcohol use and sickness absence in four cohort studies. *Addiction*, **113** (9), 1633–1642.

EUCAM. (2011). *The Seven Key Messages of the Alcohol Industry.* (See seven_key_messages_of_the_alcohol_industry on the internet).

Falkner, C., Christie, G., Zhou, L., and King, J. (2015). The effect of alcohol price on dependent drinkers' alcohol consumption. *New Zealand Medical Journal*, **128** (1427), 9–17.

Fedirko, V., Tramacere, I., and 10 others. (2011). Alcohol drinking and colorectal cancer risk: an overall and doseresponse meta-analysis of published studies. *Annals of Oncology*, **22** (9), 1958–1972.

Fenoglio, P., Parel, V., and Kopp, P. (2003). The social cost of alcohol, tobacco and illicit drugs in France, 1997. *European Addiction Research*, **9** (1), 18–28.

Fernández, M. D., Saulyte, J., Inskip, H. M., and Takkouche, B. (2018). Premenstrual syndrome and alcohol consumption: a systematic review and meta-analysis. *British Medical Journal, Open*, **8** (3), e019490.

Ferris, J., Puljević C., Labhart, F., Winstock, A., and Kuntsche, E. (2019). The role of sex and age on pre-drinking: an exploratory international comparison of 27 countries. *Alcohol and Alcoholism*, doi:10.1093/alcalc/agz040.

Florenzano, R., Huepe, G., and Barr, M. (2016). Harm to others from alcohol: the role of socio-cultural variables. *Acta Bioethica*, **22** (1), 71–79.

Fortune, S., Watson, P., Robinson, E., Fleming, T., Merry, S., and Denny, S. (2010). *Youth07: The health and wellbeing of secondary school students in New Zealand: Suicide behaviours and mental health in 2001 and 2007*. Auckland: The University of Auckland, New Zealand.

Foster, S. E., Vaughan, R. D., Foster, W. H., and Califano, J. A. (2006). Estimate of the commercial value of underage drinking and adult abusive and dependent drinking to the alcohol industry. *Archives of Pediatrics and Adolescent Medicine*, **160** (5), 473–478.

Foxcroft, D. (2005). ICAPs latest report on alcohol education: a flawed peer review process. *Addiction*, **100**, 1066–1068.

Fuchs, F. D., Chambless, L. E., and 5 others. (2004). Association between alcoholic beverage consumption and incidence of coronary heart disease in whites and blacks: the atherosclerosis risk in communities study. *American Journal of Epidemiology*, **160** (5), 466–474.

Gale, M., Muscatello, D. J., and 8 others. (2015). Alcopops, taxation and harm: a segmented time series analysis of emergency department presentations. *BMC, Public Health*, **15** (1), 468–476.

Gangisetty, O., Sinha, R., and Sarkar, D. K. (2019). Hypermethylation of proopiomelanocortin and period 2 genes in blood are associated with greater subjective and behavioral motivation for alcohol in humans. *Alcoholism: Clinical and Experimental Research*, **43** (2), 212–220.

Gapstur, M., Drope, J. M., and 7 others. (2018). A blueprint for the primary prevention of cancer: Targeting established, modifiable risk factors. *CA: A Cancer Journal for Clinicians*, **68** (5), 3–25.

Gelernter, J., Sun,, N., and 27 others. (2019). Genome-wide association study of maximum habitual alcohol intake in >140,000 U.S. European and African American veterans yields novel risk loci. *Biological Psychiatry*, **86** (5), 365–376.

Gil-Hernandez, S. and Garcia-Moreno, L. M. (2016). Executive performance and dysexecutive symptoms in binge drinking adolescents. *Alcohol*, **51**, 79–87.

Gil-Hernandez, S., Mateos, P., Porras, C., Garcia-Gomez,, R., Navarro, E., and Garcia-Moreno, L. M. (2017). Alcohol binge drinking and executive functioning during adolescent brain development. *Frontiers in Psychology*, **8**, 1638.

Goddard, E. (2001). Obtaining information about drinking through surveys of the general population. *National Statistics Methodology Series*, No. 24. Newport, UK: Office for National Statistics.

Gosselt, J. F., van Hoof, J. J., de Jong, M.D.T., and Prinsen, S. (2007). Mystery shopping and alcohol sales: Do supermarkets and liquor stores sell alcohol to underage customers? *Journal of Adolescent Health*, **41** (3), 302–308.

Globe. (2014). BRAZIL: An unregulated alcohol market. Issue 2, page 3.

Grace, A. (2018a). *This Naked Mind: Control Alcohol, Find Freedom, Discover Happiness & Change Your Life*. London: HarperCollins.

Grace, A. (2018b). *The Alcohol Experiment: 30 days to take control, cut down or give up for good*. London: HarperCollins.

Grant, B. F., Chou, S. P., and 9 others. (2017). Prevalence of 12-month alcohol use, high-risk drinking, and DSM-IV alcohol use disorder in the United States, 2001-

2002 to 2012-2013. Results From the national epidemiologic survey on alcohol and related conditions. *Journal of the American Medical Association Psychiatry*, **74**, 911–923.

Gray-Phillip, G., Huckle, T., and 9 others. (2018). Availability of alcohol: location, time and ease of purchase in high and middle-income countries: Data from the International Alcohol Control (IAC) study. *Drug and Alcohol Review*, **37** (Suppl. 2), S36–S44.

Greenfield, T. K., Rehm, J., and Rogers, J. D. (2002). Effects of depression and social integration on the relationship between alcohol consumption and all-cause mortality. *Addiction*, **97** (1), 29–38.

Griswold, M. G., Fullman, N., and many collaborators (2018). Alcohol use and burden for 195 countries and territories, 1990-2016: a systematic analysis for the Global Burden of Disease Study 2016. *Lancet*, **392**, 1015–1035.

Grube, J. (2007). Alcohol regulation and traffic safety: An overview. In Transportation Research Circular: No. E-C123 (pp. 1330). Washington, DC: Transportation Research Board of the National Academies.

Gruenewald, P., Treno, A., Ponicki, W., Huckle, T., Yeh, L.-C., and Casswell, S. (2015). Impacts of New Zealand's lowered minimum purchase age on context-specific drinking and related risks. *Addiction*, **110** (11), 1757–1766.

Gulland, A. (2016). People lack awareness of link between alcohol and cancer, survey finds. *British Medical Journal, Clinical Research*, **353**, i1881.

Gunasekara, F. and Wilson, N. (2010). Very cheap drinking in New Zealand: some alcohol is more affordable than bottled water and nearly as cheap as milk. *New Zealand Medical Journal*, **123** (1324), 103–107.

Hachinskia, V., Einhäupl, K., and 24 others. (2019). Preventing dementia by preventing stroke: The Berlin Manifesto. *Alzheimer's and Dementia: The Journal of the Alzheimer's Association*, **15** (7), 961–984.

Haggard H. W. and Jellinek, E. M. (1942). *Alcohol Explored*. New York: Doubleday.

Hall, W. and Chikritzhs, T. (2011). The Australian alcopops tax revisited. *Lancet*, **377** (9772), 1136–1137.

Hallgren, M., Lundin, A., Zeebari, Z., and Rehm, J. (2018). Collectivity of drinking or collective thinking? Policy implications of polarised alcohol consumption trends. *Drug and Alcohol Review*, **37** (Suppl. 1), S470–S471.

Hansen, C.E., Kwasniewski, M.T., and Sacks, G.L. (2012). Decoupling the effect of heating and flaming on chemical and sensory changes during flambé cooking. *International Journal of Gastronomy and Food Science*, **1** (2), 90–95.

Hartz, S. M., Oehlert, B., and 12 others. (2018). Daily drinking is associated with increased mortality. *Alcoholism: Clinical and Experimental Research*, **42** (11), 2246–2255.

Hashibe, M., Brennan, P., and many others. (2009). Interaction between tobacco and alcohol use and the risk of head and neck cancer: pooled analysis in the International Head and Neck Cancer Epidemiology Consortium. *Cancer Epidemiology, Biomarkers and Prevention*, **18** (2), 541–550.

Hay, G. C., Whigham, P. A., Kypri, K., and Langley, J. D. (2009). Neighbourhood deprivation and access to alcohol outlets: A national study. *Health and Place*, **15** (4), 1086–1093.

Health Promotion Agency. (2015a). *Objecting to a Licence to Sell or Supply Alcohol: A Guide to Objections and Hearings*. Wellington: Health Promotion Agency.

Health Promotion Agency. (2015b). *Alcohol and Older People: What You Need to Know*. Wellington: Health Promotion Agency.

Health Promotion Agency. (2018). *Trends in Affordability of Alcohol in New Zealand*. Wellington: Health Promotion Agency.

Heikkinen, N., Niskanen, E., and 7 others. (2016). Alcohol consumption during adolescence is associated with reduced grey matter volumes. *Addiction*, **112** (4), 604–613.

Higuchi, S., Matsushita, S., and Osaki, Y. (2006). Drinking practices, alcohol policy and prevention programmes in Japan. *International Journal of Drug Policy*, **17** (4), 358–366.

Hingson, R., Zha, W., and Smyth, D. (2017). Magnitude and trends in heavy episodic drinking, alcohol-impaired driving, and alcohol-related mortality and overdose hospitalizations among emerging adults of college ages 18-24 in the United States, 1998-2014. *Journal of Studies on Alcohol and Drugs*, **78**, 540–548.

Holmes, J., Meng, Y., and 7 others. (2014). Effects of minimum unit pricing for alcohol on different income and socioeconomic groups: a modelling study. *Lancet*, **383** (9929), 1655–1664.

Holmes, M. V., Dale, C. E., and many others. (2014). Association between alcohol and cardiovascular disease: Mendelian randomisation analysis based on individual participant data. *British Medical Journal*, **349** (7966), pp. 12.

Huakau, J., Asiasiga, L., and 5 others. (2005). New Zealand Pacific peoples' drinking style: too much or nothing at all? *New Zealand Medical Journal*, **118** (1216), 1491-1501.

Huckle, T., Casswell, S., and Greenway, S. (2011). The impact of alcohol-related presentations in the emergency department and the wider policy debate. *New Zealand Medical Journal*, **124** (1336), 7–9.

Huckle, T., Casswell, S., and 17 others. (2018). The International Alcohol Control study: Methodology and implementation. *Drug and Alcohol Review*, **37** (S2), S10–S17.

Huckle, T., Gruenewald, P., and Ponicki, W. R. (2016). Context-specic drinking risks among young people. *Alcoholism Clinical and Experimental Research*, **40** (5), 1129–1135.

Huckle, T., Huakau, J., Sweetsur, P., Huisman, O., and Casswell, S. (2008). Density of alcohol outlets and teenage drinking: living in an alcogenic environment is associated with higher consumption in a metropolitan setting. *Addiction*, **103**, 1614–1621.

Huckle, T. and Parker K. (2014). Long-term impact on alcohol-involved crashes of lowering the minimum purchase age in New Zealand. *American Journal of Public Health*, **104** (6), 1087–1091.

Huckle, T., Pledger, M., and Casswell, S. (2012). Increases in typical quantities consumed and alcohol-related problems during a decade of liberalizing alcohol policy. *Journal of Studies on Alcohol and Drugs*, **73** (1), 53–62 .

Huckle, T. and Romeo, P. (2018). Patterns of social supply of alcohol over time in New Zealand. Wellington: Health Promotion Agency.

Huckle, T., Sweetsur, P., Moyes, S., and Casswell, S. (2008). Ready to drinks are associated with heavier drinking patterns among young females. *Drug and Alcohol Review*, **27**, 398–403. any

Huckle T., Wong, K., Parker, K., and Casswell, S. (2017). Increased use of police and health-related services among those with heavy drinkers in their lives in New Zealand. *New Zealand Medical Journal*, **130** (1455), 102–110.

Huckle, T., You, R. Q., and Casswell, S. (2011). Increases in quantities consumed in drinking occasions in New Zealand 1995-2004. *Drug and Alcohol Review*, **30** (4), 366–371.

Jackson, N. (2016). A review of Territorial Authority progress towards Local Alcohol Policy development. Auckland: Alcohol Healthwatch.

Jarl, J., Gerdtham, U. G., and Selin, K. H. (2009). Medical net cost of low alcohol consumption - a cause to reconsider improved health as the link between alcohol and wage? *Cost Effectiveness and Resource Allocation*, **7**, 17–25.

Jernigan, D. H. and Rushman, A. E. (2014). Measuring youth exposure to alcohol marketing on social networking sites: Challenges and prospects. *Journal of Public Health Policy*, **35** (1), 91–104.

Jiang, H., Livingston, M., Room, R., and Callinan, S. (2016). Price elasticity of on- and off-premises demand for alcoholic drinks: A Tobit analysis. *Drug and Alcohol Dependence*, **163**, 222–228.

Jones, K. L., Smith, D. W., Ulleland, C. W., and Streissguth, A. P. (1973). Pattern of malformation in offspring of chronic alcoholic women. *Lancet*, **301** (7815), 1267–1271.

Jones, S. C. and Donovan, R. (2001). Messages in alcohol advertising targeted to youth. *Australian and New Zealand Journal of Public Health*, **25**, 126–131.

Jones, S. C. and Gregory, P. (2009). The impact of more visible standard drink labelling on youth alcohol consumption: helping young people drink (ir)responsibly? *Drug Alcohol Review*, **28** (3), 230–234.

Jones, S. C., Robinson, L., Barrie, L., Francis, K., and Lee, J. K. (2016). Association between young Australian's drinking behaviours and their interactions with alcohol brands on facebook: results of an online survey. *Alcohol and Alcoholism*, **51** (4), 474–480.

Jung, S., Wang, M., and 28 others. (2018). Alcohol consumption and breast cancer risk by estrogen receptor status: in a pooled analysis of 20 studies. *International Journal of Epidemiology*, **45** (3), 916–928.

Juonala, M., Viikari, J. S. A., and 9 others. (2009). Alcohol consumption is directly associated with carotid intimamedia thickness in Finnish young adults: The cardiovascular risk in young Finns study. *Atherosclerosis*, **204**, e93–e98.

Kalant, H. (2005). Effects of food and body composition on blood alcohol levels. In V. R. Preedy and R. R. Watson (Eds), *Comprehensive Handbook of Alcohol Related Pathology*, vol.1,87–102. Elsevier Academic Press.

Kalinin, S., González-Prieto, M. and 7 others. (2018). Transcriptome analysis of alcohol-treated microglia reveals downregulation of beta amyloid phagocytosis. *Journal of Neuroinflammation*, **15** (1), 141–152.

Kalinowski, A. and Humphreys, K. (2016). Governmental standard drink definitions and low-risk drinking guidelines in 37 countries. *Addiction*, **111**, 1293–1298.

Kanda, J., Matsuo, K., and 9 others. (2009). Impact of alcohol consumption with polymorphisms in alcohol-metabolizing enzymes on pancreatic cancer risk in Japanese. *Cancer Science*, **100** (2), 296–302.

Kaner, E., Newbury-Birch, D., Avery, L., Jackson, K., Brown, N., and Mason, H. (2007). Liver disease – A rapid review of epidemiology, treatment and service provision. *Institute of Health and Society, Newcastle University*, commissioned by the Department of Health. Based on WHO Mortality Database, 2007, "Standardized mortality rated for diseases of the liver years with available data between 1950-2004".

Karády, J., Szilveszter, B., and 11 others. (2016). Alcohol consumption and presence of coronary heart disease. *European Heart Journal*, **37** (Suppl. 1), 1136.

Keric, D. and Stafford, J. (2018). Proliferation of 'healthy' alcohol products in Australia: implications for policy. *Public Health, Research and Practice*, Online early publication. (https://doi.org/10.17061/phrp28231808).

Kerr, W. and Greenfield, T. (2007). Distribution of alcohol consumption and expenditures and the impact of improved measurement on coverage of alcohol sales in the 2000 National Alcohol Survey. *Alcoholism: Clinical and Experimental Research*, **31**, 1714–1722.

Key, J., Hodgson, S., and 6 others. (2006). Meta-analysis of studies of alcohol and breast cancer with consideration of the methodological issues. *Cancer Causes Control*, **17**, 759–770.

Klatsky, A. L. (2015). Alcohol and cardiovascular diseases: where do we stand today? *Journal of Internal Medicine*, **278**, 238–250.

Klatsky, A. L. and Udaltsova, N. (2013). Abounding confounding: sick quitters and healthy drinkers. *Addiction*, **108**, 1544–1553.

Klatsky, A. L, Udaltsova, N., Li, Y., Baer., D, Nicole, Tran H., and Friedman, G. D. (2014). Moderate alcohol intake and cancer: the role of underreporting. *Cancer Causes Control*, **25**, 693–699.

Koehnke, M. D., Schick, S., and 5 others. (2002). Severity of alcohol withdrawal symptoms and the T1128C polymorphism of the neuropeptide Y gene. *Journal of Neural Transmission (Vienna)*. **109** (11), 1423–1429.

Kranzler, H. R. and Soyka, M. (2018). Diagnosis and pharmacotherapy of alcohol use disorder: A review. *Journal of the American Medical Association*, **320** (8), 815–824.

Kunzmann, A. T., Coleman, H. G., Huang, W.-I., and Berndt, S. I. (2018). The association of lifetime alcohol use with mortality and cancer risk in older adults: A cohort study. *PLoS Medicine*, **15** (6), p.e1002585.

Kuo, M. C., Heeb, J. L,. Gmel, G., and Rehm, J. (2003). Does price matter? The effect of decreased price on spirits consumption in Switzerland. *Alcoholism: Clinical and Experimental Research*, **27**, 720–725.

Kypri, K., and McCambridge, J. (2018). Alcohol must be recognised as a drug. *British Medical Journal*, **362**, k3944.

Kypri, K., Davie, G., McElduff, P., Connor, J., and Langley, J. (2014). Effects of lowering the minimum alcohol purchasing age on weekend assaults resulting in hospitalization in New Zealand. *American Journal of Public Health*, **104** (8), 1396–1401.

Kypri, K., Maclennan, B., Cousins, K., and Connor, J. (2018). Hazardous drinking among students over a decade of university policy change: controlled before-and-after evaluation. *International Journal of Environmental Research and Public Health*, **15** (10), 2137.

Kypri, K., Maclennan, B, Langley J. D., and Connor, J. L. (2011). The Alcohol Reform Bill: more tinkering than reform in response to the New Zealand public's demand for better liquor laws. *Drug and Alcohol Review*, **30** (4), 428–433.

LaBrie, J. W., Boyle, S., Earle, A., and Almstedt, H. C. (2018). Heavy episodic drinking is associated with poorer bone health in adolescent and young adult women. *Journal of Studies on Alcohol and Drugs*, **79** (3), 391–398.

Lachenmeier, D. W., Przybylski, M. C., and Rehm, J. (2012 ). Comparative risk assessment of carcinogens in alcoholic beverages using the margin of exposure approach. *International Journal of Cancer*, **131** (6), pp. E995-E1003.

Lam, T., Liang, W., Chikritzhs, T., and Allsop, S. (2014). Alcohol and other drug use at school leavers' celebrations. *Journal of Public Health*, **36** (3), 408–416.

Lange, S., Probst, C., Gmel, G., Rehm, J., Burd, L., and Popova, S. (2017). Global prevalence of fetal alcohol spectrum disorder among children and youth: a systematic review and meta-analysis. *JAMA Pediatrics*,**171** (10), 948–956.

Langley, J. D., Kypri, K., and Stephenson, S. C. (2003). Secondhand effects of alcohol use among university students: computerised survey. *British Medical Journal*, **327** (7422), 1023–1024).

Lanis, R., McClure R., and Zirnsak, M. (2017). Tax aggressiveness of alcohol and bottling companies in Australia. Canberra: Foundation for Alcohol Research and Education. (http://fare.org.au/wp-content/uploads/Tax-aggressiveness-of-alcohol-and-bottling-companies-in-Australia_FINAL_04052017.pdf).

Lebel, C., Roussotte, F., and Sowell, E. (2011). Imaging the impact of prenatal alcohol exposure on the structure of the developing human brain. *Neuropsychology Review*, **21** (2), 102–118.

Li, Y., Jiang, Y., Zhang, M., Yin, P., Wu, F., and Zhao, W. (2011). Drinking behaviour among men and women in China: the 2007 China Chronic Disease and Risk Factor Surveillance. *Addiction*, **106** (11), 1946–1956.

Liang, W. and Chikritzhs, T. (2013). The association between alcohol exposure and self-reported health status: the effect of separating former and current drinkers. *PLoS One*, **8** (2), e55881.

Lim, S., Han, C. E., Uhlhaas, P. J., and Kaiser, M. (2013). Preferential detachment during human brain development: age- and sex-specific structural connectivity in diffusion tensor imaging (dti) data. *Cerebral Cortex*, **25** (6), 1477–1489,

Lim, S. S., Vos, T., and many others. (2012). A comparative risk assessment of burden of disease and injury attributable to 67 risk factors and risk factor clusters in 21 regions, 1990-2010: a systematic analysis for the Global Burden of Disease Study 2010. *Lancet*, **380**, 2224–2260.

Lin, E.-Y., Casswell, S., You, R. Q., and Huckle, T. (2012). Engagement with alcohol marketing and early brand allegiance in relation to early years of drinking. *Addiction Research and Theory*, **20** (4), 329–338.

Lippi, G., Franchini, M., and Guidi, G. C. (2010). Red wine and cardiovascular health the "French Paradox" revisited. *International Journal of Wine Research*, **2**, 1–7.

Livingstone, M. and Callinan, S. (2015). Underreporting in alcohol surveys: Whose drinking is underestimated? *Journal of Studies on Alcohol and Drugs*, **76** (1), 158–164.

Lonsdale, A. J., Hardcastle, S. J., and Hagger, M. S. (2012). A minimum price per unit of alcohol: a focus group study to investigate public opinion concerning UK government proposals to introduce new price controls to curb alcohol consumption. *BMC Public Health*, **12**, 1023–1086.

Lundberg, G. (2018). Are you an alcoholic? *Medscape*, October 12.

Lyons, A., McCreanor, T., and 6 others. (2014). Flaunting it on Facebook: Young adults, drinking cultures and the cult of celebrity. Wellington, NZ: Massey University School of Psychology.

Lyons, A., McCreanor, T., Goodwin, I., and Moewaka Barnes, H., (Eds). (2017). *Youth Drinking Cultures in a Digital World: Alcohol, Social Media and Cultures of Intoxication*. London: Routledge.

Lyons, A., McNeill, A., and Britton, J. (2014). Alcohol imagery on popularly viewed television in the UK. *Journal of Public Health*, **36** (3), 42–434.

Maheswaran, R., Green, M. A., Strong, M., Brindley, P., Angus, C., and Holmes, J. (2018). Alcohol outlet density and alcohol related hospital admissions in England: a national small-area level ecological study. *Addiction*, **113** (11), 2051–2059.

Maier, S. and West, J. (2001). Binge drinking in pregnancy and risk of fetal death. *Alcohol Research and Health*, **25** (3), 168–174.

Manthey, J., Shield, K. D., Rylett, M., Hasan, O. S. M., Probst, C., and Rehm, J. (2019). Global alcohol exposure between 1990 and 2017 and forecasts until 2030: a modelling study. *Lancet*, **393** (10190), 2493–2502.

Marshall, S. J. and Chambers, G. K. (2005). Genetic aspects of alcohol metabolism: An overview. In V. R. Preedy and R. R. Watson (Eds), *Comprehensive Handbook of Alcohol Related Pathology*, vol.1, 31–48. Elsevier Academic Press.

Marten, R., Kadandale, S., plus 25 others (2018). Sugar, tobacco, and alcohol taxes to achieve the SDGs. *Lancet*, **391** (10138), 2400–2401.

Martino, F. P., Miller, P. G., Coomber, K., Hancock, L., and Kypri, K. (2017). Analysis of alcohol industry submissions against marketing regulation. *PLoS ONE*, **12**(1), e0170366.

Mateus, G. Ferreira, I. M. P. L. V. O., and Pinho, O. (2011). Headspace SP-MEGC/MS evaluation of ethanol retention in cooked meals containing alcoholic drinks. *Food Chemistry*, **126** (3), 1387–1392.

Mattick, R. P., Clare, P. J., and 10 others. (2018). Association of parental supply of alcohol with adolescent drinking, alcohol-related harms, and alcohol use disorder symptoms: a prospective cohort study. *Lancet, Public Health*, **3** (2), e64–e71.

May, P. A., Chambers, C. D., and 27 others. (2018). Implications of higher than expected prevalence of fetal alcohol spectrum disorders. *Journal of the American Medical Association*, **319** (5), 474–482.

McCreanor, T., Lyons, A., Griffin, C., Goodwin, I., Moewaka Barnes, H., and Hutton, F. (2013). Youth drinking cultures, social networking and alcohol marketing: Implications for public health. *Critical Public Health*, **23** (1), 110–120.

McEwan, B., Campbell, M., and Swain, D. (2010). New Zealand culture of intoxication: Local and global influences. *New Zealand Sociology*, **25** (2), 15–37.

McFadyen, T., Tindall, J., and 8 others. (2018). Alcohol management practices in community sporting clubs: Validation of an online self-report tool. *Drug and Alcohol Review*, **37** (5), 580–587.

McGovern, P. E., Zhang, J., and 11 others. (2004). Fermented beverages of pre- and proto-historic China. *Proceedings of the National Academy of Sciences of the United States of America*, **101** (51), 17593–17598.

McLellan, A. T., Lew, D. C., O'Brien, C. P., and Kleber, H. D. (2000). Drug dependence, a chronic medical illness: implications for treatment, insurance and outcomes evaluation. *Journal of the American Medical Association*, **284**, 1689–1695.

M.E. Consulting (2018). *New Zealand alcohol supply and demand structures: Research report*. Wellington: Health Promotion Agency. For research reports by the Health Promotion Agency see http://www.hpa.org.nz/research-library/research-publications.

Meiklejohn, J., Connor, J., and Kypri, K. (2012). The effect of low survey response rates on estimates of alcohol consumption in a general population survey. *PLoS ONE*, **7** (4), e35527.

Meier P., S., Purshouse, R., and Brennan, A. (2010). Policy options for alcohol price regulation: the importance of modelling population heterogeneity. *Addiction*. **105** (3), 383–393.

Menéndez, P., Kypri, K., and Weatherburn, D. (2017). The effect of liquor licensing restrictions on assault: a quasi-experimental study in Sydney, Australia. *Addiction*, **112** (2), 261–268.

Michaels, D. (2008). *Doubt is Their Product: How Industry's Assault on Science Threatens Your Health*. Oxford, New York: Oxford University Press.

Miech, R. A., Johnston L. D., O'Malley P. M., Bachman J. G., and Schulenberg J. E. (2016). Monitoring the Future national survey results on drug use, 19752015: Volume I, Secondary school students. Ann Arbor, MI: Institute for Social Research, The University of Michigan.

Miller, P. G., Palmer, D., and 9 others. (2011). Dealing with alcohol-related problems in the night-time economy: a study protocol for mapping trends in harm and stakeholder views surrounding local community level interventions. *BMC Research Notes*, **4** (204), 10–20.

Millwood, I. Y., Walters, G. W., and 19 others. (2019). Conventional and genetic evidence on alcohol and vascular disease aetiology: a prospective study of 500,000 men and women in China. *Lancet*, **303** (10183), 1831–1842.

Milne, D. (2002). Alcohol consumption in Japan: different culture, different rules. *Canadian Medical Association Journal*, **167** (4), 388-388.

Ministry of Health. (2007). *Alcohol Use in New Zealand: Analysis of the 2004 New Zealand Health Behaviours Survey—Alcohol Use*. Wellington: Ministry of Health.

Ministry of Health. (2009). *Alcohol Use in New Zealand Key results of the 2007/08 New Zealand Alcohol and Drug Use Survey*. Wellington: Ministry of Health.

Ministry of Health. (2010). *Alcohol and Pregnancy: A practical Guide for Health Professionals*. Wellington: Ministry of Health.

Ministry of Health. (2015). *Taking Action on Fetal Alcohol Spectrum Disorder (FASD): A discussion document*. Wellington: Ministry of Health.

Ministry of Health. (2016a). *Health Loss in New Zealand 1990-2013: A report from the New Zealand Burden of Diseases, Injuries and Risk Factors Study.* Wellington: Ministry of Health.
(See http://www.health.govt.nz/system/files/documents/publications/health-loss-in-new-zealand-1990-2013-aug16.pdf).

Ministry of Health. (2016b). *Annual update of key results 2015/16: New Zealand health survey.* Wellington: Ministry of Health.
(See https://www.health.govt.nz/publication/annual-update-key-results-2015-16-new-zealand-health-survey).

Ministry of Health. (2017). *Annual Data Explorer 2016/17: NZ Health Survey.* Wellington: Ministry of Health.
http://minhealthnz.shinyapps.io/nz-health-survey-2016-17-annual-data-explorer/.

Ministry of Justice. (2014). *The Effectiveness of Alcohol Pricing Policies. Reducing harmful alcohol consumption and alcohol-related harm.*
(http://www.justice.govt.nz/publications/global-publications/e/the-effectiveness-of-alcohol-pricing-policies).

Miquel, L.,López-Pelayo, H.,and 6 others. (2018). Barriers to implement screening for alcohol consumption in Spanish hypertensive patients. *Family Practice*, **35** (3), 295–301.

Moodie, R., Stuckler, D., and 6 others. (2013). Profits and pandemics: prevention of harmful effects of tobacco, alcohol, and ultra-processed food and drink industries. *Lancet*, **381** (9867), 670–679.

Moore, A. A., Beck, J. C., Babor, T. F., Hays, R. D., and Reuben, D. B. (2002). Beyond alcoholism: identifying older, at-risk drinkers in primary care. *Journal of Studies on Alcohol*, **63**, 316–324.

Moore, A. A., Giuli, L., and 5 others. (2006). Alcohol use, comorbidity, and mortality. *Journal of the American Geriatrics Society*, **54**, 757–762.

Morojele, N. K, Lombard, C., Burnhams, N. H., Williams, P. P., Nel, E., and Parry, C. D. H. (2018). Alcohol marketing and adolescent alcohol consumption: Results from the International Alcohol Control study South Africa. *South African Medical Journal*, **108** (9), 782–788.

Morton, S. M. B., Atatoa Carr, P. E., and 12 others. (2010). The Growing Up in New Zealand (GUiNZ) study: a longitudinal study of New Zealand children and their families. Report 1: before we are born. University of Auckland, Auckland; 2010. (See https://cdn.auckland.ac.nz/assets/growingup/research-findings-impact/report01.pdf).

Mota, N., Parada M., and 6 others. (2013). Binge drinking trajectory and neuropsychological functioning among university students: a longitudinal study. *Drug Alcohol Dependence*, **133** (1), 108–114.

Mounga, V. and Maughan, E. (2012). Breast cancer in Pacific Islander women. *Nursing for Women's Health*, **16** (1), 26–35.

Muggli, E., O'Leary, C., and 9 others. (2016). "Did you ever drink more?" A detailed description of pregnant women's drinking patterns. *BMC Public Health*, **16**, 683–696.

Naimi, T. S, Brown, D., and 9 others. (2005). Cardiovascular risk factors and confounders among nondrinking and moderate-drinking U.S. adults. *American Journal of Preventive Medicine*, **28** (4), 369–373.

Naimi, T. S., Stockwell, T., Saitz,R., and Chikritzhs, T. (2017). Selection bias and relationships between alcohol consumption and mortality. *Addiction*, **112** (2), 220–221.

Naimi, T. S., Xuan, Z., Brown, D. W., and Saitz, R. (2012). Confounding and studies of 'moderate' alcohol consumption: the case of drinking frequency and implications for low-risk drinking guidelines. *Addiction*, **108**, 1534–1543.

Nayak, M. B., Patterson, D., Wilsnack, S. C., Karriker-Jaffe, K. J., and Greenfield, T. K. (2019). Alcohol's secondhand harms in the United States: New data on prevalence and risk factors. *Journal of Studies on Alcohol and Drugs*, **80**, 273–281.

Nelson, J. P. and McNall, A. D. (2016). Alcohol prices, taxes, and alcohol-related harms: A critical review of natural experiments in alcohol policy for nine countries. *Health Policy*, **120**, 264–272.

Neufeld, M. and Rehm, J. (2018). Effectiveness of policy changes to reduce harm from unrecorded alcohol in Russia between 2005 and now. *International Journal of Drug Policy*, **51**, 1–9.

New Zealand Law Commission (2009). *Alcohol in Our Lives: An Issues Paper on the Reform of New Zealand's Liquor Laws.* Issues paper 15. Wellington, New Zealand. (https://www.lawcom.govt.nz/sites/default/files/projectAvailableFormats/NZLC IP15.pdf).

New Zealand Law Commission (2010). *Alcohol in Our Lives: Curbing the Harm.* Report 114. Wellington, New Zealand. (See http://www.alcoholaction.co.nz/wp-content/uploads/Law-Commission-Report.pdf).

New Zealand Medical Association. (2011). Health equity position statement. New Zealand Medical Association. *New Zealand Medical Journal*, **124** (1329), 89.

Nielsen (2016). New Zealand Media Trends Report. (https://www.nielsen.com/nz/en/insights/reports/2016/new-zealand-media-trends-2016.html.)

Nippert, M. (2018). Top multinationals pay almost no tax in New Zealand. *New Zealand Herald*, 7 June. (www.nzherald.co.nz/business/news/article.cfm?c_id=3&objectid=11607336).

Noel, J. K. and Babor, T. F. (2018). Alcohol advertising on facebook and the desire to drink among young adults. *Journal of Studies on Alcohol and Drugs*, **79** (5), 751–760.

Norström, T. and Rossow, I. (2016). Alcohol consumption as a risk factor for suicidal behavior: A systematic review of associations at the Individual and at the population level. *Archives of Suicide Research*, **20** (4):489–506.

Nutt, D. J., King, L. A., and Phillips, L. D. (2010). Drug harms in the UK: a multicriteria decision analysis. *Lancet*, **376** (9752), 1558–1565.

NZIER. (2019). Impacts of local alcohol policies: Analysis of changes in spending following local changes in trading hours. Wellington: Health Promotion Agency.

Obad, A., Peeran, A., Little, J. I., Haddad, G. E., and Tarzami, S. T. (2018). Alcohol-mediated organ damages: heart and brain. *Frontiers in Pharmacology*, **9**, 81.

O'Brien K., Ferris J., and 5 others. (2014). Alcohol industry sponsorship and hazardous drinking in UK university students who play sport. *Addiction*, **109**, 1647–1654.

O'Brien, K. and Kypri, K. (2008). Alcohol industry sponsorship and hazardous drinking among sportspeople. *Addiction*, **103**, 1961–1966.

O'Brien, K., Lynott, D., and Miller P. (2013). Alcohol industry sponsorship and alcohol-related harms in Australian university sportspeople/athletes. *Drug Alcohol Review*, **32**, 241–247.

Odgers, C. L., Caspi, A., and 7 others. (2008). Is it important to prevent early exposure to drugs and alcohol among adolescents? *Psychological Science*, **19** (10), 1037–1044.

O'Donnel, A., Anderson, P., and 5 others. (2014). The impact of brief alcohol interventions in primary healthcare: A systematic review of reviews. *Alcohol and Alcoholism*, **49** (1), 66–78.

Oldham, M., Holmes, J., Whitaker, V., Fairbrother, H., and Curtis, P. (2018). *Youth Drinking in Decline*. The University of Sheffield's Alcohol Research Group. (See https://medicalxpress.com/news/2018-09-sharp-decline-england-youth.html).

O'Leary, C. M., Nassar, N., and 5 others. (2010). Prenatal alcohol exposure and risk of birth defects. *Pediatrics*, **126** (4), e843–850.

Parackal, S. M., Parackal, M. K., and Harraway,, J. A. (2013). Prevalence and correlates of drinking in early pregnancy among women who stopped drinking on pregnancy recognition. *Maternal and Child Health Journal*, **17** (3), 520–529.

Parackal, S. M., Parackal, M. K., and Harraway, J. A. (2019). Associated factors of drinking prior to recognising pregnancy and risky drinking among New Zealand women aged 18 to 35 years. *International Journal of Environmental Research and Public Health*, **16** (10), 1822.

Parfitt, T. (2009). Russia's health promotion efforts blossom. *Lancet*, **373** (9682), 2174–2176.

Park, J.-E., Ryu, Y., and Cho, S.-I. (2017). The association between health changes and cessation of alcohol consumption. *Alcohol and Alcoholism*, **52** (3), 344–350.

Parry, C., Burnhams, N. H., and London, L. (2012). A total ban on alcohol advertising: presenting the public health case. *South African Medical Journal*, **102** (7), 602–604.

Parry, C. D. H., Londani, M., and 7 others. (2018). Support for alcohol policies among drinkers in Mongolia, New Zealand, Peru, South Africa, St Kitts and Nevis, Thailand and Vietnam: Data from the International Alcohol Control Study. *Drug and Alcohol Review*, **37** (Suppl. 2), S72–S78.

Parry, C. D. H., Trangenstein, P., Lombard, C., Jernigan, D. H., and Morojele, N. K. (2018a). Support for alcohol policies from drinkers in the city of Tshwane, South Africa: Data from the International Alcohol Control study. *Drug and Alcohol Review*, **37** (S1), S210–S217.

Parry, C. D. H., Trangenstein, P., Lombard, C., Jernigan, D., and Morojele, N. (2018b). Screening for alcohol problems among adults in South Africa: Findings from the International Alcohol Control Study. *International Journal of Mental Health and Addiction*, **13** (1), 1–17.

Partanen, J. (2006). Spectacles of sociability and drunkenness: on alcohol and drinking in Japan. *Contemporary Drug Problems*, **33**2, 177-204, 175.

Patel, K. R., Scott, E., Brown, V. A., Gescher, A. J., Steward, W. P., and Brown, K. (2011). Clinical trials of resveratrol. *Annals of the New York Academy of Sciences*, **1215**, 161–169.

Patil, S., Winpenny, E. M., Elliott, M. l. N., Rohr, C. and Nolte, E. (2014). Youth exposure to alcohol advertising on television in the UK, the Netherlands and Germany. *European Journal of Public Health*, **24** (4), 561–565.

Patra, J., Giesbrecht, N., Rehm, J., Bekmuradov, D., and Popova, S. (2012). Are alcohol prices and taxes an evidence-based approach to reducing alcohol-related harm and promoting public health and safety? A literature review. *Contemporary Drug Problems*, **39**, 7–48.

Paul, C. A., Au, R., and 5 others. (2008). Association of alcohol consumption with brain volume in the Framingham study. *Archives of Neurology*, **65** (10), 1363–1367.

Pavlic, M. and Grubwieser, P. (2005). Breath and blood alcohol. In V. R. Preedy and R. R. Watson (Eds), *Comprehensive Handbook of Alcohol Related Pathology*, vol.1, 75–87. Elsevier Academic Press.

Peacock, A., Leung, J., and 15 others. (2018). Global statistics on alcohol, tobacco and illicit drug use: 2017 status report. *Addiction*, **113** (10), 1905–1926.

Pennay, A., Holmes, J., Törrönen, J., Livingston, M., Kraus, L., and Room, R. (2018). Researching the decline in adolescent drinking: The need for a global and generational approach. *Drug Alcohol Review*, **37**, S115–S119.

Petticrew M., Maani Hessari, N., Knai, C., and Weiderpass, E. (2018). How alcohol industry organisations mislead the public about alcohol and cancer. *Drug Alcohol Review*, **37**, 293–303.

Piano, M. R. (2017). Alcohol's effects on the cardiovascular system. *Alcohol Research: Current Reviews*, **38** (2), 219–241.

Piano, M. R., Burke, M., Kang, M., and Philips, S. A. (2018). Effects of repeated binge drinking on blood pressure levels and other cardiovascular health metrics in young adults: National health and nutrition examination survey, 2011-2014. *Journal of the American Heart Association*, **7** (13), e008733.

Pierce, H., Stafford, J., Pettigrew, S., Kameron, C., Keric, D., and Pratt, I. S. (2019). Regulation of alcohol marketing in Australia: A critical review of the Alcohol Beverages Advertising Code Scheme's new Placement Rules. *Drug and Alcohol Review*, 38 (1), 16–24.

Plant, M. (1985). *Women, Drinking and Pregnancy*. London and New York: Tavistock Publications.

Popova, S., Lange, S., Shield, K., Burd, L., and Rehm, J. (2019). Prevalence of fetal alcohol spectrum disorder among special subpopulations: a systematic review and meta-analysis. *Addiction*, **114** (7), 1150–1172.

Praud, D., Rota, M., and 6 others. (2016). Cancer incidence and mortality attributable to alcohol consumption. *International Journal of Cancer*, **138**, 1380–1387.

Probst, C., Parry, C. D. H., Wittchen, H. U., and Rehm, J. (2018). The socioeconomic profile of alcohol-attributable mortality in South Africa: a modelling study. *BMC Medicine*, **16** (1), 97.

Puddey, I. B., Rakic, V., Dimmitt, S. B., and Beilin, L. J. (1999). Influence of pattern of drinking on cardiovascular disease and cardiovascular risk factors—a review. *Addiction*, **94** (5), 649–663.

Randerson, S., Casswell, S., and Huckle, T. (2018). Changes in New Zealand's alcohol environment following implementation of the Sale and Supply of Alcohol Act (2012). *New Zealand Medical Journal*, **131** (1476), 14–23.

Randerson, S., Casswell, S., and Rychert, M. (2019). Diminished inclusivity in public space: How alcohol reduces people's use and enjoyment of public places literature review. Wellington: Health Promotion Agency

Reeve, B. and Gostin, L. O. (2019). "Big" food, tobacco, and alcohol: reducing industry influence on noncommunicable disease prevention laws and policies: Comment on "Addressing NCDs: challenges from industry market promotion and interferences." *International Journal of Health Policy and Management*, **8** (7), 450–454.

Rehm, J. (2011). The risks associated with alcohol use and alcoholism. *Alcohol Research and Health*, **34** (2), 135–143.

Rehm, J., Baliunas, D., and 12 others. (2010). The relation between different dimensions of alcohol consumption and burden of disease: an overview. *Addiction*, **105** (5),817–843.

Rehm, J. and Ferreira-Borges, C. (2018). Risk factor policies, morbidity, and mortality in Russia. *Lancet*, **392** (10153), 1094–1095.

Rehm, J., Gmel, G. E., and 10 others. (2017). The relationship between different dimensions of alcohol use and the burden of disease—an update. *Addiction*, **112** (6), 968–1001.

Rehm, J., Guiraud, J., Poulnais, R., and Shield, K. D. (2018). Alcohol dependence and very high risk level of alcohol consumption: a life-threatening and debilitating disease. *Addiction Biology*, **23** (4), 961–968.

Rehm, J., Mathers, C., Popova, S., Thavorncharoensap, M., Teerawattananon, Y., and Patra, J. (2009). Global burden of disease and injury and economic cost attributable to alcohol use and alcohol-use disorders. *Lancet*, **373** (9682), 2223–2233.

Rehm, J., Patra, J., and Popova, S. (2007). Alcohol drinking cessation and its effect on esophageal and head and neck cancers: a pooled analysis. *International Journal of Cancer*, **121** (5), 1132–1137.

Rehm J., Taylor B., and 5 others. (2010). Alcohol as a risk factor for liver cirrhosis: a systematic review and meta-analysis.*Drug Alcohol Review.* **29** (4), 437–445.

Rehm, J., Zatonski W., and Taylor, B. (2011). Epidemiology and alcohol policy in Europe. *Addiction*, **106** (Suppl. 1), 11–19.

Richardson, E. A., Hill, S. E., Mitchell, R., Pearce, J., and Shortta, N. K. (2015). Is local alcohol outlet density related to alcohol-related morbidity and mortality in Scottish cities? *Health Place*, **33**, 172–180.

Richardson, S. K., Grainger, P. C., Ardagh, M. W., and Morrison, R. l. (2018). Violence and aggression in the emergency department is under-reported and under-appreciated. *New Zealand Medical Journal*, **131** (1476), 50–58.

Rigaud, A. and Craplet, M. (2004). The "Loi Evin": a French exception. (See http://www.ias.org.uk/What-we-do/Publication-archive/The-Globe/Issue-2-2004-amp-1-2004/The-Loi-Evin-a-French-exception.aspx).

Roberts, E. and Drummond, C. (2019). Alcohol related hospital admissions: Locking the door after the horse has bolted. *BMJ opinion*, July 30.

Roberts, E., Morse, R., Epstein, S., Hotopf, M., Leon, D., and Drummond, C. (2019). The prevalence of wholly attributable alcohol conditions in the United Kingdom hospital system: a systematic review, meta-analysis and meta-regression. *Addiction*, **114** (10), 1726-1737.

Robertson, K. and Tustin, K. (2018). Students who limit their drinking, as recommended by national guidelines, are stigmatized, ostracized, or the subject of peer pressure: Limiting consumption is all but prohibited in a culture of intoxication. *Substance Abuse: Research and Treatment*, **12**, 1–9.

Rodgers, B., Korten, A. E., Jorm, A. F., Jacomb, P. A., Christensen, H., and Henderson, A. S. (2000). Non-linear relationships in associations of depression and anxiety with alcohol use. *Psychological Medicine*, **30**, 421–432.

Roerecke, M., Greenfield, T. K., Kerr, W. C., Bondy, S., Cohen, J., and Rehm, J. (2011). Heavy drinking occasions in relation to ischaemic heart disease mortality— an 11–22 year follow-up of the 1984 and 1995 US National Alcohol Surveys. *International Journal of Epidemiology*, **40** (5), 1401–1410.

Roerecke, M., Kaczorowski, J., Tobe, S. W., Gmel, G., Hasan, O. S. M., and Rehm, J. (2017). *Lancet Public Health*, **2** (2), e108–e120.

Roerecke, M. and Rehm, J. (2010). Irregular heavy drinking occasions and risk of ischemic heart disease: a systematic review and meta-analysis. *American Journal of Epidemiology*, **171** (6), 633–644.

Roerecke, M. and Rehm, J. (2012). The cardioprotective association of average alcohol consumption and ischaemic heart disease: a systematic review and meta-analysis. *Addiction*, **107** (7), 1246–1260.

Roerecke, M., Tobe, S. W., and 7 others. (2018). Sex-specific associations between alcohol consumption and incidence of hypertension: a systematic review and meta-analysis of cohort studies. *Journal of the American Heart Association*, **7** (13), e008202.

Romieu, I, Scoccianti, C., and many others. (2015). Alcohol intake and breast cancer in the European prospective investigation into cancer and nutrition. *International Journal of Cancer*, **137** (8), 1921–1930.

Room, R. (2005). What to expect from a 'social aspects' organization, and what to expect from school-based alcohol education. *Addiction*, **100**, 1069–1073.

Rossen, F., Newcombe, D., and 7 others. (2018). Alcohol consumption in New Zealand women before and during pregnancy: findings from the Growing Up in New Zealand study. *New Zealand Medical Journal*, **131** (1479), 24–34.

Rossow, I. and Nörstrom, T. (2012). The impact of small changes in bar closing hours on violence. The Norwegian experience from 18 cities. *Addiction*, **107** (3), 530–537.

Rout, J. and Hannan, T. (2016). Consumer awareness and understanding of alcohol pregnancy warning labels. Wellington: Health Promotion Agency. (http://ndhadeliver.natlib.govt.nz/delivery/DeliveryManagerServlet?dps_pid= IE26781497).

Rutherford, D. (2013). Beware of the alcohol industry bearing gifts. *Globe*, (3), 3–7.

Ryan-Hughes, N. (2018). *Sale and Supply of Alcohol Act (2012) Community Experience Survey.* Wellington: Health Promotion Agency. (See https://www.hpa.org.nz/research-library/research-publications.)

Ryapushkina, J., Skovenborg, E., and 5 others. (2016). Cooking with beer: How much alcohol is left? *International Journal of Gastronomy and Food Science,* **5-6**, 17–26.

Saitz, R. (2018). Medications for alcohol use disorder and predicting severe withdrawal. *Journal of the American Medical Association,* **320** (8),766–768.

Saitz, R., Heeren, T. C., Zha, W., and Hingson, R. (2019). Transitions to and from at-risk alcohol use in adults in the United States. *Journal of Substance Use,* **24** (1), 41–46.

Samokhvalov, A. V., Irving, H. M., and Rehm, J. (2010). Alcohol consumption as a risk factor for atrial fibrillation: a systematic review and meta-analysis. *European Journal of Cardiovascular Prevention and Rehabilitation,* **17** (6), 706–712.

Sassi, F., Belloni, A., and 8 others. (2018). Equity impacts of price policies to promote healthy behaviours. *Lancet,* **391**, 2059–2070.

Schelleman-Offermans, K., Knibbe, R. A., Kuntsche, E., and Casswell, S. (2012). Effects of a natural community intervention intensifying alcohol law enforcement combined with a restrictive alcohol policy on adolescent alcohol use. *Journal of Adolescent Health,* **51**, 580–587.

Schutte, R., Huisman, H., and 9 others (2019). Iron loading, alcohol and mortality: A prospective study. *Clinical Nutrition,* **38** (3), 1262–1268.

Schütze, M., Boeing, H., and many others,. (2011). Alcohol attributable burden of incidence of cancer in eight European cuntries based on results from prospective cohort study. *British Medical Journal,* **342**, d1584.

Schwarzinger, M., Pollock, B. G., Hasan, O. S. M., Dufouil, C., and Rehm, J. (2018). Contribution of alcohol use disorders to the burden of dementia in France 2008–13: a nationwide retrospective cohort study. *Lancet, Public Health,* **3** (3), e124–e132.

Scocciantia, C., Cecchini, M., and 10 others. (2015). European code against cancer 4th Edition: Alcohol drinking and cancer. *Cancer Epidemiology,* **45**,181–188.

Scott, S. and Kaner, E. (2014). Alcohol and public health: heavy drinking is a heavy price to pay for populations. *Journal of Public Health,* **36** (3), 396–398.

Secretan, B., Straif, K., and 9 others. (2009). A review of human carcinogens—Part E: tobacco, areca nut, alcohol, coal smoke, and salted fish. *Lancet Oncology,* **10** (11), 1033–1034.

Seitz, H. K. and Becker, P. (2007). Alcohol metabolism and cancer risk. *Alcohol Research and Health,* **30**, 38—47.

Seitz, H. K. and Mueller S. (2015). Alcohol and cancer: an overview with special emphasis on the role of acetaldehyde and cytochrome P450 2E1. *Advances in Experimental Medicine and Biology,* **815**, 59–70.

Seitz, H. K., Pelucchi, C., Bagnardi, V., and La Vecchia, C. (2012). Epidemiology and pathophysiology of alcohol and breast cancer: Update 2012. *Alcohol and Alcoholism,* **47** (3), 204–212.

Sellman, D. (2010). The 10 most important things known about addiction. *Addiction,* **105** (1), 6–13.

Sellman, D., Adamson, S., Foulds, J., Beaglehole, B., and Mulder, R. (2019). Another government ignores a recommendation to strengthen alcohol regulations. *New Zealand Medical Journal*, **132** (1498), 7922.

Sellman, D. and Connor, J. (2009). In utero brain damage from alcohol: a preventable tragedy. *New Zealand Medical Journal*, **122** (1306), 6–8.

Sellman, D., Connor, J., Robinson, G., and Jackson, R. (2009). Alcohol cardioprotection has been talked up. *New Zealand Medical Journal*, **122** (1303), 97–101.

Sellman, D., Connor, J., Robinson, G., and McBride, S. (2017). Alcohol reform—New Zealand style: Reflections on the process from 1984 to 2012. *Psychotherapy and Politics International*, **15** (1), e1398, 12 pages.

Sellman, D., Connor, J., Robinson, G., McBride, S., and Farrell, T. (2018). Law, liquor and love. *Policy Quarterly*, **14** (1), 44–49.

Seo, S., Chun, S., Newell, M., and Yun, M. (2015). Korean public opinion on alcohol control policy: A cross-sectional International Alcohol Control study. *Health Policy*, **119** (1), 33–43.

Shaper A. G. (2011). Alcohol consumption decreases with the development of disease. *Addiction*, **106**, 1023–1025.

Sharma, M., Anyimukwu, C., Kim, R. W., Nahar, V. K., and Ford, M. A. (2018). Predictors of responsible drinking or abstinence among college students who binge drink: A multitheory model approach. *Journal of the American Osteopathic Association*, **118** (7), 519–530.

Sherafatmanesh, S., Ekramzadeh, M., and Akbarzadeh, M. (2017). The carcinogenicity of alcoholic beverages: A review. *International Journal of Nutrition Sciences*, **2** (1), 2–9.

Silins, E., Horward, L. J., and 16 others. (2018). Adverse adult consequences of different alcohol use patterns in adolescence: an integrative analysis of data to age 30 years from four Australasian cohorts. *Addiction*, **113** (10), 1811–825.

Sinclair, J., McCann, M., Sheldon, E., Gordon, I., Brierley-Jones, L., and Copson E. (2019). The acceptability of addressing alcohol consumption as a modifiable risk factor for breast cancer: a mixed method study within breast screening services and symptomatic breast clinics. *BMJ Open*, **9**(6), e027371.

Sinner, M. F., Drobesch, C., and 5 others. (2018). Acute alcohol consumption and effects on cardiac excitation, conduction, and repolarization. Results from the MunichBREW Study. *EP Europace*, **20** (suppl. 1), 16.

Skog, O. J. (1985). The collectivity of drinking cultures: a theory of the distribution of alcohol consumption. *British Journal of Addiction*, **80**, 83–99.

Slack, A., Nana G., et al. (2009). Costs of harmful alcohol and other drug use. *Report to Ministry of Health and ACC, NZ*, Wellington, BERL. (http://www.justice.govt.nz/justice-sector/drivers-of-crime/documents/BERL_-July_2009-_Costs_of_Harmful_Alcohol_and_Other_Drug_Use-1.pdf).

Smith, A. H., Ovesen, P. L., and 12 others (2018). Risk locus identification ties alcohol withdrawal symptoms to SORCS2. *Alcoholism: Clinical and Experimental Research*, **42** (12), 2337–2348.

Smyth, A, Teo, K. K., and 24 others. (2015). Alcohol consumption and cardiovascular disease, cancer, injury, admission to hospital, and mortality: a prospective cohort study. *Lancet*, **386** (10007), 1945–1954.

Starodubov, V. I., Marczak, L. B., and 15 others. (2018). The burden of disease in Russia from 1980 to 2016: a systematic analysis for the Global Burden of Disease Study 2016. *Lancet*, **392**, 1138–1146.

Starkman, B. G., Sakharkar, A. J., and Pandey, S.. C. (2012). Epigenetics—Beyond the genome in alcoholism. *Alcohol Research: Current Reviews*, **34** (3), 293–305.

Stewart, D. and McCambridge, J. (2019). Alcohol complicates multimorbidity in older adults. *British Medical Journal*, **365**, 14304.

Stewart, R., Das, M., and 8 others. (2014). The impact of alcohol-related presentations on a New Zealand hospital emergency department. *New Zealand Medical Journal*, **127** (1400), 23–38.

Stockwell, T., Auld, M. C., Zhao, J., and Martin, G. (2012). Does minimum pricing reduce alcohol consumption? The experience of a Canadian province. *Addiction*, **107** (5), 912–920.

Stockwell, T. and Chikritzhs, T. (2013). Commentary: Another serious challenge to the hypothesis that moderate drinking is good for health? *International Journal of Epidemiology*, **42** (6), 1792–1794,

Stockwell, T., Zhao, J., and Macdonald, S. (2014). Who under-reports their alcohol consumption in telephone surveys and by how much? An application of the "yesterday method" in a national Canadian substance use survey. *Addiction*, **109** (10), 1657-1666.

Stockwell, T., Zhao, J., Panwar, S., Roemer, A., Naimi, T., and Chikritzhs, T. (2016). Do "moderate" drinkers have reduced mortality risk? A systematic review and meta-analysis of alcohol consumption and all-cause mortality. *Journal of Studies on Alcohol and Drugs*, **77** (2), 185–198.

Stockwell T., Zhao, J., Sherk, A., Rehm, J., Shield, K., and Naimi, T. (2018). Underestimation of alcohol consumption in cohort studies and implications for alcohol's contribution to the global burden of disease. *Addiction*, **13** (12), 2245–2249.

Stokowski, L. A. (2015). Alcohol and Cancer: Drink at Your Own Risk. *Medscape*, Nov 23, 2015.

Stoolmiller, M., Wills, T. A. and 5 others. (2012). Comparing media and family predictors of alcohol use: a cohort study of US adolescents. *BMJ OPEN*, **2**, e000543.

Strandberg-Larsen, K., Nielsen, N. R., Grønbæk, M., Andersen, P. K., Olsen, J., and Andersen, A.-M. N. (2008). Binge drinking in pregnancy and risk of fetal death. *Obstetrics and Gynecology*, **111** (3), 602–609.

Sullivan, T., Edgar, F., and McAndrew, I. (2019). The hidden costs of employee drinking: A quantitative analysis. *Drug and Alcohol Review*, **38** (5), 543–553.

Summers L. H. (2018). Taxes for health: evidence clears the air. *Lancet*, **391**, 1974–1976.

Tael-Öeren, M., Naughton, F., and Sutton, S. (2019). The relationship between parental attitudes and children's alcohol use: a systematic review and meta-analysis. *Addiction*, **114** (9),1527–1546.

Tangcharoensathien, V., Chandrasiri, O., Kunpeuk, W., Markchang, K., & Pangkariya, N. (2019). Addressing NCDs: Challenges from industry market promotion and interferences. *International Journal of Health Policy and Management*, **8** (5), 256–260

Teachout, R. P. (1980). *The use of "Wine" in the Old Testament*. ThD thesis. Dallas Theological Seminary.

Thamarangsi, T. (2006). Thailand: alcohol today. *Addiction*, **101**, 783–787.

The Lancet, editorial. (2007). A framework convention on alcohol control. *Lancet*, **370** ( 9593), 1102–1102.

Tinawi, G., Gray, T., and 6 others. (2018). Highly deficient alcohol health warning labels in a high-income country with a voluntary system. *Drug and Alcohol Review*, **37** (5), 616–626.

Tobin, C. L., Moodie, R., and Livingstone, C. (2011). A review of public opinion towards alcohol controls in Australia. *BMC Public Health*, **11** (58), 1–9.

Toomey, T. L., Erickson, D. J., and 5 others. (2012). Is the density of alcohol establishments related to nonviolent crime? *Journal of Studies on Alcohol and Drugs*, **73** (1), 21–25.

Torjesen, I. (2019). Exclusive: Partnering with alcohol industry on public health is not okay, WHO says. *British Medical Journal, online*, **365**, I1666.

Toumbourou, J. W., Rowland, B., Ghayour-Minaie, M., Sherker, S., Patton, G. C., and Williams, J. W. (2018). Student survey trends in reported alcohol use and influencing factors in Australia. *Drug and Alcohol Review*, **37**, S58–S66.

Towers, A., Sheridan, J., Newcombe, D., and Szabo, A. (2018). The longitudinal patterns of alcohol use in older New Zealanders. Wellington: Health Promotion Agency (natlib-primo.hosted.exlibrisgroup.com).

University of Sheffield (2008). Independent review of the effects of alcohol pricing and promotion: Part B Modelling the Potential Impact of Pricing and Promotion Policies for Alcohol in England: Results from the Sheffield Alcohol Policy Model Version 2008.

Vartolomei, M. D., Kimura, S., and 6 others. (2018). The impact of moderate wine consumption on the risk of developing prostate cancer. *Clinical Epidemiology*, **10**, 431–444.

Vasiljevic, M., Coulter, L., Petticrew, M., and Marteau, T. M. (2018). Marketing messages accompanying online selling of low/er and regular strength wine and beer products in the UK: a content analysis. *BMC Public Health*, **18**, 147.

Viet Cuong, P., Casswell, S., and 9 others. (2018). Cross-country comparison of proportion of alcohol consumed in harmful drinking occasions using the International Alcohol Control Study. *Drug and Alcohol Review*, **37** (S2), S45–S52.

Voskoboinik, A., Costello, B.T., and 13 others. (2018). Atrial fibrillation population: a cross-sectional MRI-based study. *JACC: Clinical Electrophysiology*, **4** (11), 1451–1459.

Voskoboinik, A., Pradhu, S., Ling, L.-H, Kalman, J. M., and Kistler, P. M. (2016). Alcohol and atrial fibrillation: a sobering review. *Journal of the American College of Cardiologists*, **68**, 2567–2576.

Voskoboinik, A., Wong, G., Lee, G,, and 10 others. (2019). Moderate alcohol consumption is associated with atrial electrical and structural changes: Insights from high-density left atrial electroanatomic mapping. *Heart Rhythm*, **16**, 251–259.

Wagenaar, A. C., Maldonado-Mollna, M. M., and Wagenaar, B. H. (2009). Effects of alcohol tax increases on alcohol-related disease mortality in Alaska: time-series analyses from 1976 to 2004. *American Journal of Public Health*, **99** (8), 1464–1470. *Erratum: American Journal of Public Health*, (2012), **102** (4), 584.

Wagenaar, A. C., Salois, M. J., and Komro, K. A. (2009). Effects of beverage alcohol price and tax levels on drinking: a meta-analysis of 1003 estimates from 112 studies. *Addiction*, **104** (2), 179–190.

Wagenaar, A. C., Tobler, A. L., and Komro, K. A. (2010). Effects of alcohol tax and price policies on morbidity and mortality: a systematic review. *American Journal of Public Health*, **100** (11), 2270–2278.

Wall, M. and Casswell, S. (2013). Affordability of alcohol as a key driver of alcohol demand in New Zealand: a cointegration analysis. *Addiction*, **108** (1), 72–79.

Wall, M. and Casswell, S. (2017). Drinker types, harm, and policy-related variables: Results from the 2011 international alcohol control study in New Zealand. *Alcoholism: Clinical and Experimental Research*, **41** (5), 1044–1053.

Wall, M., Casswell, S., and 5 others. (2018). Alcohol taxes' contribution to prices in high and middle-income countries: Data from the International Alcohol Control Study. *Drug and Alcohol Review*, **37** (Suppl. 2), S27–S35.

Wall, M., Casswell, S., and Yeh, L.-C. (2017). Purchases by heavier drinking young people concentrated in lower priced beverages: Implications for policy. *Drug and Alcohol Review*, **36**, 352–358.

Wallack, L. (1992). WARNING: The alcohol industry is not your friend? *British Journal of Addiction*, **87** (8), 1109–1111.

Wallack, L. (1993). Some proposals for the alcohol industry. *Addiction*, **88** (2), 174–178.

Wannamethee, S. G., Whincup, P. H., Lennon, L., Papacosta, O., and Shaper, A. G. (2015). Alcohol consumption and risk of incident heart failure in older men: a prospective cohort study. *Open Heart*, **2**, e000266.

Warrington, R. (2018). *Sober Curious: The Blissful Sleep, Greater Focus, Limitless Presence, and Deep Connection Awaiting Us All on the Other Side of Alcohol.* HarperOne.

Wells, J. E., Baxter, J., and Schaaf, D. (Eds). (2007). *Substance Use Disorders in Te Rau Hinengaro: The New Zealand Mental Health Survey.* Wellington: Alcohol Advisory Council of New Zealand. https://psychiatry-training.wiki.otago.ac.nz/images/e/ec/ALAC_Substance_Abuse _Report.pdf.

Wells, S., Graham, K., and Purcell, J. (2009). Policy implications of the widespread practice of pre-drinking or pre-gaming before going to public drinking establishments-are current prevention strategies backfiring? *Addiction*, **104**, 4–9.

Westberg, K., Stavros, C., Smith, A. C. T., Munro, G., and Argus, K. (2018). An examination of how alcohol brands use sport to engage consumers on social media. *Drug and Alcohol Review*, **37**, 28–35.

Westman, J., Wahlbeck, K., and 6 others. (2015). Mortality and life expectancy of people with alcohol use disorder in Denmark, Finland and Sweden. *Acta Psychiatrica Scandinavica*, **131** (4), 297–306.

WHO Executive Board. (2008). Strategies to reduce the harmful use of alcohol. Geneva: World Health Organization, EB122.R2.

WHO. (2019). Risk reduction of cognitive decline and dementia: WHO guidelines. Geneva: World Health Organization.

Wicki, M. and Gmel, G. (2011). Hospital admission rates for alcoholic intoxication after policy changes in the canton of Geneva, Switzerland. *Drug Alcohol Dependence*, **118** (2–3), 209–215.

Wilkinson, C., Livingston, M., and Room, R. (2016). Impacts of changes to trading hours of liquor licences on alcohol-related harm: a systematic review 2005-2015. *Public Health Research and Practice*, **26** (4), e2641644.

Wilkinson, R. and Marmot, M. (Eds). (2003). *Social Determinants of Health: The Solid Facts*, 2nd edit. Regional Office for Europe of the World Health Organization, Denmark.

Wilson, J., Ogeil, R. P., and 10 others. (2018). Re-thinking pre-drinking: Implications from a sample of teenagers who drink in private settings. *International Journal of Drug Policy*, **52**, 20–24.

Wilson, N. and Blakely, T. (2015). The high health burden from alcohol in New Zealand and the need for an appropriate government response. *New Zealand Medical Journal*, **128** (1409), 6–8.

Wilson, P. (1981). Improving the methodology of drinking surveys. *Statistician*, **30** (3), 159–167.

Winpenny, E., Marteau, T., and Nolte, E. (2013). Exposure of children and adolescents to alcohol marketing on social media websites. *Alcohol and Alcoholism*, **9** (2), 154–159.

Wood, A. M., Kaptoge, S., and many others. (2018). Risk thresholds for alcohol consumption: combined analysis of individual-participant data for 599,912 current drinkers in 83 prospective studies. *Lancet*, **391** (10129), 1513–1523.

Wood, E., Albarquoni, L., and 6 others (2018). Will this hospitalized patient develop severe alcohol withdrawal syndrome?: The rational clinical examination systematic review. *Journal of the American Medical Association*, **320** (8), 825–833

World Health Organization. (2007). WHO Technical Report Series 944. WHO expert committee on problems related to alcohol consumption.

World Health Organization. (2013). Global action plan for the prevention and control of noncommunicable diseases 2013-2020. Geneva.

World Health Organization. (2014). Global status report on alcohol and health, 2014. *World Health Organization*.

World Health Organization. (2018). *Global Status Report on Alcohol and Health 2018*. V. l. Poznyak and D. Rekve (Eds).
https://www.who.int/substance_abuse/publications/global_ alcohol_report/en/.

Worldwide Brewing Alliance. (2007). *Global Social Responsibility Initiatives*, 2nd edit. London, UK: British Beer and Pub Association.
http://ec.europa.eu/health/ph_determinants/life_style/alcohol/Forum/docs/alcohol_lib6_en.pdf.

Yeung, S. L. A. and Lam T.-H. (2019). Unite for a framework convention for alcohol control. *Lancet*, **393** (10183),1778–1779.

Yoon, S. and Lam, T.- H. (2013). The illusion of righteousness: corporate social responsibility practices of the alcohol industry. *BMC Public Health*, **13** (1), 630.

Zaridze, D., Lewington, S., and 14 others. (2009). Alcohol and mortality in Russia: prospective observational study of 151,000 adults. *Lancet*, **383** (992), 1465–1473.

Zeigler D. W., Wang, C. C., plus 5 others (2005). The neurocognitive effects of alcohol on adolescents and college students. *Preventive Medicine*, **40** (1), 23–32.

Zeisser, C., Stockwell, T. R., and Chikritzhs, T. (2014). Methodological biases in estimating the relationship between alcohol consumption and breast cancer: the role of drinker misclassification errors in meta-analytic results. *Alcoholism: Clinical and Experimental Research*, **38** (8), 2297–2306.

Zerhouni, O., Bégue, L., and O'Brien, K. S. (2019). How alcohol advertising and sponsorship works: Effects through indirect measures. *Drug Alcohol Review*, **38**, 391–398.

Zhang, C., Paolozza, A., Tseng P.-H., Reynolds, J. N., Munoz, D. P., and Itti, L. (2019). Detection of children/youth with fetal alcohol spectrum disorder through eye movement, psychometric, and neuroimaging data. *Frontiers in Neurology*, **10**, article 80. (https://doi.org/10.3389/fneur.2019.00080).

Zhang, J., Casswell, S., and Cai, H. (2008). Increased drinking in a metropolitan city in China: a study of alcohol consumption patterns and changes. *Addiction*, **103**, 416–423.

Zhao, J., Stockwell, T., Roemer A., and Chikritzhs, T. (2016). Is alcohol consumption a risk factor for prostate cancer? A systematic review and meta–analysis. *BioMed Central Cancer*, **16** (1), 845. DOI: 10.1186/s12885-016-2891-z.

Zhao, J., Stockwell, T., Roemer, A., Naimi, T., and Chikritzhs, T. (2017). Alcohol consumption and mortality from coronary heart disease: an updated meta-analysis of cohort studies. *Journal of Studies on Alcohol and Drugs*, **78** (3), 375–386.

Zeigler, D. W., Wang, C. C., and 5 others (2005). The neurocognitive effects of alcohol on adolescents and college students. *Preventive Medicine*, **40** (1), 23–32.

Zhou, Y., Zheng, J., Li, S., Zhou, T., Zhang, P., and Li, H.-B. (2016). Alcoholic beverage consumption and chronic diseases. *International Journal of Environmental Research and Public Health*, **13** (6), 522–549.

REFERENCES

## OTHER BOOKS FROM GEORGE A. F. SEBER:

Seber is also the author or co-author of seventeen books on statistics.

**Counseling Issues**

A comprehensive handbook covering the major issues a counselor, chaplain or psychotherapist might meet in the counseling room.

ISBN: 978-0-473-50816-6

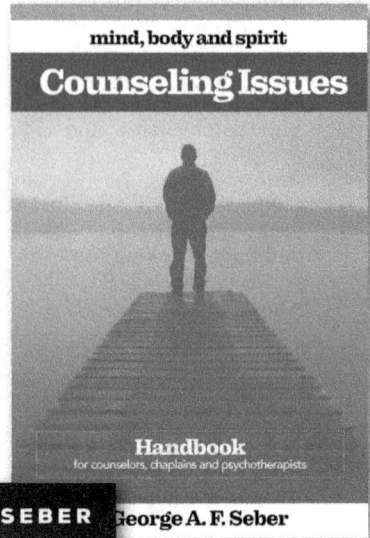

**mind, body and spirit**
**Counseling Issues**

**Handbook**
for counselors, chaplains and psychotherapists

George A. F. Seber

**Can We Believe It?**

Science-based evidence for Christianity.

ISBN:
978-1-4982-8919-1

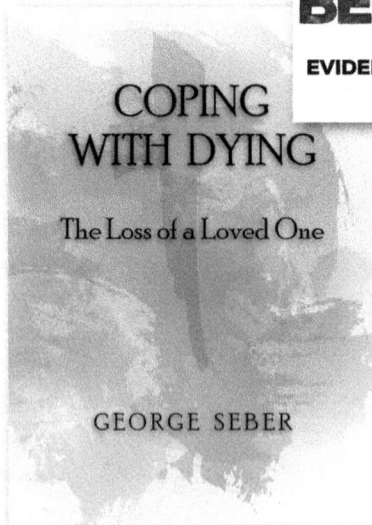

GEORGE A. F. SEBER

**CAN WE BELIEVE IT?**

**EVIDENCE FOR CHRISTIANITY**

COPING WITH DYING

The Loss of a Loved One

GEORGE SEBER

**Coping with Dying**

A valuable booklet which describes in detail what a caregiver can expect when a person is dying.

ISBN:
978-0-995-11177-6

**Visit www.george-af-seber.com for George's blog and other info.**